POLITICAL JUSTICE AND RELIGIOUS VALUES

Political Justice and Religious Values explores the impact of theological interpretations of God, the individual, society, church, and government on attitudes toward procedural and distributive justice. Combining theories with evidence, the volume focuses on individual beliefs and national conditions that explain policy views about political justice. It blends information from diverse fields: political science, religion, sociology, psychology, and history. The approach clarifies ways that the U.S. context influences religious values and preferences for civil liberties, women's rights, and economic equality.

Charles F. Andrain is Professor Emeritus of Political Science at San Diego State University.

Professor of Religion at Northwestern University, and Laura Olson, Professor of Political Science at Clemson University, provided comprehensive reviews filled with thoughtful recommendations, enlightened comments, and specific suggestions for clarifying interpretations. Stephen D. Rutter, sociology publisher at Routledge, gave the encouragement, support, and practical advice that authors seek. Routledge Production Editor, Alfred Symons, and Copy-editor, Andy Soutter, transformed the manuscript into a book. For over twenty years Anne L. Leu has prepared manuscripts for me. She not only processed this book with expertise, rapport, and patience but also served as a valued scholar and friend.

1
INTERPRETATIONS OF POLITICS AND RELIGION

> I . . . spent years in looking for men wise enough to solve the problems that puzzled me, not in religion or politics so much as along the wavy line between the two.
>
> (Lord John Acton)

During the mid-nineteenth century, Herman Melville portrayed the ties that linked political and religious values. For him, many Americans infused the nation with spiritual values. As he commented in *White-Jacket or The World in a Man-of-War*: "We Americans are the peculiar, chosen people—the Israel of our time. . . . The political Messiah . . . has come in us, if we would but give utterance to his promptings. . . . To be efficacious, Virtue must come down from aloft, even as our blessed Redeemer came down to redeem our whole man-of-war world; to that end, mixing with its sailors and sinners as equals" (Melville 2002:151, 229). In his later novel, *Moby Dick*, Melville held that the individual owed a higher loyalty than to the national ship of state engaged in warfare, injustice, and oppression. Preaching to congregants in the New

Bedford, Massachusetts chapel, Father Mapple concluded his sermon about the sailor Jonah with this hosanna: "Delight,—top gallant delight is to him who acknowledges no law or lord but the Lord his God, and is only a patriot to heaven" (Melville 1961:64). Horrified by the injustices reflected in the "bloody massacres" and national wars, Melville recognized the gap between the "wisdom of heaven" taught by Jesus and the "practical wisdom of earth" implemented by government officials (Melville 2002:324). Echoing Jesus' teachings, he asserted that citizens' identity rested mainly on ultimate spiritual values that assumed a universal perspective, not loyalty to the nation-state.

Political Attitudes and Religious Values

Just as during the nineteenth century, so today the impact of religious values has attracted extensive attention in the United States. Issues of justice linked to war, nationalism, and legal rights stimulate divergent interpretations. Disputes arise about the meaning of procedural and distributive justice. Threats to national security jeopardize support for civil liberties. Legalization of rights to abortion and homosexual relationships provokes controversies among churches and political parties. Procedures for expanding gender equality arouse disagreements about women's rights. On matters of distributive justice, ideological differences split those who favor government policies for greater income equality from groups that prefer more promarket programs.

This book explores the diverse ways that religious values influence political attitudes toward procedural and distributive justice. Whereas procedural justice emphasizes the means to achieve goals, distributive justice pays greater attention to the results, especially to the actual allocation of income and wealth. Both religion and politics place high importance on the laws, rules, and norms that regulate human interactions. Distributive justice involves the link between individual interests and the common good. Equitable treatment of the poor, marginals, and outcasts forms a major issue considered by religious and political texts.

Three related questions become crucial to the analysis of justice. First, why do individuals and groups hold distinctive theological views about spiritual justice, and why do these beliefs change? Second, in what ways do theological interpretations influence concepts of political justice? Third, how and why do these perceptions of justice shape political preferences held by religious liberals and conservatives, both among the elite as well as the mass public? Despite a few differences elaborated in Chapters 3, 4, and 5, the Social Gospel and New Thought best represent liberal positions toward politics and theology. Table 1.1 illustrates the crucial variables explaining political attitudes. These explanations include the historical context, theological assumptions about spiritual justice, and orientations toward political justice.

How do theological interpretations of God, the individual, and society shape beliefs about spiritual justice? Hierarchy, individualism, egalitarianism, and fatalism represent four types of justice. To what degree do persons stress deference to authority versus opposition to hierarchy? Do they give priority to individual autonomy or to personal interdependence with the community? When interacting with others, some people prefer inclusive, egalitarian relationships, whereas others lean toward more elitist, exclusive connections. How fatalistic or efficacious do individuals feel about changing the status quo? If efficacious feelings dominate, faith, righteous beliefs, good works, obedience to law, prayer, and education comprise possible ways to achieve personal salvation and societal redemption (see Andrain and Smith 2006:94–103; Douglas and Ney 1998:96–185; Lockart 2003; Thompson et al. 2006; Wildavsky 1998).

What explanations lie behind the links between theological interpretations and concepts of political justice? A functional theory of attitudes at the micro (individual) level, a meso approach to church organizations and their ties to political parties, and a macro concern for the historical context—cultural values, political and economic structures—provide some tentative explanations. Interacting with the structural situation, religious beliefs can fulfill several needs: the search for meaning, the establishment of community solidarity, and defense against threats (Smith et al. 1956). These beliefs then influence interpretations of political justice about the interactions among the church, government, and individual.

How do interpretations of political justice influence specific attitudes toward procedural and distributive justice, particularly preferences for civil liberties, legal abortion, gender equality, and economic equality? Particularly when religious values become closely aligned with ideological identifications, prospects rise for the political importance

Table 1.1 Explanations for political attitudes

Historical context	→	Theological views about spiritual justice	→	Concepts of political justice	→	Political attitudes toward procedural and distributive justice
Cultural values ↕ Distribution and use of political power ↕ Distribution and use of income and wealth		hierarchy, individualism, egalitarianism, fatalism God ↔ individual ↕ society ↔ individual		hierarchy, individualism, egalitarianism, fatalism church ↔ individual ↕ government ↔ individual		civil liberties, sexual freedom, gender equality, economic equality

of religious issues. Liberals and conservatives articulate different concepts of justice. Conservatives who affirm hierarchy, individual freedom for property-owners, unequal economic outcomes, and resignation to established traditions will probably give lower support to civil liberties, sexual choice, gender equality, and activist government programs intended to promote greater income equality. By contrast, most liberals express opposite beliefs about justice. They reject hierarchical authority, prefer more equal distribution of resources, feel high personal efficacy, and uphold individual liberty from domination by government, corporate, and ecclesiastical bureaucracies. According to liberals, public policy officials should support civil liberties, legal abortion, gender equality, and egalitarian government programs that provide comprehensive, generous social services. Under these polarizing ideological conditions, liberal and conservative activists in churches, business firms, unions, political parties, and social movements link their theological beliefs to public attitudes. Activists who can mobilize the most cohesive networks and form alliances with powerful government officials attain the greatest influence over the public policy agenda.

These questions about religious values and political justice pose important issues that pertain to everyone's life. Despite the "wavy line" separating religious values from political ideologies, both discourses highlight similar issues, feature a similar structure of thought, and fulfill the same functions. Even if specific interpretations differ, major topics of communication revolve around justice, equality, liberty, civic virtue, the public good, and ethical behavior. However divergent their orientations, theologians and political leaders stress hierarchy, individualism, egalitarianism, and fatalism as key perspectives toward justice. Politics and religion also focus on power. Whereas government officials accumulate and use power to make public decisions, many New Thought adherents view God as Omnipotence, infinite power, and creative, ultimate energy (Cady 1995:29–31).

The structure of thoughts elaborated by political and religious adherents show similar structural dimensions: coherence, consistency, and interdependence of ideas. These vary according to the degree of an individual's active involvement. Political leaders and activists express a greater coherence than do more passive party supporters and voters among the general public. Similarly, whereas theologians and ministers often articulate coherent beliefs, the laity, especially inactive members diverse groups. Minimal hostility emerges between "pure" ingroups and "decadent" outgroups. Civic solidarity promotes support for democratic principles. Yet often religious solidarity rests on adversarial relations with different groups. Dominant loyalty attaches to a monolithic, homogeneous religious institution. Instead of building bridges, the religious group remains a separate island with hostile attitudes toward other groups that fail to support their dominant beliefs. Even if conflict with outgroups intensifies intragroup solidarity, it lessens enthusiasm for such notions of procedural justice linked to civil liberties, individual rights for all citizens, and political equality (Andrain and Smith 2006:76–84).

Particularly when conflictual interactions strengthen solidarity, defense against threats becomes a crucial function of both political and religious beliefs. All over the world, individuals face many threats to their security. Some arise from their own fear of death or the actual deaths of loved ones. Threats from marginal groups—homosexuals, AIDS victims, drug addicts, people of a minority ethnic or religious association—often pose dangers to those feeling insecure. National unemployment, declining wages, growing poverty, and high inflation cause widespread worries about economic well-being. The dysfunctional aspects of modernization, globalization, and neoliberalism —rising joblessness, increased poverty, heightened income inequality, rapid changes in economic growth—often produce the threats that lead to membership in a religious community promising reassurance against all these perceived dangers. When domestic violence, wars, famines, hurricanes, and earthquakes strike a nation, the defensive urge rises. If defense against threats becomes a dominant motive, religious polarization may combine with political polarization to exacerbate conflict (Cesari 2005; Leustean 2005; Yamane 2007).

However important the resemblances between political and religious beliefs, they reveal crucial differences. A key dissimilarity stems from political leaders' greater concern for mundane, incremental, pragmatic issues that yield to compromise and accommodation. By contrast, religion stresses more transcendental, ultimate ends that provide meaning to human experiences, strengthen solidarity, and offer reassurance against threats. Particularly if these transcendental standards apply to all aspects of life, "true believers" cannot easily make compromises for fear of contaminating the purity of their spiritual interpretations. Regardless of these differences, the major focus of this book highlights the interaction—the reciprocal influence—that politics exerts on religion. How do religious values shape concepts of political justice? In what ways do political developments affect general interpretations of justice and their links to specific policy preferences?

POLITICAL AND SPIRITUAL JUSTICE

Interpretations of religious and political justice focus on three dimensions: the content (meaning) of justice, the methods for gaining knowledge about justice, and the application of this general knowledge to specific attitudes, such as civil liberties, gender equality, sexual freedom, and economic equality. In each of these dimensions, we can distinguish divergent liberal and conservative views most often assumed by well-educated activists, academicians, and theologians.

Meaning of Justice

Mary Douglas and Aaron Wildavsky formulated four types of justice that shape theological perspectives and political outlooks. They include hierarchy, individualism, egalitarianism, and fatalism (Douglas and Ney 1998:96–153; Wildavsky 1998). These four worldviews depend on the strength of group ties over the individual as well as the acceptance of role differentiation and externally-imposed rules. Hierarchy gives precedence to strong group ties, deference to rules imposed by elites, and norms that accord high-status persons the greatest privileges. Individualism ranks lower on group cohesion and rules imposed by external authorities. Rather than deferring to hierarchs' interpretation of rules, individualists in small groups negotiate the specific implications of general rules, so that they adjust to changing, ad hoc conditions. Competition becomes important as a way to motivate incentives for productive achievement and to allocate unequal rewards based on the degree of performance. Unlike individualists, egalitarians affirm the need for more equal rights to participation and resources. They want individuals to participate in communal networks where widespread, inclusive participation prevails among people who conduct discourse about rules for reconciling conflicts. Fatalism takes an atomized outlook on the world. Cynicism, social distrust, and alienation toward others deter individuals from group cooperation. Perceiving change as futile, fatalists resign themselves to accepting rules imposed by hierarchical institutions. Apathy and minimal participation in either a political or religious association result. In general, whereas liberals place priority on egalitarian, individualist concepts of justice, conservatives give greater emphasis to hierarchy and the need to obey the dictates of the collective ethos upheld by family and church heads.

Examining the main goals of justice, the sources of injustice, and ways for attaining greater justice, we can better comprehend the meaning of these four worldviews. The conservative hierarchs uphold order, loyalty, and harmony as primary goals. Injustice derives from deviations from the rules imposed by established institutions. Disobedience toward traditional ethical standards produces decadence, disorder, impurity, and moral anarchy. To strengthen justice, society must strengthen the traditional established institutions: the church, family, military, police, and courts. Besides educating the masses in ethical, spiritual standards, these institutions impose sanctions on individuals who deviate from customary rules. Society operates as an organic community based on loyalty to the established traditional order. Government assistance to church and patriarchal families strengthens social harmony.

Unlike hierarchs, who value order, libertarian individualists equate justice with the innovative freedom to compete and achieve success. For them, the main goals focus on performance, efficiency, and productivity: entrepreneurial values. This utilitarian view assumes that a just society grants higher rewards—income, promotion, status—to individuals who have made the greatest contribution to beneficial outcomes. The causes of injustice stem from both structural inequities and personal failings. An oppressive bureaucratic government may wield extensive control over business enterprises, so that individuals retain few choices. Social groups can discriminate against persons with high talents, abilities, and skills. Laziness, drug addiction, alcoholism, and irresponsibility may deter individuals from taking advantage of existing opportunities or creating new opportunities for achievement. Rather than egalitarian public policies administered by a bureaucratic government, voluntary associations and personal effort become the major strategies for attaining a more just society where benefits depend on individual contributions. Stable contracts, secure property rights, privatization, deregulation, flexible wages, and education in productive skills and attitudes that promote personal responsibility become crucial programs for securing procedural fairness. Under these policies, equal opportunities, however extensive, usually lead to unequal economic rewards.

By contrast, leftist egalitarians seek to enhance all dimensions of equality: cultural, economic, and political. Cultural equality focuses on treating all persons, whatever their social status, with respect and dignity. Economic equality connotes not only enhanced opportunities for everyone but a narrower gap separating rich from poor. Political equality encompasses equal treatment before the law, access to the government decision process, and equal influence over the policy agenda. Injustice emerges from structural domination: political repression, economic exploitation, and cultural humiliation by authoritarian churches, oppressive governments, and gigantic corporations. For egalitarians, the most effective strategies for obtaining justice involve more inclusive popular participation in decentralized governments, small-scale councils, consumer groups, nonbureaucratic unions, mass political parties, populist movements, and religious associations such as *comunidades eclesiales de base* (Christian local communities teaching liberation theology). Upholding the need for equality between men and women, young and old, rich and poor, saints and sinners, these populist organizations campaign for universalist, inclusive public policies that grant social services to all persons, regardless of income, social status, political power, ethnicity, or religion. By implementing policies in a fair, nonarbitrary, nondiscretionary way, government administrators secure procedural justice. Distributive justice thrives when policies produce egalitarian consequences in a caring, sharing society.

Unlike the egalitarians, fatalists place little faith in ever securing either procedural or distributive justice. For them, justice seems futile, however desirable. Survival becomes a major goal. Injustice arises from conditions beyond one's personal control—luck, chance, accidents, karma, maybe even God or Satan. Life appears unfair, random, unpredictable, uncontrollable, and chaotic. Perceiving life as a lottery, fatalists have low personal and political efficacy. They rely on cleverness and manipulation, key strategies for survival. Although their sense of political impotence discourages active public participation, fatalists may support powerful patrons and charismatic leaders who promise immediate but dictatorial solutions to their personal frustrations about perceived injustice. Playing the public lottery often gives marginals the rare if random chance to win a fortune and alleviate deprivations stemming from unjust conditions.

Neither one individual nor the same society consistently upholds only a single worldview; divergent values compete for dominance and often combine to influence theological and political orientations. For example, corporate elites often synthesize individualism with hierarchy to justify their class rule. When the Swedish Social Democrats initially gained power, they blended organizational hierarchy with egalitarian social service benefits. Whereas the Social Gospel prophet Walter Rauschenbusch linked economic equality to collectivism, New Thought students in Unity and Religious Science harmonize cultural equality with individualism. If fatalism combines with equality, high alienation emerges against the elitist establishment; yet the radical dissidents lack the efficacy to engage in collective political action. The merger of hierarchy with fatalism reflects marginalization by right-wingers who see themselves victimized by leftist oppression but feel powerless to organize for sociopolitical change (Grendstad 2003).

The four worldviews shape theological outlooks on spiritual justice, which revolve around interactions among God, the individual, and society. Hierarchs view God as the sovereign authority over the individual and society. Perceived as a personal patriarch, God punishes those who disobey the divine commandments and attach their allegiance to nongodly objects. Living in sin, individuals must become responsive to redemption by God. Faced with disorder, chaos, and anarchy, society also needs divine redemption. From the hierarchical perspective, society represents an organism with the top organs—the head, brains, reason—dominating the lower organs, such as the feet. For example, Roman Catholic hierarchs see society as the body of Christ, with the pope serving as the vicar of Christ on earth. The cardinals, archbishops, and bishops enforce his will. At the foot of the hierarchy the laity obey the will of God and his representatives on earth. A high functional unity binds members together. Even though each organ performs a different function, shared spiritual values secure harmony among the diverse organs. Spiritual justice ensues when individuals obey the divine commandments interpreted and enforced by ecclesiastical authorities.

Unlike hierarchical views, individualist interpretations of spiritual justice rest on greater autonomy for the individual vis-à-vis God and society. According to them, God plays a nurturant role as a partner with specific individuals, who also enjoy some independence from society. They regard society more as a mechanism than an organic corporate body. Instead of a natural organism, society functions as an artificial entity constructed by individuals. An aggregate of parts, modern society requires a differentiation between the public and private spheres. Spiritual values help mediate conflicts in the private religious sector. Reason and laws arbitrate conflicts in the public sector. By coordinating actions of their members, voluntary associations of churches can bring greater order to society. Spiritual justice emerges when all individuals retain the freedom to follow their reason and conscience about ethical behavior. God, not a personal hierarch, serves as a key source of enlightenment for autonomous individuals (Rasmussen and Brown 2005).

Among the four worldviews, egalitarianism places the highest priority on egalitarian relationships among God, the individual, and society. Most egalitarians, especially those in New Thought movements, conceive of God as creative energy that nurtures life, love (*agape*), and enlightenment. God represents not only these transcendent spiritual principles but also an indwelling spirit. Rather than burdened with original sin, individuals have a "light within," the spark of divinity that reflects the divine image. Spiritual justice occurs when individuals align their thoughts and actions with the spiritual essence, so that they get "in tune with the infinite," as Ralph Waldo Trine (2002) wrote at the end of the nineteenth century. Enlightened self-consciousness leads to social harmony and justice. Compared with the New Thought theologians, egalitarian Social Gospelers place higher stress on the need to redeem society, not just save the individual from false thinking. From their outlook, sin stems not just from personal attitudes and actions but also from collective sources: government oppression, economic exploitation, and cultural humiliation. Justice will emerge only when social movements can change these unjust structural conditions through fomenting conflict with the establishment. Justice denotes egalitarian outcomes in the society. Just as individuals enjoy an egalitarian, cooperative relationship with God, the same equality should pervade social interactions on earth.

Fatalists, however, take a more futile attitude toward the possibilities of ever securing justice on earth. For them, God demonstrates an arbitrary will incomprehensible to "mere mortals." Rather than order, harmony, or justice, randomness and chaos result from his will. Fatalists hence distrust other individuals as well as social institutions. Except perhaps for such primary groups as family, friends, and neighbors, society remains a source of cynical distrust. Disdainful of collective action, fatalists' concept of spiritual reality deters them from taking any efforts to mobilize for greater political justice.

The interpretations of political justice partly flow from these concepts of spiritual reality. Probing the meanings of political justice, we concentrate on the power relationships among the church, individual, and government. How much control does each exert over the others? Of all the four worldviews, hierarchy seeks the greatest power of the established Church over the individual and government. During the European Middle Ages the Roman Catholic Church wielded hierarchical authority over individuals and governments. According to St. Thomas Aquinas, the whole universe reflects a hierarchical order filled with varying degrees of power and authority. Within the Church the pope governs. Within the government the monarch rules. Both pope and king need to exert their power based on reason, virtue, and the will of God. Just as in the human body reason should govern the appetites, so in the Church—the mystical body of Christ on earth—as well as in the political institutions, justice emerges when reason supersedes the passions, the common good triumphs over private interests, and people attain a virtuous life. Because of the fallen state of humans, Aquinas believed in the need for eternal, natural laws to restrain arbitrary acts by rulers. The king's laws should derive from propositions rationally deduced from the just principles that flow from God. Because few government leaders demonstrate perfect civic virtue, Aquinas preferred a mixed, pluralist government ruled by a king with assistance from virtuous aristocracy. When just rulers implement rational laws, unity, order, peace, and harmony result. An unjust ruler, however, produces disorder when he rules arbitrarily, rejects legal restraints, and pursues his private desires. Yet in this conservative hierarchical system affirming the primacy of order, Aquinas perceived that disobedience and rebellion, even against unjust governments, endanger political order. Hence, the Roman Catholic Church as the institution representing God on earth bears the responsibility to restrain the power of both governments and individuals (Aquinas 1953, 1960, 1988; Wolin 2004:118–23).

By contrast to medieval theologians like Aquinas, John Locke took a more liberal, individualist view of political justice. From his perspective, the church should function as a voluntary association. Governing by persuasion, not coercion, it promotes spiritual activities but refrains from monopolizing society or truth. Because no ecclesiastical officials can ever fully comprehend the ambiguous, uncertain nature of God, society needs a separation between political and religious activities. Human beings, not God, artificially construct both church and state. Several independent churches proclaim alternative, diverse opinions about truth and the need for general faith in God. Rather than focusing on achieving spiritual salvation or societal redemption, governments should give priority to more pragmatic, concrete benefits: physical security, life, liberty, and private property rights. From Locke's nonhierarchical, tolerant, pluralist outlook, government needs a balance of powers between a strong legislature and a weaker monarch. Justice results when government officials rule by legal restraints. Rejecting paternalistic, absolutist rule, Locke believed that citizens, especially property-owners, have the equal intellectual capabilities to help decide political options. Rather than deprived, fallen sinners, they can play an active role in making rational choices about their leaders and public policies. Political justice prevails when independent churches, consensual governments, and rational individuals remain committed to laws that protect life, liberty, and property (Locke 2003:193–209; Owen 2007; Stanton 2006).

Prophets of the Social Gospel, such as Walter Rauschenbusch, gave greater priority to egalitarian interpretations of political justice than did Locke. Writing during the first two decades of twentieth-century America, Rauschenbusch interpreted justice to mean greater political and economic equality. Like Locke, he favored a strict separation of the voluntary churches from government control. Opposed to ecclesiastical, bureaucratic institutions, he wanted churches to reject public funds as well as efforts by government officials to select religious leaders or enforce particular doctrines. Ideally, the church should proclaim the highest ethical ideals and strive not only to redeem individuals but to realize the Kingdom of God on earth. By maintaining a decentralized system with extensive popular participation, governments will achieve political justice. Along with churches, they have the responsibility to secure a more egalitarian, just society. Injustice stems from both individual and especially collective sins found under a capitalist economy. Based on selfishness, class conflict, and private greed, capitalism brings the inequalities linked to low wages, high profits, long working hours, pollution, and unsafe, unhealthy conditions. Rauschenbusch felt that socialist policies would liberate workers from their oppression, expand equality for the poor, and promote greater political rights for the marginals. In this egalitarian society, justice would entail a communal spirit based on the spiritual ideals of sacrificial love (*agape*), service, and justice (Rauschenbusch 1991, 1997).

Fatalists express little hope about realizing the Kingdom of God on earth. Instead, theologians like John Calvin believed that because of original sin and extensive evil in the human condition, individuals lack the free will to act with virtue or to choose between good and evil. Instead, the "bondage of sin" motivates them toward evil actions. They tend to serve the self but rebel against God. Acting through the Holy Spirit, only the grace of God, not human achievement, can secure personal salvation, inspire people to seek goodness, and lead them to obey the laws of God, not the laws of sin. Like Augustine and Thomas Aquinas, Calvin assumed that God as Sovereign Authority predestines the chosen elect for eternal life and degenerates for eternal damnation. God invests government officials with "sacred majesty." Hence, no one has the right to rebel against unjust rulers who oppress the poor, coerce the humble, and extort widows. Even the tyrant brings some justice, however limited. God alone has the authority to establish justice based on obedience to the eternal laws found in sacred scripture.

Given Calvin's views about the seditious tendencies of the wicked, he prescribed extensive power to political and religious institutions to preserve order, cohesion, harmony, and obedience. Church and government need to harmonize their activities. The powerful church exerts widespread control over individuals. Pastors give sermons, elucidate divine law, and administer the sacraments of baptism and the Lord's supper. Reassuring the "chosen elect" about their salvation, they urge them to show God's love toward others. As theological monists, teachers who impose spiritual doctrines on the laity allow only one interpretation of truth. Elders preserve discipline. Deacons give alms to the poor. The office of magistrate secures its jurisdiction from God; government officials owe obedience to God, not to the citizenry. God's word mandates that political leaders enforce decency, modesty, honor, and piety as well as punish those guilty of impiety, immodesty, heresy, and blasphemy. These groups included Catholics ("papists"), Anabaptists, and Libertines (mystical Gnostics). When Calvin assumed the dominant role in Geneva from 1536–38 through 1541–64, not only consensual political education but imprisonments, occasional executions, and excommunication from the church maintained this monistic rule. Institutional hierarchy, group conformity, inequality that split the predestined elect from the unsaved, and fatalism about the prospects for secure relief from injustice impeded peaceful religious and political change.

Yet Calvin granted merchants the opportunity to make money, earn a profit, and produce for the common good. Called to serve God and gain reassurance about their predestined salvation, entrepreneurs felt motivated to save their money, invest capital, and practice rational self-control. Even if Calvin's notions about fatalism reinforced political order, his economic ideas about entrepreneurial efficacy contributed to the rise of capitalist change (see Calvin 1982, 1996, 2001; C. Campbell 2006; Elwood 2002; Helm 2004:159–83; Mansbach 2006; O'Donovan and O'Donovan 1999:662–84; Pellerin 2003; M. Weber 2002; Wolin 2004:148–74).

Sources of Knowledge about Justice

Interpretations of justice stem from several sources: the individual, scripture, tradition, and scholarly investigations. Liberal and conservative outlooks take a divergent position toward these bases of authority. For the liberals, the individual conscience and scholarly historical investigations assume priority as the basis for understanding spiritual justice. Following John Locke, they stress reason, logic, and empirical inquiry. New Thought adherents focus not merely on reason but also personal prayer, meditation, intuition, dreams, and visions. Whether done by Social Gospel or New Thought scholars, historical investigations of the biblical context become an important method for comprehending the meaning of spiritual reality. Rather than viewing the Bible as an inerrant, infallible text open to literal interpretation, liberals perceive the Hebrew Bible and the Greek New Testament in a symbolic way. Filled with ethical standards, myths, stories, and diverse spiritual principles, these scriptures convey their truths through metaphors, analogies, parables, and visions. Their meaning depends on a specific historical context. Because the books of both the New Testament and especially the Hebrew Bible were compiled by several contributors over hundreds of years, the original intent of the authors becomes difficult to ascertain. Oral teachings merge with written texts, which contain inconsistencies, ambiguities, paradoxical conclusions, and missing passages. Scribes copied the dictated messages of the biblical author; often they made a few changes to the original text. Hence, contemporary readers cannot easily apply the original scriptural teachings to the present situation. Several different meanings of the same passage abound. Neither tradition nor the canons of the church fathers offer much assistance. Individuals must choose those scriptural passages viewed as most important. Guided by historical scholarship, they supply their own interpretations of justice under contemporary conditions.

Liberals also take an individualist view of political justice. Each person has the reason to make political judgments, whether in the voting booth or a jury. Instead of seeking the original intent of constitutional authors, liberals perceive the constitution as an ever-changing document dependent for its meaning on a particular historical context. They want individuals to seek advice from intellectuals and scholars for ways to interpret the legal foundations of justice (Berlinerblau 2005; Helmer 2005a, 2005b, 2005c, 2005d, 2006).

Conservatives place higher priority on tradition as a method for acquiring knowledge about justice. For example, Roman Catholics with close ties to the Vatican look to the canonical teachings of the church fathers as found in such texts as the Apostles' Creed, the Nicene Creed, the books by St. Augustine and St. Thomas Aquinas, papal encyclicals, the *Catechism of the Catholic Church* (1997), and the *Compendium of the Social Doctrine of the Church* (Pontifical Council for Justice and Peace 2004). For many Protestant evangelicals, the traditional basis of authority rests with clergy who regard the Bible as the inerrant, infallible, literal Word of God applicable to all aspects of life, not just to the ethical-spiritual sphere but also to science. They disdain empirical historical investigations that seem to cast doubt on the literal meaning of the Bible. Peer group conformity in a cohesive congregation, not rational scholarship in a seminar or university, produces the dominant interpretations of justice, whether religious or political. Rigidity, closure to new information, and a monistic outlook shape fundamentalist preferences, especially on such issues as abortion and homosexual rights (Greeley and Hout 2006).

Application of Spiritual Principles to Public Policies

Influenced by the four worldviews of justice, liberals and conservatives apply general principles to specific public attitudes toward procedural and distributive justice. These policy issues include civil liberties, sexual freedom, gender equality, prison reform, ecology, world peace, and income distribution. On all these issues, liberals rather than conservatives adopt a more optimistic, individualistic, and egalitarian perspective but show lower deference to established authority. As a result, they give greater support to civil liberties, gender equality, sexual choice, economic equality, and policies for expanding the scope of government authority to provide social service benefits for health care, urban assistance, and poverty reduction. By contrast, conservatives take a more pessimistic, hierarchical, elitist, communal outlook on these public issues. Social institutions, especially the church and family, wield communal control over individual will. Opposed to disorder, chaos, and anarchy, they show greater faith in hierarchical elites: men, elders, clergy, and the wealthy. However great the ideological consistency affirmed by conservative activists, class differences often split the conservative movement. Whereas wealthier members oppose government attempts to increase income equality, poorer conservatives show stronger support. Hence, public attitudes toward economic equality will probably reveal fewer differences than opinions about civil liberties, gender equality, and particularly abortion (Collins 1993; Grafton and Permaloff 2005; Greeley and Hout 2006:84–90, 121–27).

Given the diversity of meanings attached to religious concepts, notions of spiritual reality do not always congrue with interpretations of just policies. The most consistent stands occur among those who share a similar outlook toward spiritual and political justice. For example, William Sloane Coffin, John Shelby Spong, and Rabbi Michael Lerner all favor civil liberties, procedural democracy, gender equality, and more equal economic outcomes. Perceiving God as loving, nurturant spirit, they view biblical truths in a symbolic, metaphorical, pluralist way. By contrast, Protestant fundamentalists like Pat Robertson, James Dobson, Tim LaHaye, and dominant Southern Baptist ministers take a self-styled "conservative" perspective on politics and religion. Compared with liberal clergy, they give less support to legalized abortion, homosexual rights, women's equality with men in church or government, and government programs to secure greater economic equality. Interpretations of truth rest on a monistic, literal reading of the Bible, regarded as an inerrant, infallible foundation of personal behavior, legal decrees, and even conclusions about evolution. For them, God plays a punitive role, judging sinners and punishing the wicked. Reflecting a polarized view, these fundamentalist leaders believe divine nurturance extends only to "born-again" Christians who have accepted Jesus Christ as their personal savior.

Other religious leaders adopt less consistent perspectives toward politics and spiritual values. The founder of Sojourners, a national network that works for world peace, poverty reduction, and social justice, Protestant evangelical Jim Wallis holds "orthodox" theological doctrines derived from the Apostles' Creed. Although he displays limited enthusiasm for abortion and homosexual rights, he strongly backs public policies to secure expanded civil liberties, gender equality, and especially economic equality. Dorothy Day, the cofounder of the Catholic Worker movement, affirmed the theological concepts in the Apostles' Creed, the Nicene Creed, the seven sacraments of the Church, and the proclamations of the Vatican II Council. She remained actively committed to economic equality, women's rights, political dissent, and world peace yet took a skeptical stand toward sexual permissiveness, abortion, and homosexual behavior. Although Unity and Religious Science adherents affirm homosexual rights, they hold more conservative positions toward economic policies that uphold individual initiative, not government laws, as the better way to overcome poverty. Yet New Thought shares a liberal outlook on the spiritual interpretations of God, the individual, and society. Perceiving God as the spiritual principle of life, light, and love, it places a high value on individual education, prayer, and meditation as effective ways to raise people's consciousness and thereby revitalize social conditions. Discourse becomes a crucial method for educating the public.

Religious Discourse and Political Change

Discourse analysis helps clarify the complex impact of beliefs about justice on public attitudes toward justice. Several related questions deserve attention. Why do individuals, both citizens and leaders, find meaning in discourse? Why does the content of discourse change? Under what conditions can a religious group secure greater influence over the policy process and thereby produce change in society?

The meanings attributed to discourse revolve around the three "i"s: ideas, institutions, individuals (Palier and Surel 2005). If religious values prove salient to individuals—offer clarity, coherence, and plausibility—they will adopt them. This acceptance particularly occurs when these ideas portray a vision of justice, virtue, hope, and redemption that gives meaning, cements social solidarity, and provides reassurance against threats to the self, group, and society. Effective discourse facilitates this importance, which most often prevails when powerful, cohesive institutions propagate the teachings. Governments, political parties, churches, popular social movements, and especially the mass media play a crucial role. With sufficient resources, networks, and cohesion, they can use both oral and written texts to mobilize supporters, demobilize opponents, and gain defections from rivals. Priests, ministers, pastors, rabbis, and imams function as key religious figures framing spiritual values. Political party leaders and government officials articulate their visions of the public interest. Entrepreneurs use economic resources to spread the message. Mass media personnel who communicate through radio, television, newspapers, magazines, and the Internet may reach a broad audience in modern societies. If audience members form a discourse community with relatives, friends, neighbors, and workmates, then the prospects rise for accepting the dominant interpretations of religious values as well as their application to specific policy issues (Besecke 2005).

Conflict stimulates changing interpretations. Inversionary discourse challenges the hegemonic, dominant concepts of authority with oppositional interpretations. Powerful sociopolitical networks communicate beliefs about justice that draw sharp contrasts between present empirical conditions and transformative ideals, such as equality, respect for marginals, and service to others. Inversionary discourse advocates profound role reversals. The last become first. Outsiders come inside. Marginals join the inner circle. Sinners gain redemption.

Justice, righteousness, hope, efficacy, and life replace injustice, corruption, despair, fatalism, and decay. Conflicts between opposing ideas, competitive institutions, and different individuals facilitate the acceptance of inversionary discourse. Conflicting standards of justice produce changed meanings. When hierarchical, elitist, fatalistic views yield to greater stress on opposition to hierarchy, egalitarian interactions among all people, and personal efficacy, individuals will more likely adopt a liberal inversionary discourse. Particularly when structural conflicts wrack the society, opposing standards of justice intensify. Wars, depressions, floods, hurricanes, and earthquakes cause conflicts. Rapid modernization often produces dysfunctional consequences—rising poverty, higher unemployment, greater income inequality, more interpersonal violence, and cultural humiliation of outcast groups. Under these structural conditions, high risks result. A perceived loss in political power, wealth, and status often leads deprived individuals to reject the interpretations upheld by the establishment. Angered by injustice, they may turn to a religious or political group that promises hope for a better future. Personal leaders mobilize support behind the inversionary discourse. Charismatic heroes, populists, and radical prophets communicate messages that deconstruct old meanings, construct new orientations, and reinterpret formerly-dominant values. Only when leaders develop a powerful organization, gain widespread support, and weaken the sanctions imposed by the dominant establishment do the changed meanings actually produce egalitarian social change (Apter 2005, 2006a; Apter and Saich 1994; Mansbridge 2005; Wald et al. 2005).

From a dialectical perspective, contradictory values often produce social movements seeking either a restoration of the previous order or a new transformed society. For example, in the United States the original fundamentalist movement of the 1914–1920 era arose against the growing popularity of Progressivism, with its Enlightenment priority on rationality, empirical evidence, scientific skepticism, evolutionary progress, cultural relativism, and functional differentiation, under which no single, powerful established church controls the government. Immediately before World War I, Protestant evangelicals published a series of paperback books titled *The Fundamentals: A Testimony to the Truth*. They rejected theological and sociopolitical modernism: historical biblical criticism, the social gospel, secular humanism, evolution, liberalism, socialism, and communism. Instead, the fundamentalists affirmed such traditionalist tenets as the trinitarian God, the deity of Jesus Christ, the virgin birth, his bodily resurrection, the second coming, and the literal inerrancy of the Bible. Faced with a depression, World War II, and postwar reconstruction, most evangelicals withdrew from active political participation from the late 1920s through 1960. Located primarily in the South, they mainly supported Democratic Party candidates for economic reasons. With the election of a Catholic president, John F. Kennedy, in 1960 and increased government support for liberal stands on issues linked to cultural values (abortion, gay rights, racial integration, opposition to prayer in public schools), evangelicals became disenchanted with liberal Democrats. Allying with the Republican Party during the Reagan administration (1981–88), political and religious conservatives rejected the secularized, modern, urban lifestyle that they equated with moral decadence, permissiveness, hedonism, and cultural relativism. Using modern communications media, they sought public policies that would curtail abortion, same-sex marriage, and rights for homosexuals but expand government expenditures for private religious schools and "faith-based initiatives." This evangelical activism peaked during the 1996–2006 period when Republicans dominated first the national legislature and then the presidency. The evangelicals' rise to policy influence stimulated more liberal churches to reinvolve their members in political activity, with primary attention placed on world peace, poverty, civil liberties, gender equality, and ecology. In the dialectical synthesis, closer ties with liberal Democrats recurred (Andrain and Apter 1995:28–30, 48–53; Cesari 2005).

As this example of cultural polarization illustrates, discourses on justice not only assert conservative positions but also propose liberal public policies for changing social conditions. Composed mainly of traditionalist Catholics and evangelical Protestants, "pro-life" groups view abortion as a legal injustice that they equate with murder. The more liberal National Council of Churches combats government oppression, militarism, poverty, income inequality, environmental pollution, racism, and restrictions on sexual freedom. Conflicts among rival political parties, different churches, and opposed ideologies propel demands for public policy changes.

If religious or political activists aim to enact policies for social change, they need an innovative vision, a powerful organization, and the public support that comes from effective mobilization. The idealistic vision arouses interest and highlights the importance of specific policy issues that focus on current problems. Material interests become congruent with moral-spiritual values that bring benefits to the self, group, and nation. Mass media transmit a shared language about the policy relevance of such issues as reproductive choice, gender equality, civil liberties, and economic redistribution. If electoral campaigns stress these issues and provoke conflict between competing political parties, public attentiveness grows. Churches, unions, and parties can mobilize higher participation among concerned citizens. Particularly when individuals perceive the discourse as cognitively believable, emotionally appealing, and relevant to their need for meaning, social solidarity, and reassurance against perceived threats, these persons will support the policy message for social change (Hutchings 2003; Mühlhäusler and Peace 2006).

Beginning with the Protestant reformations in the sixteenth century and extending to the present time, societies have become more modernized, differentiated, and open to conflicts that generate a changed discourse. Mobilizers pursuing an egalitarian, efficacious, individualist form of justice forge several struggles: economic conflicts, cultural struggles over legitimacy, and political competition to shape public policy performance. By forming unions, consumer associations, and other populist movements, formerly-excluded classes claim that the dominant classes pursue injustice, corruption, and private interests. In the religious sphere, conflicting symbols delegitimize the ecclesiastical authorities. Prophets who promise innovation struggle against religious officials who seek continuity with tradition. These prophets articulate a new discourse that deconstructs established hierarchical authority. Through dialogues with the public, the unjust absurdities of political life become unmasked. Particularly during crisis times when disasters, war, and economic stagnation threaten the society, prophetic heroes articulate new messages that promise the hope of change. Resignation yields to efficacy. The possible becomes probable. Improvement of worldly conditions appears feasible now, not in some future heaven. Structural crises bring the decay in traditions that used to legitimize the sociopolitical hierarchy. As the class and religious conflicts mount, change appears in the political sphere. Religious heresy leads to political dissent. Rhetorical appeals rally activists around a campaign for social justice, liberation, and equality. Combined with inclusive political organizations, the innovative discourse mobilizes liberal supporters (Bourdieu 1998a, 1998b; Engler 2003; Verter 2003).

Given the present conditions in the United States, the prospect for liberal churches securing fundamental transformations appears limited. Although several religious leaders articulate an innovative vision, they lack a national centralized organization to realize that vision. Since the 1968 assassination of the Reverend Martin Luther King, Jr., no charismatic prophet has arisen to mobilize a mass membership behind a spiritual campaign for social change. Most liberal church members, whether Unitarian, Congregational, or New Thought, come from high-status backgrounds with advanced formal education. Despite the calls for greater inclusiveness, few poor people belong to these churches. These denominations give lower priority to economic equality than to cultural freedom for women, homosexuals, abortion-seekers, and political dissidents. Their rational approach to the Bible downplays emotional commitment to a spiritual faith. Compared with orthodox Roman Catholics and especially fundamentalist-evangelical Protestants, liberal Christians and Jews display a weaker commitment to their religious values. For New Thought adherents, individual activities like prayer, meditation, and education take precedence over collective political mobilization. Like most other Americans, they perceive no feasible alternative to the current economic or political system. Preferring incremental change, individuals who share a Social Gospel–New Thought ethos believe that an alliance with liberal Democrats will most effectively achieve civil liberties, gender equality, reproductive choice, reduced poverty, and a peaceful world (Taussig 2006).

Conclusion

Focusing on the four worldviews of justice, the book analyzes several interpretations of procedural and distributive justice. The second chapter probes the inversionary discourses of Jesus and Paul, especially the impact of their teachings on the Social Gospel and New Thought. Chapters 3 and 4 compare the meanings of justice expounded by Social Gospel advocates. Walter Rauschenbusch served as a leading prophet of the Social Gospel movement from 1890 to 1914. After World War II Jim

Wallis, William Sloane Coffin, John Shelby Spong, Dorothy Day, and Michael Lerner reformulated many Social Gospel assumptions about justice originated by Rauschenbusch. These two chapters indicate the ways that their interpretations differ from those held by conservative theologians. After the fifth chapter examines those who influenced New Thought, it explores Religious Science and the Unity School of Christianity. Comparisons of Social Gospel and New Thought adherents emphasize the political implications of their religious values, their organizational resources, and their influence over the policy agenda. Chapter 6 explains why religious liberals wielded less policy influence than religious conservatives during the 1996–2006 era. Not only their more unified spiritual vision, but also the local networks and individual support they rallied behind their cause, explain conservatives' enhanced influence on political leaders, especially in the Republican Party.

Using General Social Survey (GSS) data for 1998–2004, the concluding chapter examines the American public's attitudes toward several policy issues linked to procedural and distributive justice. Procedural justice involves preferences for civil liberties and sexual choice, including the right to a legal abortion. Distributive justice concentrates on government efforts to expand income equality and increase social service benefits. Gender equality refers to similar opportunities for women and men to become paid employees and political leaders. It entails aspects of both procedural and distributive justice. Comparing liberal with conservative stands on these four issues, Chapter 7 uses the four worldviews of justice—hierarchy, individualism, egalitarianism, fatalism—and the three needs fulfilled by religious values (meaning, solidarity, defense against threats) to explain the survey results. Insights from the Social Gospel and New Thought perspectives suggest relevant hypotheses. The GSS provides clues about the explanatory importance of holding a nurturant concept of God, assuming a symbolic, non-literal interpretation of the Bible, affirming the need for children's independence, and expressing an optimistic outlook.

2
PERSPECTIVES ON BIBLICAL JUSTICE

> Learn to do good. Seek justice, rescue the oppressed, defend the orphan, plead for the widow.
>
> (Isaiah 1:17)
>
> Seek first God's reign and God's justice, and all these things will be given to you as well.
>
> (Matthew 6:33)
>
> We have our citizenship in heaven; from there, we eagerly await the coming of our Savior Jesus Christ.
>
> (Philippians 3:20)

Writing poems from 1770 through 1820, William Blake envisioned an unorthodox conception of the Bible. His topsy-turvy world of inversionary discourse transformed biblical images. From his iconoclastic perspective, the gates of hell seemed more welcoming than the doors of heaven. Jesus as a human being became more impressive than Christ as a pre-existent Word of God. Although he obeyed God, he disobeyed his family. Humble toward God, he was haughty toward both political and religious rulers, denouncing them for their injustice. Charity toward the people contrasted with the sharp distinction drawn between the sheep and goats. For Blake, these conflicting images produced change as individuals disputed the meaning of scriptural passages. As he wrote in *The Everlasting Gospel*, "Both read the Bible day and night, but thou read'st black where I read white" (Blake 1989:853–68).

INTERPRETATIONS OF THE SCRIPTURES

We can best explain the divergent meanings attributed to the Bible by focusing on three key dimensions of the historical context: structural conditions, cultural values, and behavioral interactions among leaders and followers. Structures encompass the political, economic, and cultural sectors. What power relationships exist between the rulers—those who make the key decisions for a society—and the less active ruled? The degree of coercion, centralization, coordination, pluralism, and scope of power represents basic aspects of political interactions. Economically, the rigidity of the class structure affects interpretations of justice. Whereas the upper class seeks to legitimate its status by claiming to uphold a just social order, the marginals often view the class system as perpetuating injustice. From their perspective, exploitation, not the grace of God, shapes the economic system. Often political repression and economic exploitation reinforce the cultural humiliation of outcasts, whom the ruling elites view as inferior subjects. In more egalitarian societies, however, less polarized images of justice emerge. Justice merges with empathy. Dominant views perceive that all people, whatever their political power, wealth, or status, deserve respect for sharing a common humanity.

Cultural values also shape biblical interpretations. They communicate both normative rules of behavior as well as prescribed roles. Scripts frame key issues about justice. In this connection, language becomes crucial for understanding the scriptures. Before it became a written text, the Bible originated as oral traditions. Later compositors translated the oral dialogues into written languages. The Hebrew Bible developed over an 800-year period from 800 BCE through 100 BCE. Around 200 BCE, Jewish scholars translated it into the dominant Greek language. Paul relied on this Septuagint version. Later Christian clergy translated the Septuagint and the Greek New Testament into Latin. Protestant reformers like Martin Luther, John Calvin, and William Tyndale translated the Latin vernacular into their national languages, such as German, French, and English. Yet all these linguistic transformations often obscured the meaning of the texts. For example, written Hebrew has no vowels, only consonants. The original Hebrew contained no punctuation or divisions between words. Unclear tenses confused translators who pondered if a verb referred to the past, present, or future tense. When Jesus preached his message during the period before 30 CE, Jews spoke Aramaic, not Hebrew. Translation of spoken Aramaic into written Greek brought further interpretive problems. For these linguistic reasons, multiple meanings of the same passage arose over the centuries as the Bible became translated into thousands of different languages. To understand the meaning of the original text, analysts master the art of sociohermeneutics, which links the meaning of a text to sociological and historical issues (see Berlinerblau 2005: 78–83, 112–14; Pelikan 2005).

Linguistic discourse relates to the behavioral interactions between religious leaders and their followers. Political rulers, priests, prophets, teachers, healers, and messianic figures have spoken to their followers about the imperatives of justice. Even if contemporary scholars cannot fathom the precise ways that the hearers understand the message of their mentor, knowledge of sociohermeneutics enables us to comprehend, however imperfectly, the meaning behind the stories, parables, poems, and historical narratives. Effective prophets with charisma—the gift of grace—attained resonance with their followers, who became faithful disciples and teachers to others. Later adherents who relied on the written biblical text then interpreted scriptural passages by ascribing literal, allegorical, and ethical meanings to a specific passage (Andrain and Apter 1995:4–10; Horsley 2005a).

Although a historical, sociological, and linguistic analysis of a biblical text may supply meaning of its context, what relevance does the Bible have for contemporary readers who seek to relate the scriptures to their personal and social situation? The writings of the eighteenth-century minister, professor, and theologian Friedrich Schleiermacher (1768–1834) offer valuable insights. Like William Blake he drew contrasts between polar opposites. His dialectic method perceived the reconciliation of reason and intuition as the best way to comprehend the Bible. Influenced by the Enlightenment tradition, he used reason, logic, linguistics, and historical analysis to provide a critical interpretation of the New Testament. According to him, the scriptures reveal no fixed, unchanging, eternal meaning. Instead, their meaning depends not only on the historical context of the original text but on the contemporary situation and personal religious experiences of the reader, particularly on her experience with faith in Jesus as the Redeemer. From his perspective, theologians need to link the historical experiences of Jesus to present conditions, so that his prophetic message about the infinite Spirit becomes incorporated into finite minds when readers gain awareness of the indwelling Christ presence. By linking the continuity of the original biblical text to changing situations, individuals recognize how ideas expressed in words take form as "food for thought" that revitalizes spiritual life. Through intuition and comprehension of metaphorical symbols, they interpret the mysteries behind ultimate reality.

Not only methodologically but substantively as well, Schleiermacher synthesized apparent contradictions. To achieve redemption, Christians need to merge mind with body, thoughts with feelings, and especially their self-consciousness with God consciousness, defined as the complete dependence on God. Socially, he assumed a dependence of the individual on the society. For him, sin derived from false beliefs: the notion that individuals are independent of both God and each other and that the bodily self takes precedence over the spirit. As the embodiment of the God consciousness, Jesus inaugurated the reign of God—the new spiritual community based on divine love, which perfects wisdom. Rejecting Calvin's pessimistic view of eternal damnation for degenerates, Schleiermacher held that the Christian church must redeem (regenerate) all humanity. His belief in universal election led him to assume that God has selected everyone for eventual blessedness, even if at present all persons have yet to demonstrate their regeneration. At least, they have the potential for goodness. Affirming a congruence between justice and divine love, Schleiermacher believed that individual and societal redemption will eventually occur when justice merges with holiness (communion with God). Christians thus have the obligation to strive actively toward achieving the spiritual reign of God in this world, although its full realization remains incomplete.

Schleiermacher's interpretations of the New Testament have contemporary relevance for New Thought students and Social Gospel supporters. The two groups share his view that justice involves non-hierarchical relations, personal efficacy, and individualism. Within the church he sought a partnership between laity and clergy as well as extensive participation in decisionmaking. Opposing state censorship and repressive power by the Prussian secret police, he upheld civil liberties, a free press, citizenship rights for Jews, expanded freedom for peasants, high participation in political issues, a constitutional monarchy, church independence from state control, and governmental institutions that restrained each other's power. Rather than resignation to the status quo, personal efficacy shaped his views about the prospects for improving society. Accepting the dominant views of early nineteenth-century Germany, he remained less enthusiastic about gender equality as the basis for justice. Although he regarded men and women as sharing a common spiritual gender, he proposed that women incarnated divine feelings whereas men embodied cognition: thoughts, comprehension, and logic. The twin dimensions should complement and harmonize the others. Yet he stressed women's dominant role in the private domestic sphere where they raised a family and cared for children. For him, men must play the key role in government.

By contrast, New Thought and the Social Gospel place greater attention on the egalitarian basis of justice. New Thought students accept several individualist ideas of Schleiermacher. For them, thought becomes the guide to personal spiritual behavior when the individual merges the self-consciousness with the universal God consciousness. Rather than having any human characteristics, God represents an impersonal spirit of divine love and wisdom. Orthodox doctrines about Jesus' physical resurrection, his descent into hell, the ascent to heaven, his second coming, and the last judgment become for both Schleiermacher and New Thought adherents theologically invalid interpretations of the New Testament. Instead, they distinguish between Jesus as a historical human being and the living Christ presence that indwells each person as the Holy Spirit. The latter brings vitality, health, and harmony not only to the individual but also to society.

Social Gospelers focus attention on the communal dimensions of Schleiermacher's theology. They stress the political activities of Schleiermacher, who participated as a member of Berlin's Poverty Directorate, opposed the French occupation of Prussia (1806–13), served as editor of a political newspaper the *Prussian Correspondent* from 1813 to 1814, and challenged the king for pursuing unjust policies. Schleiermacher emphasized the need to redeem society not only from individual sins—self-deception, self-delusion about independence from God—but also from the collective sins inherited from previous generations that transmitted false consciousness via families, clans, tribes, nations, governments, and churches. The Christian church has a key role to play as a redemptive institution that regenerates society. Cooperating with laity, the clergy educate the public about the need to base justice on divine love and wisdom. As the expression of God's Spirit, Jesus for both Schleiermacher and Social Gospel theologians functions as a teacher, healer, prophet, and redeemer (see Crouter 2005:177–91; DeVries and Gerrish 2005; Helmer 2005a, 2005b, 2005c, 2005d; Mariña 2004, 2005; Schleiermacher 1963, 2003; Thandeka 2005; Tice 2005, 2006; Vial 2005; Wyman 2005).

Jesus, Justice, and the Challenge to Elitist Rule

In his calls for justice, Jesus mounted a challenge to elitist rule. When he proclaimed the "good news" about the reign of God to his followers during the early first century CE, the Roman empire fused political, economic, and cultural power. Politically, the ruling class comprised several groups. Roman conquerors at the top and below them their allies in the Herodian dynasty dominated the society. The priestly aristocrats governed the Jerusalem temple. At the bottom the scribes and Pharisees interpreted the Torah. Brutal coercion maintained the system, as evidenced by executions, imprisonment, massacres of peasant revolts by Roman troops, and crucifixions that brought a shameful death to poor people, slaves, and political rebels who threatened Rome's imperial rule. Although policy formation occurred in Rome, indirect rule delegated policy implementation to regional officials, such as prefects in Judea and the Herodian family in Galilee. Some pluralism enabled the Jews to retain their religious observances, so long as they showed minimal loyalty to the empire. Bureaucrats and military officers coordinated this global empire that extended throughout parts of Southern Europe, North Africa, and the Middle East. Despite the extensive coercion, the government's scope of power remained limited in this agricultural society. Whereas the state focused on defense, security, tax collection, and construction of an infrastructure (roads, communications, some urban construction), villages had the responsibility to provide local social services to rural residents, who comprised around 90 percent of the population.

The class system reflected the same gap that split the rulers from the ruled. The same groups that wielded political dominance—Roman officials, chief priests, the Herodian family dynasty—also retained key economic resources, including finances, land, and access to patrons' wealth. Landed elites exploited the peasantry, especially tenant farmers and unskilled day laborers who worked for the landlords. High taxes, tribute, and tithes paid to Rome, the priestly temple aristocracy, and the Herodian dynasty impoverished the farmers. Dysfunctional consequences resulted from some urban development and elite attempts behind commercialized agriculture. Herod the Great (40–4 BCE) and his son Herod Antipas who ruled Galilee from 4 BCE to 39 CE built luxurious palaces, temples, new cities (Tiberias, Sepphoris), and massive fortresses. These urban construction projects widened the income gap between the cities and villages. Taxes needed to finance the incipient modernization impoverished the people. Suffering from high taxes and interest charges, many small farmers faced debt and loss of their land. Beggars and unskilled day laborers became numerous among the destitute. The call for food and release from debt resounded among rural and urban poor.

Widespread cultural humiliation pervaded the Roman empire. The Romans viewed their subjects as inferior people—illiterate peasants with no knowledge of Roman and Greek civilization. State cults of priests cemented loyalty to Caesar, whom they regarded as divine Lord and Savior who brought peace, justice, and order. Temples, rituals, and festivals encouraged the populace to worship Caesar as their protector. Even the Jewish temple priests in Jerusalem had to make sacrifices not only to Yahweh but to Caesar as well (Friesen 2005; Horsley 2005a, 2005b; Horsley and Silberman 1997:9–42).

Challenging this elitist system, Jesus played several roles that exemplified an alternative vision. As prophet, he declared God's will for justice, specified the ethical basis of a redeemed community, and denounced the hypocrisy of religious leaders allied with the Roman bureaucracy. Following in the footsteps of Moses, Jesus renewed the Mosaic covenant, reinterpreting it for his time. According to this covenant declared to Moses on Mount Sinai, Yahweh commanded the

Jewish people to articulate their sacred beliefs to the world, obey God's will, and demonstrate this obedience in their law, ethical actions, and care for others. In exchange, Yahweh would grant them the blessings of land, abundance (milk and honey), peace, and justice. Jesus reiterated this message by blessing the righteous but denouncing hypocrites who venerated power, wealth, and status. As a teacher of wisdom, Jesus the rabbi used parables and aphorisms to make his ethical principles comprehensible to illiterate peasants. For him, the knowledge of God's will deriving from Wisdom reflects the eternal light that illuminates the fallible mind about the meaning and purpose of life. As a healer, Jesus cured the sick and exorcised demons. Signifying his resistance to Roman rule, he identified the evil spirits ("demons") with the Roman legions, the military forces that dominated society. As a "suffering servant" mentioned by the prophet Isaiah (53:50), Jesus embodied the suffering Israel who would also redeem other nations. Jesus' followers saw him as a faithful witness to God's will—one whom God will vindicate (Herzog 2000, 2005a).

Jesus affirmed spiritual values that contradicted the dominant ideology of the Roman empire. Service took precedence over domination. Egalitarianism toward the poor and other marginals supplanted elitist rule by foreign kings and priestly aristocrats. Cooperation and fellowship in a new spiritual community—the reign of God inaugurated by Jesus—replaced the competitive individualism and search for material gain under Roman rule. Personal efficacy based on faith in God assumed priority over fatalism and resignation to the status quo. Rejecting the notion of a warrior God, Jesus proclaimed nonviolence as the most effective, desirable way to change structural conditions (Freyne 2004:97–114; Herzog 2005a, 2005b; Krause 2005).

Jesus' rejection of hierarchy became expressed in his opposition to Roman rulers and their collaborators—the Herodian dynasty and the Jerusalem priestly aristocracy. For him, liberation meant a commitment to love and service, not hatred and domination. The story of the exodus from Egyptian oppression, as well as the prophetic teachings of the prophet Micah, influenced Jesus' attitude toward authority. Justice, mercy, and humility before Yahweh represent the prime spiritual/political virtues. As Micah (6:8) asked: "What does the Lord require of you but to act justly, to love kindness, and to walk humbly with your God?" Denouncing Herod Antipas as a "fox"—a sly but dangerous tetrarch—Jesus urged his disciples to serve others, not dominate them:

> You know that among the Gentiles rulers lord it over their subjects and the great make their authority felt. It shall not be so with you. Among you, whoever wants to be great must be your servant, and whoever wants to be first must be the slave of all—just as the Son of Man did not come to be served but to serve and to give his life as a ransom for many.
> (Matthew 20:25–28)

Service based on *agape* (divine sacrificial love), not coercive force, would pervade interpersonal relations in the Kingdom of God, which Jesus had inaugurated during the present and would emerge more fully in the future. Under this new spiritual reign, everyone would show loyalty to God, not to any human king like Caesar. Rather than urging Jews to pay taxes to Rome, Jesus gave an ambiguous reply: "Pay Caesar what belongs to Caesar and God what belongs to God" (Mark 12:17). The denarius coin used to pay the Roman poll tax carried the images of the emperor Tiberius and this inscription: "Tiberius Caesar, Son of the divine Augustus." Jesus implied that Caesar deserved only a puny coin with his image. The primary loyalty should go toward God, who created human beings in the divine image. Jesus clashed not only with the Roman rulers but with their Jewish clients the Herodians and chief priests. The cleansing of the Jerusalem temple challenged the power of the corrupt priests who managed currency exchanges, regulated temple trade, and exploited the poor, particularly destitute widows. In the reign of God, however, abundance and sharing of economic resources prevail (Crossan 2007:97–142; Herzog 2004, 2005a:182–92).

The inversionary discourse of Jesus upset dominant role relationships, so that role reversals occurred. Defying the usual hierarchical authority in first-century Palestine, he affirmed the need for the last to become first and for the humble to become exalted (Mark 9:35; Luke 14:11). In the topsy-turvy parable about the feisty widow (Luke 18:1–8), women gained equal rights with men to exert public pressure for justice. Conventional norms dictated that women defer to elites, rarely appear in public courts, and remain confined to their private family roles. The parable, however, challenged these conventional obligations. The assertive widow with no political power, wealth, or status confronted the corrupt, unjust judge. Only after public pleading did the judge grant the woman legal protection. Bound by convention, he feared loss of social esteem from male elites. Jesus' parable suggested that even though God grants justice to powerless persons like widows, they must act to receive this justice (Cotter 2005).

The teachings of Jesus highlighted the egalitarian role transformations that reflected his interpretations about justice. Inclusiveness took precedence over an exclusive interpretation about those groups who merited justice. He particularly appealed to the marginals and outcasts: women, children, the poor, beggars, lepers, the disabled, prostitutes, tax collectors, and Samaritans—those regarded as impure sinners by the religious and political establishment. Denouncing the rich who served Mammon, not God, Jesus proclaimed the need for greater economic equality. He reiterated passages from Leviticus 15–16, Deuteronomy, and Isaiah 60–61 about Jubilee and Sabbath obligations. According to the Mosaic covenant, leaders have the duty to aid the poor, secure Sabbath rest for all, cancel debts, charge no high-interest loans, free slaves, grant land to the original familial owners, and secure the restoration of the land to Israel from their oppressors. Even if the Jewish rulers failed to honor these obligations every seven or fifty years, they remained valuable standards for evaluating the leaders' actual behavior. Jesus indicated that both the Romans and their Jewish collaborators had violated these ethical criteria of justice by living in luxury. His concept of the reign of God envisioned economic abundance, sharing of economic resources, and messianic banquets attended by even the contemporary outcasts who heard his message and followed his teachings (Cook 2003; Grassi 2000; Hellerman 2000; Hendriks 2005, 2006: 1–73, 132–44, 319–32; Knauth 2004).

Jesus' inclusive outlook extended to women's rights and family relationships. Including women in his movement and welcoming them to his meals, he viewed men and women as sharing a common humanity that owed loyalty to only one divine father, not to any human father, lord, or emperor. He rejected divorce that favored men who regarded their wives as personal property. Reflecting his elevation of the spiritual family over the traditional married family, Jesus in Matthew 19:12 even praised stigmatized eunuchs—those with an ambiguous sexual identity—as welcome in the Kingdom of God (Corley 2002; Hester 2005; Talbott 2006).

The inclusiveness of Jesus' interpretation also appeared in his notion that the reign of God applied to all peoples, not only to Jews. Although preaching mainly to village Galileans, he included in the Kingdom of God Gentiles who accepted his message. As the prophetic agent of God, he appealed first to the lost sheep of Israel. From his conception, Gentiles would form a part of the reconstituted Israel (Bird 2005).

Instead of emphasizing self-interest and competitive individualism, Jesus, like the Hebrew prophets, reaffirmed spiritual communalism. His followers formed a new spiritual family united by a dedication to follow God's will. As servants of God, they imitated the life of Jesus by showing total dependence on God. In the transformative kingdom of God that Jesus had initiated, solidarity derived from a renewed covenant that linked spiritual personhood to a focus on cooperation, reciprocity, generosity, and mutual support. Service to God blended with service to others as the ideal standards of justice.

Rather than fatalism, apathy, and resignation, personal efficacy accompanied the stress on communal justice. The four Gospels record Jesus' rejection of self-blame and his praise for personal efficacy based on trust in God. Showing grace (free gifts) to all, God makes the sun rise on both good and evil people and sends the rain to fall not only on the just but also on the unjust (Matthew 5:45). Peasant poverty stems from neither divine disfavor nor personal laziness but from actions by arbitrary landlords (Matthew 20:1–15). Jesus promises many concrete benefits to those who demonstrate their faith in God. Instead of behaving like a punitive warrior-king, Yahweh operates as an active creator God who brings enlightenment to people who obey divine will and accept his free gifts. Although individuals often act in a sinful way by becoming alienated from the spirit, God created them in a divine spiritual image; hence, they have the potential for good behavior and through repentance can actively change their conditions. God grants food and clothing to those who give priority to the Kingdom of God and its justice (Luke 12:22–31). Faith in God can move mountains and heal the sick (Matthew 17:20; Mark 5:34). Salvation comes even to the rich through divine power: "With God all things are possible" (Mark 10:27). The Gospel of John highlights the key role that Jesus plays to his followers. Through active cooperation with God and belief in Jesus' words, individuals can attain great achievements: "The one who believes in me will also do the works that I do and, in fact, will do greater works than these, because I am going to the Father. . . . If in my name you ask for anything, I will do it" (John 14:12, 14).

Despite these promises about the personal efficacy that will come to those showing faith in God and Jesus, the crucifixion brought temporary despair to his disciples. Some expected a messiah who would act as a victorious warrior-king marching into Jerusalem on a stallion and triggering the overthrow of Roman oppression. Instead, Jesus entered Jerusalem on a donkey and experienced the fate of a suffering servant who endured a shameful execution by crucifixion. Political liberation, economic well-being, and cultural dignity seemed impossible to secure. Faced with the dire situation, Jesus' followers needed to gain reassurance against the threats, to secure meaning behind the political injustices, and to secure social support for their beliefs. For despair to transform into hope, they had to reframe the issue and change the Roman script. The several Jesus movements that emerged after the crucifixion expressed divergent interpretations. Nearly all perceived the cross not as a sign of Roman humiliation but a symbol of spiritual victory that overcame or "crossed out" oppression. Taking an apocalyptic view, many looked for the imminent return of Jesus the Messiah, the restoration of Israel, and the establishment of the Kingdom of God on earth. John's Gospel saw the reign of God as dwelling within specific persons and among the assemblies of believers. To many followers, after his death Jesus as a historical person became less important than the living Christ presence. As the movements expanded beyond Galilee and Jerusalem to include other parts of the Roman empire, they gathered social support not only from Greek-speaking Jews but also from Gentiles. With the growing support, despair weakened. Even when suffering from Roman persecution, especially during the last four decades of the first century CE, believers gained reassurance from these political threats. Causal attributions gave new meaning to the crucifixion. Followed by the resurrection, it signified spiritual victory over supposed defeat, nonviolent justice over violent injustice. For the Jews who believed in Jesus as the promised Messiah, the resurrection symbolized the redemption of Israel from oppression. To the Gentiles, it meant eternal life for his followers (Hurtado 2004; McGrath 2006).

Paul, Justice, and Citizenship in Heaven

Twenty years after the crucifixion, the apostle Paul emerged as the major interpreter of the new faith. After the Roman destruction of Jerusalem from 65 to 70 CE, he replaced the original disciples of Jesus as the authoritative foundation for the religious assemblies emerging throughout the Roman empire, especially the Middle East, North Africa, Asia Minor (Asian Turkey), and Southern Europe. A Pharisee, Paul knew Greek and perceived his role as a Jewish envoy who proclaimed his interpretation of Jesus' mission to Gentiles, especially those who attended synagogue services on the Sabbath. Paul's mystical vision portrayed Jesus as the Christ (Messiah, the Anointed One). He reflected the wisdom of God. To his followers, the Holy Spirit imparted the mystical, mysterious teachings of Wisdom. Paul saw Christ Jesus mediating between heaven and earth. The Heavenly Man made in the image of God became incarnated in the Messiah on earth. As the second Adam, he brought salvation and eternal life not only to the Jews but to the whole world. By supplying solidarity to his believers, the heavenly Christ became more important to Paul than the historical person Jesus, whom he had never met (Andrain and Apter 1995:77–79; Witherington 2000:293–333).

Jesus and Paul shared many similar beliefs. Challenging the dominant religious and political orthodoxies, they sought fundamental transformations of individual behavior and sociopolitical conditions. Opposed to power and materialism, they affirmed the priority of humility, generosity, service, compassion, and justice over pride, greed, domination, injustice, and hatred of enemies. Both drew a sharp contrast between the Roman empire and the spiritual realm: the Kingdom of God for Jesus, the commonwealth in heaven for Paul. Love of God and neighbors formed the essence of the Law (Wills 2006).

Despite these similarities, Jesus and Paul took a different perspective toward God, the individual, society, and government. Whereas Jesus focused his activities on Galilean villagers, Paul communicated his letters to several cities throughout the Roman empire: Rome, Corinth, Thessalonica, and Philippi. Jesus appealed to the outcasts of Jewish society; however, Paul concentrated on urban Jews and Gentiles who worshiped in the synagogues and who had assimilated Greek culture (Crossan 2007:152–58; Stark 2006:119–37). Jesus stressed the need for a total commitment to God. Paul highlighted the redeeming role of Jesus as savior of all humanity. Even if Jesus recognized the sinful behavior of those who "missed the mark" and needed to change their behavior, he saw great potentiality in his followers who pledged their faith in God. From a more pessimistic outlook, Paul placed greater emphasis on human evil, wickedness, and sin. Jesus not only denounced religious authorities for their hypocrisy and self-righteousness but voiced a less deferential attitude toward Roman political authority than did Paul. Avoiding entrapment about the obligation to pay taxes to Rome, Jesus implied that Caesar deserved only a puny dinarius, not loyalty or acceptance of his divine right to rule. Feeling vulnerable to the political disorder and tax riots that Roman officials blamed on Jewish and Christian communities, Paul pragmatically urged his followers to obey government authorities. God had instituted them. Ideally, they functioned as God's agents, punishing criminals and promoting the common good. Political obedience also involved paying personal and property taxes, as Romans 13:1–7 mandated. Yet for Paul divine love within the emerging Christian assemblies took priority over reverence for Roman authority (Engberg-Pedersen 2006; Horrell 2002; Voskuilen 2005).

In his letters, Paul stressed the basic differences between the kingdom of Caesar and the heavenly commonwealth of Christ Jesus. Whereas the Roman empire upheld a punitive, retributive, coercive form of justice, the spiritual reign of Christ affirmed procedural justice based on fairness, equity, goodness, and peace. For the Romans, peace emerged through conquest, war, and death. A rigid hierarchy maintained sharp distinctions that separated Roman citizens from noncitizens, masters from slaves, and divergent ethnic/religious groups from each other. Imperial cults legitimated this coercive, hierarchical rule. Patron-client ties viewed Caesar as the Patron of all Rome, the father of his country, and a human god who functioned as lord and savior for all. Images in temples, shrines, statues, and festivals signified loyalty to Caesar. Seeking domination over conquered peoples, Roman soldiers undertook sacrifices to gain victory for Rome—the *Pax Romana*. Inequality accompanied the focus on coercion and hierarchy. Even if female citizens secured rights to own property, end a marriage, testify in court, and even hold public office, wealthy men sexually exploited poorer women and teenage boy slaves. Prostitution, pornography, and nudity elevated the physical body above the spiritual being. Lower-status groups felt little efficacy about overcoming their dire conditions. Fatalism reinforced acquiescence to Roman rule.

Paul's epistles challenged these Roman images with a less hierarchical, elitist, and fatalistic interpretation of justice. His inversionary discourse communicated sharp role reversals and values. From the Pauline perspective, peace emerged from justice through the grace of God and the sacrificial role of Christ Jesus. The crucified and resurrected Jesus secured eternal life for believers. Through the cross, the dishonorable became honorable. God transformed the shameful injustice into divine justice. Despite Roman intentions, the execution of Jesus led to the victory of divine foolishness, humility, and apparent weakness over Roman laws, pride, and military power. Religious assemblies organized by Paul viewed Christ as their redeemer, lord, and savior. God, not Caesar, functioned as their patron. Rather than paying for services, the clients—believers in Christ—received their benefits as free gifts of God. They owed ultimate loyalty to God and the Messiah Jesus. Grace and faith would eventually regenerate both the individual and society from contemporary evils.

The sharp contrasts that Paul drew between human laws and divine justice illustrate his transformative position toward the Roman political system. As a Pharisee who interpreted the Hebrew scriptures (the Greek Septuagint) for the first century CE, he regarded the Mosaic legal obligations as superior to the Roman laws. Yet the latter especially revealed the limitations of human justice that had legitimated Jesus' execution. According to Paul, Roman laws rested on coercive power and violence. Corrupt outcomes ensued when Roman officials used their power to oppress the weak and vulnerable, as indicated by frequent crucifixions of innocent victims. A punitive orientation enacted retribution against those found guilty. Retaliation tried to deter legal violations. Human justice applied to a limited segment of the population, mainly citizens and free persons, not aliens or slaves—the vulnerable members of Roman society. Roman law thus sought to reinforce the dominant political order. By contrast, divine justice of God transcends imperfections of human justice based on the Mosaic and particularly Roman laws. Divine justice stems from God's love as expressed in love of neighbors, strangers, and even enemies. Rather than based on good deeds (compliance), it comes to everyone as a free gift from God. Generosity and harmony supersede the competitive struggle for scarce goods. Faithful obedience to divine justice occurs when believers incorporate the mind of Christ Jesus in their own bodies and imitate the deeds of their Messiah—the exemplar for their own behavior. In the organic community that remains faithful to Christ Jesus, a new creation, both individual and social, emerges. Paul expects that the unchanging, absolute ideals of divine justice will transform the whole world. The redeemed Israel will include Jews, Gentiles, all nations, and every religion. According to Paul's renewed covenant, redemption extends not only to Jews but also to Gentiles, who no longer have to accept the Mosaic laws about circumcision and diet. Instead, their commitment to Christ Jesus secures their salvation within the reconstituted Israel (Wright 2005:108–29).

Paul's organic metaphors drew parallels between the human body and the spiritual body. He perceived the personal body as a temple of the Holy Spirit. Hence, it must avoid sexual impurities linked to incest, prostitution, rape, and exploitive sex between men and boys (1 Corinthians 5:11, 6:19, 7:1–39; Romans 1:26–27). Unlike Romans who regarded fertility as the major reason for marriage, Paul believed that celibacy represents the ideal, given the imminent end of the world and its transformation into a spiritual community. Married partners should treat each other with mutual respect. The same functional interdependence and empathy must unite the followers of Christ Jesus. Paul perceived believers as a messianic body formed around the Messiah Jesus:

> All of you are God's children because of your faith in Christ Jesus. And when you were baptized, it was as though you had put on Christ in the same way that you put on new clothes. Faith in Christ Jesus is what makes each of you equal with each other, whether you are a Jew or a Greek, a slave or a free person, a man or a woman. So if you belong to Christ, you are now part of Abraham's family, and you will be given what God has promised.
>
> (Galatians 3:26–29)

Baptism and the Eucharist supplied cohesion to the organic community. Through the baptismal ritual of purification, members shared the death of the old person, a spiritual rebirth, and union with Christ. The Eucharist celebrated Christ's presence and expressed hope for his early return. Whereas temple feasts under the imperial cult offered food to different people at different times and places, the Eucharist meal gave the same food to all people at similar times—a practice that symbolized egalitarian inclusiveness. Sharing of economic resources also remained the ideal for the religious assemblies organized by Paul. From these organic communities—the forerunner of the heavenly commonwealth—he saw emerging a new spiritual person who shows empathy for other people, not only a concern for the self (Philippians 2:4). Community well-being thus took precedence over an interpretation of justice based on self-interest and individual merit.

Even if Paul's interpretation of the social body rested on an inclusive orientation, he expressed ambivalence about the status of slaves and women. On the one hand, he advocated their egalitarian inclusion in the spiritual community. The letter to Philemon (1:15) called the slave Onesimus a "beloved brother." Women played key leadership roles as apostles, prophets, and teachers in the early religious assemblies, such as those in Corinth and Rome. Examples included Prisca, Junia, Mary, Tryphaena, Tryphosa, Phoebe, Julia, Olympas, and Chloe (1 Corinthians 1:11; Romans 16:1–15). On the other hand, Paul accepted some local hierarchical customs about slaves and women. The letter to Philemon gave no explicit instructions that urged him to release Onesimus from slavery. Local customs dictated the need for women to wear a head covering when they prophesied. Yet some women in the Corinthian assemblies refused to follow that tradition, which presumably implied a refusal to acknowledge men's superior authority (Wills 2006:89–104). Paul recommended that the Corinthians show respect for each other's feelings, peacefully resolve the dispute, and remember that God created all humans. Both men and women should unite in their commitment to God and Christ Jesus: "In Christ, woman is not different from man, and man is not different from woman. Woman may come from man [Genesis 2:23], but man is born of woman. And both come from God" (1 Corinthians 11:11–12).

Paul's acquiescent stance toward the Roman political system also reflected his ambivalence toward hierarchical authority. For him, believers in Christ had begun to live in a divine community outside the Roman empire. He never assumed that loyalty to the state took precedence over loyalty to God. Worship of the state meant idolatry. Yet, for prudential reasons, he urged respect for political rulers, who bring some degree of order, however imperfect. Rome had established a worldwide communications and transportation network that enabled

Paul and other apostles to spread their message to Gentiles throughout Southern Europe, the Middle East, North Africa, and Asia Minor. He assumed an imminent collapse of the Roman empire. Jesus Christ would soon return, abolish all government powers, and establish the Kingdom of God ruled by God and Jesus the Messiah (1 Corinthians 15:20–25).

During the interim period, Paul sketched a clear distinction between members of the spiritual community and outsiders. Insiders expressed a spiritual transformation, mental renewal, and ethical regeneration. Their lives manifested spiritual values: eternal life, light, and love. Although they struggled against mortal sins, harmony pervaded the organic community. Justice revolved around service to God and neighbors. In contrast, those outside the organic community remained under the spell of the material world: death, darkness, and sin. Violence and evil brought injustice based on punitive retribution (see Belleville 2005; Berlinerblau 2005:106–08; Blumenfeld 2001; Crossan and Reed 2004; Heen 2004; Jeffers 2002; Segal 2006; Wright 2005).

Conclusion

This conflict between two different orders—the secular vs. the sacred, the coercive vs. the consensual—continued to shape theological interpretations after Paul's death during the early 60s CE. After the Romans destroyed Jerusalem in 70 CE, the Jesus movement relocated to Rome. Ties to Judaism weakened, as many Jews refused to accept Jesus as the Messiah. The synagogues split into factions that viewed Jesus as the promised Anointed One and those that disagreed. Intense conflicts also occurred between Jews and Gentiles who accepted Jesus as the Messiah. After Roman troops destroyed the Jewish temple in Jerusalem, the Gentiles gained supremacy. As Roman persecution, especially under emperors Nero (54–68) and Domitian (81–96), mounted against both Jews and the followers of Jesus in household gatherings, Gospel writers downplayed Roman responsibility for Jesus' crucifixion. Instead, they stressed disputes with the Pharisees, who actually shared many spiritual principles voiced by Jesus. As the first century ended, many believers in Christ Jesus no longer expected his immediate return, the abolition of the Roman political regime, and the establishment of the Kingdom of God on earth. Some Roman officials began accepting the new Christian faith. The bishop in Rome gradually consolidated his power over other bishops and became the pope—the holy father.

The Roman Catholic Church developed a hierarchical structure that diverged from the more spontaneous, egalitarian assemblies formed by earlier Jesus movements. Ecclesiastical bureaucratic offices superseded functional activities performed by diverse individuals, especially women. In 324 Constantine unified his control over the disintegrating Roman empire and became the first Christian emperor. A year later he instituted a council at Nicea that formulated basic Christian doctrines accepted as authoritative by the Church. During the era from 200 CE to 400, the Apostles' Creed and later the Nicene Creed became Church doctrines that proclaimed the holy catholic Church, the trinitarian God, the virgin birth of Jesus, his ascent into heaven, his second coming, and the resurrection of the dead. By the end of the fourth century, the Church recognized most of the books in the present New Testament as official canon. Along with secular government rulers, Catholic clergy emerged as the ruling elite. With an educated background, the clergy had the literacy to translate the Bible from Greek to Latin as well as to instruct the laity about biblical teachings. The Church gained state support and subsidies, including tax exemptions, land, funds for construction, and participation in state bureaucratic posts. The Roman government secured ecclesiastical authority for its rule. Whereas the early Jesus movements had stressed personal holiness, decentralization, and egalitarian interactions among members, the institutionalized Roman Catholic Church provided salvation through the priestly administration of the sacraments, operated a more hierarchical, centralized organization, and combined elitist rule with an inclusive, universal membership (Andrain and Apter 1995:79–80; Pottenger 2007:53–56).

Despite the bureaucratization of the Christian movement, the ideas of Jesus and Paul continued to shape later interpretations about justice. The contrasts between the Roman empire and the spiritual community, whether the Kingdom of God stressed by Jesus or the heavenly commonwealth portrayed by Paul, particularly influenced theologians. Shortly after the death of Constantine, the Christian theologian Augustine (354–430) portrayed a vision of two distinct societies—the Heavenly City and the earthly city—that resembled Paul's contrast between the Roman empire and the heavenly commonwealth. For Augustine, the City of God became a Christian utopia freed from all the evils Paul attributed to Roman political life: conflict, struggle, instability, corruption, oppression of the vulnerable, and injustice. From his perspective, the two cities represented divergent models of society. Whereas the earthly city loves the self, the Heavenly City loves God. In the earthly city, self-love leads to conflict, coercion, "the lust for domination," rule by powerful leaders, and scarce goods. Because of this obsession with coercive power, wealth, and social status (pride), no earthly state could ever attain true justice—conceived by Augustine as the rule of God over individuals, reason over the passions, and the soul over the body. Nevertheless, like Paul, he did perceive some positive results ensured by political regimes. Even if only the invisible City of God fulfilled eternal peace, the state could maintain order, harmony, and worldly peace. By incorporating unbelievers in the Roman Catholic Church, which imperfectly embodied the Heavenly City, the state would help the Church secure the salvation of individual souls. Yet only in the Heavenly City could people find true fellowship, community consensus, abundance, service to others, eternal peace, and especially divine justice (Augustine 1984; Wolin 2004:107–18).

Although Protestants rejected the ecclesiastical authority wielded by the Roman Catholic Church, they accepted many ideas linked to Paul, Augustine, and Jesus. During the sixteenth century, Martin Luther and John Calvin upheld the Augustinian view about the wicked nature of fallen individuals and the need for the state to repress evil, promote order, and enforce religious practice. The less hierarchical visions of Jesus and Paul shaped Social Gospelers and New Thought students during the twentieth century. Protestant Social Gospel ministers revitalized the prophetic messages of Jesus who drew a sharp distinction between the Kingdom of God and the Roman empire. Not only Protestants but also Catholic liberation theologians reiterated the need for struggle against the religious/political establishment as the way to overcome collective sins: political repression, economic exploitation, and cultural humiliation. Only through struggle could Christians realize the egalitarian ideals taught by Jesus. The Pauline emphasis on the disjunction between human legal justice and divine justice also influenced Social Gospel interpretations. By contrast, New Thought adherents focused greater attention on the individual, not the collectivity, on harmony, rather than conflict. For them, Jesus exemplified the ideal teacher who healed the sick, taught wisdom, and stressed personal efficacy with God as the most effective way to transcend human vulnerabilities. Like both Jesus and Paul, New Thought disciples affirmed the priority of spiritual virtues over materialism. Justice revolves around divine love, compassion, enlightenment, and care for others. It means mental renewal—transformation of the human mind by the mind of Christ Jesus and the indwelling Christ Spirit (Philippians 2:5). New Thought stresses the spiritual gifts praised by Paul in Galatians 5:22: "love, joy, peace, patience, kindness, generosity, faithfulness, gentleness, and self-control."

The interpretations of justice attributed to Jesus and Paul have diverged over the past 2,000 years. Even their early followers during the first century CE disputed the meanings of their teachings. Today riddles, contradictions, mysteries, and paradoxes confound our understanding. Over 200 years before Jesus, Ben Sira, a wisdom teacher in Jerusalem, prescribed the obligations of the scribe, who must meditate on the mysteries of scripture, ascertain the "hidden meanings of proverbs," and explain the obscure meaning of parables (Sirach 39:2–3, 7). As an enigmatic teacher of wisdom, Jesus despaired about the failure of his disciples to comprehend the meaning of his numerous parables, even though he had explicated to them the mysteries of God's kingdom (Mark 4:13, 8:17, 21; Matthew 13:10–17). The mysteries of Paul's epistles stimulated even greater disputes. Later generations gave conflicting interpretations to scriptural messages not only because they disagreed about the precise meanings of such ambiguous concepts as justice, love, faith, and equality but because they selected different biblical passages for emphasis. To later theologians, certain texts seemed most salient to their spiritual priorities and most relevant to the structural context in which they wrote. Hence, as Friedrich Schleiermacher explained, interpretations of justice scarcely reveal only one literal meaning. Instead, the pluralist, symbolic, metaphorical interpretations change with the historical context. Language, economic stratification, the power of political institutions, the role of religious associations, the influence of the mass media that communicates biblical messages, and the importance of specific cultural values to the audience all influence spiritual meanings. These contextual variables clarify the ideas about justice elaborated by Social Gospelers and New Thought students, which the next three chapters will compare.

3

WALTER RAUSCHENBUSCH
Prophet of the Social Gospel

> Freedom, justice, solidarity are among the aims of the social gospel.... The social gospel ... feels the need of present inspiration and of living prophetic spirits in order to lead humanity toward the Kingdom of God.... Some sense of antagonism between the will of God and the present order of things is necessary to ignite the spirit of the prophet.
>
> (Walter Rauschenbusch)

In his 1909 short story "South of the Slot," Jack London narrated a tale of role reversals. A professor of sociology at the University of California in Berkeley during the early 1900s, Frederick Drummond led two lives. At the university he adopted a cold, inhibited manner toward his students and wrote dry academic treatises that celebrated capitalist efficiency, hard work, productivity, and supremacy of the corporation over the factory worker. As a skilled linguist, he tried to explicate the differences between metaphors and metonymies, between semantics and semiotics. South of the slot, however, Professor Drummond became a different person—Big Bill Totts, who used a different lingo than did Frederick. The "slot" signified a crack that ran through the center of Market Street in San Francisco. North of this crack stood the upper class, fancy hotels, expensive restaurants, and large department stores. South of the slot dwelled the working class amid slums, factories, machine shops, cheap boarding houses, and small family markets. In this part of the city, Big Bill abandoned his inhibitions, cold manner, formal speech, and stiff posture. Known at Berkeley as "Cold-Storage," Bill became famous for his warmth, emotionalism, and spontaneity. Jack London described him: "Down below he was 'Big' Bill Totts, who could drink and smoke, and slang and fight, and be an all-around favorite." As his contacts with the working class lengthened, an internal conflict arose between "Drummond, the sane and conservative sociologist, and Bill Totts, the class conscious and bellicose union workingman" (London 1986:225, 234). As Frederick Drummond, he had planned to marry Catherine Van Vorst, the wealthy daughter of the philosophy department chairman at UC. After living south of Market, Bill fell in love with Mary Condon, president of the local glove workers' union. He married her, fought police protecting scab workers, and later led a strike staged by cooks and waiters. The professor had disappeared into the labor ghetto, emerging in a new proletarian role, voicing unorthodox ideas, and speaking a different argot than found on the Berkeley campus.

Even if Walter Rauschenbusch hardly shared the socialist interpretations of Jack London, both authors rejected the injustice and economic inequalities produced by capitalist industrialization during the early twentieth century. Unlike Frederick Drummond, Walter Rauschenbusch never abandoned his academic career after he served from 1886 to 1896 as a Baptist minister to German immigrants in New York City's "Hell's Kitchen"—an experience that shaped his views about justice for low-income workers. At the end of this ministry before becoming a professor at Rochester Theological Seminary, he published two articles in the *American Journal of Sociology*. London, however, disdained the life of an academic intellectual. Although he and Rauschenbusch stressed the need for a more humanistic, compassionate, just, and egalitarian society, they disagreed about the most ethical, effective methods to attain socialism. For London, class conflict, not compromises with the capitalists, represented the appropriate way to reduce exploitation and secure proletarian strength. Based on the ideas of Darwin, Spencer, and Nietzsche, the survival of the fittest lay behind his stress on human conflict. As a Baptist prophet of the social gospel, Rauschenbusch affirmed Christian dimensions of socialism, which he regarded as an ethical movement to realize the Kingdom of God on earth and the ideals of Jesus through gradual, nonviolent procedures. He reconciled the liberal stress on science, evolutionary progress, economic equality, civil liberties, and opposition to religious dogma with a Pietist belief in the need for spiritual rebirth, personal conversion, and communion with God as the best way to regenerate society (Bowman 2007).

Capitalist Modernization and the Progressive Movement

During the period from 1890 through 1917, when Walter Rauschenbusch conducted his most important activities as minister, university professor, author, and lecturer, capitalist modernization shaped all dimensions of life in the United States. Economically, industrialization advanced as the proportion of workers employed in manufacturing and service jobs increased while the share of farmers declined from 50 percent in 1870 to 27 percent by 1913 (Maddison 1995:253). Along with the industrializing trend came greater urbanization when farmers left the rural hinterlands to seek employment in the cities. Owned by national chains, urban department stores became numerous. Expenditures on consumer goods rose. Concentrated industries expanded. Globalization of trade and capital investment brought consumer goods from overseas to the United States. Widespread immigration from Western and Eastern Europe added to the urban work force. U.S. capital investment overseas went mainly to Canada, Australia, New Zealand, Western Europe, and Latin America. Developments in communications and transportation enlarged the variety of ideas beyond the farms and small towns. The telegraph, telephone, railroad, automobile, airplane, and radio enabled people to travel and communicate farther than ever before.

Politically, modernization involved the growth of the nation-state as it expanded overseas and carried out domestic activities linked to industrialization. At both the state and national levels, governments grew more bureaucratic. Professionalized civil services began to emerge during the late nineteenth century, when the national Department of Interior, Department of Agriculture, Department of Commerce, and Department of Labor, along with regulatory agencies, promoted economic development. Although the U.S. governments still concentrated on defense, internal security, and government subsidies to businesses boosting industrial growth, the provision of social services grew slightly more important. Whereas the major national government benefits supplied veterans' pensions, the Progressive movement encouraged increased state government services such as workers' compensation and mothers' pensions.

Culturally, modernization accelerated the growth of populist and individualist values. New Thought groups stressed individual fulfillment of one's highest aspirations. Through the development of their spiritual consciousness, individuals would supposedly achieve a renewed mind leading to health, happiness, and prosperity. They needed no ecclesiastical institutions to mediate between themselves and God. The Social Gospel movement, trade unions, socialists, Populists, and Progressives placed greater attention on the collective sources of injustice, especially elitist practices. They challenged elitist rule by business conglomerates, "trusts," corrupt party machines, and religious institutions, particularly the Roman Catholic Church. The Progressives assumed that a transformed economic environment would secure the realization of people's potentialities. Yet populism and individualism extended mainly to people with a Western European background. Excluded from "the people," African Americans, Native Americans, and Asian immigrants secured fewer individual rights (Hays 1995; McGerr 2003:182–218).

What consequences arose from the economic modernization that spurred the growth of the Progressive movement during the 1890–1915 era? Between 1800 and 2000, the 1870–1913 period experienced the second highest per person growth rate: 1.82 percent compared to 2.45 percent in 1950–1973 (Maddison 2003:263). Yet along with this fairly rapid growth came busts that followed booms. Severe depressions occurred in 1873–79, 1882–85, and 1893–97. Slow growth also prevailed from 1906 through 1915. As a result, unemployment rose under the bust. There is a lack of accurate data, but joblessness rates as a share of the civilian private nonfarm labor force ranged from 10 percent to 17 percent from 1893 to 1899. During 1908–16 it averaged 10 percent a year. Whereas consumer prices declined in the 1890s, they rose in 1909–16 before U.S. government entry into World War I. Hence, the real wages of all workers, especially the unskilled, fell. People from the Northeast and Midwest who worked in such urban industries as steel, construction, coal mining, and textiles particularly suffered from declining real wages and high unemployment. As a result, the income gap separating rich from poor became severe. The top 1 percent of income holders gained the major benefits from economic growth emerging from high stock values. Several conditions contributed to the income inequalities. In 1913 regressive taxes mainly came from property and sales, not from personal income. All governmental expenditures totaled only 6.4 percent of the gross national product. Of this proportion, spending on social services (primarily veterans' pensions as well as limited retirement benefits and health) amounted to 2.7 percent of GNP. Corporations controlled government institutions and political parties. Labor unions enrolled only 11 percent of the nonfarm labor force (Carter et al. 2006:2–33, 2–56, 2–82, 2–257, 2–734, 3–25, 3–79, 3–158; Dewhurst and Associates 1955:578, 583, 627, 959; Piketty and Saez 2003; U.S. Bureau of the Census 1975:126, 211, 340–41, 1115, 1122).

The Progressive movement secured its greatest success from 1900 through 1917 when its policy proposals responded to the dysfunctional consequences of modernization, especially the high unemployment and income inequality. Progressives included various groups: socialists, unionists, social workers, economists, sociologists, and ministers like Walter Rauschenbusch. Presidents Theodore Roosevelt and Woodrow Wilson favored many Progressive programs that expanded national government power to regulate corporations and implement more social service benefits for workers. Although diverging on their stands toward specific policies, nearly all Progressives supported an egalitarian interpretation of justice (Bender 2006:246–95). Individualism merged with collectivism. Political efficacy took precedence over fatalistic resignation to the status quo. Yet aspects of hierarchy contradicted the populist rejection of deference to established authority exercised by conglomerates, party machines, and ecclesiastical institutions. For most Progressives, economic equality assumed priority over gender and particularly ethnic equality. They favored higher wages, shorter working hours, collective bargaining by unions, higher pensions, accident insurance, disability insurance, workmen's compensation, and greater worker participation in business management. All these proposals represented an attempt to humanize capitalism and expand industrial democracy. Progressive income taxes on individuals and corporations, along with government regulation of businesses, further reflected the Progressive movement to reduce corporate control over government and attain a more egalitarian income distribution. Groups like the Feminist Alliance and the Equality League of Self-Supporting Women sought female independence, day nurseries for children, maternity leave for married women, and mothers' pensions. Single women, however, gained less support from these feminist organizations. Men who dominated most Progressive associations showed even less enthusiasm for gender equality; instead, they stressed economic equality mainly for white male workers. Upholding ethnic segregation and exclusion from equal economic participation, nearly all Progressives opposed greater rights for African Americans, Native Americans, and immigrants from Asia.

Political populism combined with a hierarchical orientation. On the one hand, Progressives backed direct participation by voters in the political process, including direct election of senators, the initiative, recall, referendum, and women's suffrage. On the other hand, Progressives wanted a more bureaucratized government led by experts, managers, and educated professionals. Independent regulatory agencies, commissions, and city managers would gain the authority formerly exercised by elected government officials, whom the Progressives claimed behaved in a corrupt, partisan way. Despite their call for increased populist control over the state governments, they backed a more powerful nation-state ruled by "impartial" experts who would secure order, efficient management, and technological advances—all signs of scientific progress.

The Progressive emphasis on collectivism superseded a commitment to individualism, however important the movement for personal fulfillment. Opposed to the "rugged" individualism and ruthless competition proclaimed by capitalists, the Progressives placed priority on harmony, homogeneity, and the common good over conflict, pluralist diversity, and private interests. Sexual freedom received limited support, as exemplified by support for traditional marriage and rejection of prostitution, labeled "white slavery." According to the Progressives, men should play the dominant role in public life. Women ideally confined their main duties to the home, where they cared for their husbands and children. Particularly when the United States joined the European war in 1917, most Progressives, if not all, supported the crusade by the Wilson administration to make the world "safe for democracy." Dissenters against the war, such as the Industrial Workers of the World, anarchists, socialists, and communists, faced loss of their civil liberties to oppose the war. The 1917 Espionage Act and the 1918 Sedition Act passed under the Wilson government curtailed individual rights, especially those of radical dissidents. Under the "Red Scare" of 1919–20, the federal administration deported many opponents of war participation. Political conformity squashed individual freedom (Foner 1998:139–93; McGerr 2003).

Rather than submitting to a fatalistic orientation toward political life, Progressives voiced high efficacy, especially by middle-class, educated professionals who supported science and a powerful nation-state, if not expanded participation by radical dissenters. Hostile to fundamentalist Protestantism that rejected scientific progress, especially evolutionary theory, Christian Progressives wanted to apply the optimistic ethics of Jesus to economic issues and personal interactions. Downplaying any apocalyptic images voiced by Jesus, they sought to realize on earth some aspects of the Kingdom of God.

Even if Walter Rauschenbusch refrained from supporting all these Progressive ideas, he affirmed the stress on economic equality, personal efficacy, collective sins that caused personal misery, and the ambivalence toward hierarchy. Like most religious activists, he modified his views over time as the historical context changed. At the end of his life in 1918, he gave greater support to women's equality than he had shown during the late 1890s. Although his support for socialism declined around 1917, he remained adamant in his enthusiasm for social justice. Opposed to the powerful nationalism that backed U.S. intervention in World War I and scapegoated German Americans, by spring 1918 Rauschenbusch reluctantly voiced acceptance of that participation. Yet he warned about the dangers of militarism that caused injustice, not only in Germany but in the United States as well (C. Evans 2004:264–311).

THEOLOGICAL VIEWS ABOUT JUSTICE

Rauschenbusch's theological views revolved around the concepts of God, the individual, and society. Published in 1917, *A Theology for the Social Gospel* most fully expressed his interpretations. Rather than a punitive, hierarchical, distant monarch, God represented for him a nurturant spiritual being both transcendent and immanent. As Holy Comforter, God reflects the transcendent principles of love, light, justice, and mystical solidarity. Within each individual dwells the divine light that illuminates the way to spiritual growth. Whereas God manifests an unchanging spirit, the individual and society show evolutionary growth. Assuming the individual's tendency to sin, Rauschenbusch also perceived the potentiality for goodness. Personal sins stem mainly from collective sources linked to the "Kingdom of Evil": coercive political power, militarism, economic exploitation, inequality, graft, corruption, religious dogmatism, bigotry, and upper-class humiliation of the marginals. All these forms of injustice, not a personal Devil or punitive God, cause evil. Through personal repentance, individual regeneration, and environmental transformation, humans can grow toward perfection. Rauschenbusch also saw society evolving toward more just conditions. According to him, society functions as an organic community with high interdependence among its parts. Opposed to violent revolution, he supported peaceful evolution as the way to attain the Kingdom of God on earth. This reign of God will arrive not through an apocalyptic catastrophe but through an alliance of churches, other voluntary associations, popular movements, and political agencies that peacefully mobilize to realize the spiritual vision of Jesus.

The interactions between church, individual, and government flowed from these evolutionary notions. Sharing many ideas voiced 100 years earlier by Friedrich Schleiermacher, Rauschenbusch believed that churches had the responsibility to regenerate the individual and to redeem society. Opposed to an ecclesiastical, hierarchical, bureaucratic, monopolistic church, he favored religious pluralism and separation of churches from the government. They should maintain no close ties with government agencies and accept no public funds from them. As a Baptist, he rejected Roman Catholic political practices found in Latin America, Spain, and Italy during the early twentieth century. Rather than serving private interests of these institutions' elites, he wanted both church and state to pursue the common spiritual good articulated by Jesus and the Hebrew prophets: "The machinery of Church and State must be kept separate, but . . . their common aim is to transform humanity into the kingdom of God" (Rauschenbusch 1991:380). Unlike Protestant fundamentalists, Rauschenbusch did not perceive the Bible as inerrant or infallible. Adopting a skeptical Enlightenment interpretation, he sought to blend historical criticism of the scriptures with insights derived from the indwelling spiritual consciousness, not from ecclesiastical authorities. Instead of waiting for the second coming of Jesus or expecting immediate ascension of believers into heaven after death, Rauschenbusch envisioned a gradual, organic evolution of the spiritual kingdom. Christians should realize the heavenly qualities—love, solidarity, harmony, justice—now, not postpone their attainment until they enter a future otherworldly heaven (Rauschenbusch 1897; 1991:185–86, 207, 355, 380, 410; 1997).

The egalitarian, communal, efficacious interpretations of justice affirmed by Rauschenbusch derived from his ideas about God, the individual, society, church, and government. Commitment to economic equality took precedence over support for gender and especially ethnic equality. Attacking the inegalitarian distribution of income under capitalism, he backed public policies that would increase equal opportunities, ensure more equal respect for the poor, and narrow the gap splitting rich from poor. According to him, "Approximate equality is the only enduring foundation of democracy" (Rauschenbusch 1991:247). From his perspective, capitalism had created more economic inequalities not only for men but also for women workers who earned low wages and labored long hours. Yet until 1917 he refrained from displaying enthusiasm for gender equality outside the home. Taking an ambivalent position on women's role in society, he rejected patriarchal relations and affirmed the need for greater gender equality in religion, political life, and especially higher education. He wanted young men and women to help create a transformed society based on spiritual values. Despite these egalitarian sentiments, he believed that most women should focus greater attention on the home, where they give loving care to children, than on the public sector, where men need to assume dominance. This role division would best contribute to a happy, stable home life. Rauschenbusch felt that capitalism had weakened family stability by promoting low wages, income inequality, prostitution, alcoholism, and obscene media. Hence, the social gospel had the obligation to struggle for enhanced sexual purity. Ethnic equality for African Americans received less attention from Rauschenbusch than did gender or especially economic issues. Although rarely mentioning the widespread ethnic segregation that had increased during the early 1900s, he denounced lynching and other unjust effects of slavery—features that exemplified the inferior rights held by blacks in the United States (C. Evans 2004:205, 233–34, 251–56, 292; Fishburn 2003; Rauschenbusch 1912:264–70; 1913; 1991:134–40, 276–78, 345, 367, 412; 1997:79, 185–86).

The ambivalence shown by Rauschenbusch over gender equality also became apparent in his orientation toward hierarchy. On the one hand, he rejected deference to the authority wielded by such bureaucratic institutions as governments, corporations, and churches, especially the Roman Catholic Church. Decentralized churches would enable the laity to exert authority, unlike the situation in the Vatican hierarchy, which he viewed as a monarchical institution run by the pope. His nonhierarchical conception of God and the church influenced his plans for extending popular participation to the economy and political system. Proposals for industrial democracy opposed owners' and managers' autocratic power over workers. Instead, unions and cooperatives needed to train workers for greater participation in managing a business, so that they could secure higher wages, improved working conditions, a share of profits, and peaceful resolution of conflicts. Political programs for increased popular participation resembled the Progressive reforms: initiative, recall, direct election of U.S. senators, and nomination of candidates by direct primaries, not party conventions. He hoped that all these measures would enable workers to gain greater political power. On the other hand, like Schleiermacher, Rauschenbusch wanted educated professionals like clergy and intellectuals, but not political party leaders, to play a key role in framing issues, mediating between owners and workers, and helping to forge social change. He envisioned idealistic intellectuals forming an alliance with the industrial working class:

> Just as the Protestant principle of religious liberty and the democratic principle of political liberty rose to victory by an alliance with the middle class which was then rising to power, so the new Christian principle of brotherly association must ally itself with the working class if both are to conquer. Each depends on the other. The idealistic

movement alone would be a soul without a body; the economic class movement alone would be a body without a soul. It needs the high elation and faith that come through religion.

(Rauschenbusch 1991:409)

Rauschenbusch hoped that by synthesizing faith with work, idealism with material interests, and scientific individualism with working-class solidarity, the coalition would gradually generate a transformed society that gave priority to the spiritual values of justice proclaimed by Jesus (Rauschenbusch 1912:362; 1991:363, 409–13; 1997:169–72).

Like other Progressives, Rauschenbusch held that individuals could realize their full potentialities only under changed social conditions. According to him, capitalist incentives focused not on the common good but on private interests. Selfishness, greed, and a concern for profits as the major goal caused poverty, economic inequality, pollution, illness, war, and general injustice. Faced with corporate control over government and political parties, churches had the responsibility to not only redeem the individual but also regenerate society. Overcoming their fixation on personal salvation and "exaggerated individualism," Protestant denominations must embody the spiritual ideals of the Kingdom of God: sacrificial love (*agape*), justice, and service to others, especially the poor. Opposed to the possessive individualism stressed by capitalists, Rauschenbusch affirmed the need for greater cooperation among individuals in an organic community. Only through communal fellowship, solidarity, and collective structures could they achieve justice. Influenced but not controlled by churches, the government should give priority to the promotion of justice. Even if highlighting these collective virtues, Rauschenbusch never abandoned his belief in personal freedom and a universalist ethos that transcended narrow nationalism. Despite his emphasis on Protestant values, he maintained an ecumenical orientation that downgraded militarism but furthered a just world peace (Rauschenbusch 1991:185–88, 380; 1997:123–25).

Rather than take a fatalistic view of social change, Rauschenbusch affirmed a belief in personal efficacy. He expected that churches would actively organize behind public policies intended to attain greater social justice. Instead of resigning themselves to the deterministic "laws of the market" or awaiting the apocalyptic second coming of Jesus, Christians should strive now to help realize the reign of God on earth. Faith in a loving, just God would give them the optimism to mobilize for a transformed society. However great the hopes for a peaceful struggle, Rauschenbusch realized that this mobilization would involve protest activities and hence bring social unrest from opponents who feared the effects of Christian socialist policies (Rauschenbusch 1991:139–40; 1997:156–59, 220, 233).

Public Policy Preferences for Justice

Like his views on Christian justice, Rauschenbusch's preferences for specific public policies stressed the need for greater harmony among diverse religions, nations, and economic classes. For Christian socialism to succeed, it must reconcile the divergent interests of progressive business owners and professionals with the demands of the working class for a democratic, just economy. His version of socialism rejected the atheistic "scientific socialism" elaborated by Marx and Engels in late nineteenth-century Europe. Instead, Rauschenbusch supported a uniquely American socialism based on tolerance, pluralism, and a spiritual ethic that affirms justice, equality, dignity, wisdom, fellowship, and personal liberty (Rauschenbusch 1896; 1912:398–405).

Commitment to civil liberties flowed from his nonpunitive conception of God and his experiences as a Baptist minister who upheld individual freedom. Supporting a cooperative, consensual society, he rejected a coercive state that used torture to secure compliance and police force to suppress strikes. As illustrated by his dissent over U.S. participation in World War I, Rauschenbusch recognized the importance of free speech, free assembly, and a free press for a viable political democracy. He hoped that these freedoms would contribute to a more informed public opinion ensuring legal rights. His procedural justice extended to enhanced prisoners' rights, including opposition to capital punishment and support for rehabilitation measures that avoided contract labor controlled by corporations in prisons (Rauschenbusch 1912:466–67; 1997:175, 183, 195–96).

Opposition to capitalist practices lay behind Rauschenbusch's preference for policies that would achieve greater economic equality. Along with Progressives and socialists, he backed programs for extending public ownership, regulating corporations, implementing egalitarian expenditures, and enacting progressive taxes—all policies designed to improve the material well-being of low-income workers. Like contemporary liberation theologians, Rauschenbusch perceived that "God is on the side of the poor," so government officials should take a similar stand (Rauschenbusch 1997:168). He advocated public ownership for schools, parks, police and fire departments, urban transportation, roads, bridges, public utilities (gas, electric power facilities, water power), coal mines, and oil/natural gas wells. Small business owners, farmers, and cooperatives should have the right to manage their private firms. Consumers must own their homes, clothes, and personal savings. Rauschenbusch wanted public employment bureaus to offer information about available jobs. If private enterprises did not provide them, the public sector should supply jobs to the unemployed.

Through government regulation of private corporations, Rauschenbusch hoped to expand workers' rights, especially for women. He favored restrictions on "monopoly profits," on high prices, on long working hours, and on child labor. Industrial accident insurance, a minimum wage, higher general wages, and laws that regulated collective bargaining between labor and management represent other policies that he felt would reduce the income gap splitting capitalists from workers.

Preference for egalitarian fiscal policies resembled the Progressive stands. These included greater government spending on pensions, health care, maternity benefits, housing for the poor, and assistance to the elderly. Like Henry George, Rauschenbusch denounced land speculation and backed a high land tax on vacant land that brought unearned income to the landowner. He also supported progressive taxes like a higher inheritance tax, but favored lower protective tariffs, which raised prices on consumer imports. According to Rauschenbusch, these public fiscal measures, not private charity, would expand the workers' purchasing power and secure higher personal dignity (Rauschenbusch 1912:232, 337–38, 347–89, 412–29; 1991:238, 347–89).

If the economic policies preferred by Rauschenbusch expressed strong commitment to egalitarian distributive justice that clashed with U.S. capitalist practices during the early 1900s, his attitude toward the sexual dimensions of procedural justice upheld more traditional Christian values. Stable family life took precedence over personal sexual freedom. Yet rather than blaming prostitution, adultery, media obscenity, and erotic imagery solely on sinful individuals, he attributed their causes mainly to capitalist corporations that paid low wages to workers, harmed family life, deterred marriage, and impeded loving parent–child relations. By organizing the liquor and gambling industries, businesses destroyed family values. Profit mattered more than the sanctity of the home. The popular media portrayed sexual images that stimulated erotic desires. Opposed to "free love" and sexual relations outside marriage, Rauschenbusch never upheld censorship. Instead, he wanted religious institutions to support a harmonious, stable, egalitarian family life where parents expressed nonpunitive, loving care for their children. This interpretation of family life stemmed not only from his opposition to capitalist practices that downgraded women's status but also from his nurturant view of a democratic, loving God:

> The sense of fear which has pervaded religion has doubtless been, at least in part, a psychological result of the despotic attitude of parents, of school-masters, of priests, and of officials.... To uncounted people God has not been the great Comforter but the great Terror.... [Jesus] democratized the conception of God. He disconnected the idea from the coercive and predatory State, and transferred it to the realm of family life, the chief social embodiment of solidarity and love.
>
> (Rauschenbusch 1997:173–75)

This perception of God meant for him that gender equality pertained primarily to the home, rather than to the political arena. Yet especially after 1912 he accepted the active role that his elder daughter Winifred played at Oberlin University, where she majored in sociology and served as president of the student socialist union (C. Evans 2004: 232–39, 251–53; Rauschenbusch 1912:264–70).

Conclusion

Whereas Protestant ministers led the Social Gospel movement, which gained its greatest strength from 1900 through 1915, what relevance does it have for other religions and for the early twenty-first century? While Rauschenbusch still lived, Jews and Catholics advocated the same egalitarian perceptions of justice that he proclaimed. Liberal, reform Jews played an active role in social charities and in left-wing parties, such as the socialist parties, which attracted support from many Jewish immigrants born in Western and East-Central Europe. Like

Rauschenbusch, these liberal Jews reiterated the egalitarian ethic of the Hebrew prophets. In 1892 Pope Leo XII issued an encyclical letter, *Rerum Novarum*, which stressed the dignity of work, the rights of the poor, the need for workers to organize unions, and the deleterious effects of capitalist exploitation on labor. Although rejecting liberalism and socialism as too materialistic, it committed the Roman Catholic Church to voluntary associations that strived for improved working conditions, such as higher, more just wages and a safer, healthier environment. In the United States, Monsignor John A. Ryan (1896–1945) endorsed the *Rerum Novarum* teachings. An economist as well as theologian at the Catholic University of America, he wrote two books—*A Living Wage* and *Distributive Justice*—that applied Catholic spiritual values to the economic realm. Paternalism and hierarchy blended with an egalitarian attitude toward distributive justice (Bender 2006:272; Hays 1995:106; Pontifical Council for Justice and Peace 2004:119–20).

During the early twenty-first century, the issues emphasized by Rauschenbusch remain. Economic inequality, unemployment, poverty, war, terrorism, coercive police, punitive prison treatment, capital punishment, unstable family life, alcoholism, prostitution, gambling, government impediments to labor union formation, and especially corporate control over political institutions still bring injustice, especially to stigmatized marginals and outcasts. The Progressive reforms enacted from 1900 through 1910 weakened during the 1920s. The Democratic Party in the New Deal (1933–37) and the New Frontier–Great Society (1961–68) revived more egalitarian tax and expenditure policies. Under the Nixon administration, the Democratic Congress passed many programs, such as the Occupational Safety and Health Administration and the Environmental Protection Agency, which President Nixon approved. Since the 1980s, however, egalitarian fiscal measures have waned. Privatization and deregulation policies now receive approval, particularly from Republicans but also from Democratic legislators.

With elite support, promarket programs give priority to expanded control by private corporations over the economy. Typical programs include privatization of state-owned enterprises, private provision of social services (education, health care, pensions), deregulation, and increased foreign investment and trade. Regressive policies enact lower taxes on corporations and the wealthy but higher taxes on social security and consumption, such as sales taxes. Inegalitarian government expenditures secure higher spending on national defense and security but lower spending for personal social services like health care, public assistance, child care, and unemployment compensation. These fiscal programs not only disadvantage low-income persons but give corporate managers greater control over workers. Union influence declines. As salaries and fringe benefits of chief executive officers rise, real wages of workers fall. A larger proportion work under part-time and temporary contracts. Multinational corporations, especially financial institutions, benefit from reduced government power over the global flow of financial capital: stock market transactions, currency speculation, and trading in securities. Shareholders who earn higher dividends but pay lower taxes secure the greatest payoffs from globalization (Andrain and Smith 2006:23–31; Wade 2006).

Since World War I until the early 2000s, income inequality showed the most rapid increases during Republican administrations when private corporations wielded the greatest control over public policymaking. Peaking in 1928, the income share held by the wealthiest one percent of taxpayers fell from 1929 to 1976. This share especially declined from 1940 through 1952. Remaining fairly low during the 1960s, income inequality soared during the 1980s and early 2000s during the Republican presidencies of Ronald Reagan and George W. Bush. In the 1945–76 period, the wealthiest persons derived their income mainly from capital dividends. In the 2000s their income came mainly from high compensation and fringe benefits. In 2001 U.S. chief executive officers secured 44 times the pay of manufacturing workers. Along with reduced government expenditures for child care, health care, and education, lower taxes on corporate incomes, estates, and gifts widened the income gap between rich and poor. When private businesses reduced health care and retirement benefits but increased premiums, lower-income workers bore the costs (Aron-Dine and Shapiro 2006; Carter et al. 2006:2–656; Johnston 2007; Piketty and Saez 2003, 2006, 2007; Voscho and Fullerton 2005).

The George W. Bush administration backed the promarket policies preferred by corporate executives. Supported by a cohesive Republican Party in Congress, his presidency favored lower taxes on corporations and the wealthy, tried to abolish the estate tax affecting the wealthiest two percent of the population, and refused to eliminate the earnings ceiling on the regressive social security tax. As expenditures for national defense and internal security rose, spending on civilian social services fell, except for social security and Medicare. Bush officials supported privatization measures for education, health care, and retirement. Government funds went to private schools and to private contractors who supplied services to government agencies. Reduced government regulation of private businesses enabled timber companies, construction firms, and oil corporations to develop public lands. Regulatory agencies restricted labor union rights to collective bargaining. Private corporations obtained major benefits not only from these domestic policies but also from the prosecution of wars overseas. As a result of these promarket policies, income distribution became more unequal. During 2004 the real income of the wealthiest 1 percent grew by over 12 percent, whereas the real income of the other segments of the population rose by only 1.5 percent (Krugman 2006).

The United States now has the highest post-tax, post-transfer income inequality of any other industrialized nation. Norway, Sweden, Finland, the Netherlands, Belgium, Luxembourg, Germany, and Austria especially show more equality. From 1979 through 1999, United Kingdom and U.S. residents also experienced the greatest rise in the gap between rich and poor. Whereas Swedes and Finns have the lowest child poverty—defined as living in households with income under one half the disposable median national income—children in the United States suffer from the greatest poverty. Children of African Americans, Native Americans, and mothers who originally came from Mexico, Puerto Rico, the Dominican Republic, and Southeast Asia mainly bear the poverty burden. Single unemployed mothers endure the most poverty. Regressive taxes, limited social service expenditures, weak unions, high CEO compensation, and low wages for unskilled workers, single mothers, and those with limited formal education explain these patterns of unequal income distribution and childhood poverty in the United States (Lichter et al. 2005; Moran 2006; Osberg and Smeeding 2006:465; Smeeding 2005, 2006).

Today economic inequality exerts similar effects to those Walter Rauschenbusch denounced 100 years ago. High unemployment, low life expectancy, deficient public education, weak unions, rule by corporate oligopolies, and greater interpersonal violence plague the poorest 20 percent of the population. Low rates of political participation by low-income persons occur. Political parties reflect the policy preferences of their wealthiest activists who dominate the public agenda. Redistributive measures such as higher, more progressive taxes and egalitarian social service programs gain limited support from legislators (McCarty et al. 2006). Corporations benefit from greater emphasis on preemptive wars. U.S. soldiers who die in these wars are mainly low-income persons from rural areas. The terror scare has replaced the red scare. Appeals to national security justify increased repression of civil liberties.

Faced with these current injustices, modern exponents of the Social Gospel articulate a message that seems relevant to the contemporary situation. The next chapter explores the views on justice held by three Protestant activists: evangelical Jim Wallis, Presbyterian/Congregationalist William Sloane Coffin, and Episcopal bishop John Shelby Spong. It will also consider the interpretations of Dorothy Day, who led the Catholic Worker movement, and Rabbi Michael Lerner, who heads the Network of Spiritual Progressives. All these leaders take an egalitarian stand on justice, promote political efficacy, and uphold civil liberties and individual freedom. A collective orientation merges spiritual values with concerns about the material well-being of the poor. Issues of civil liberties, protests against war, income distribution, and sexual choice assume priority, with abortion and homosexual rights arousing the greatest disagreement among the modern Social Gospelers.

4

THE SOCIAL GOSPEL AND POLITICAL ACTION

Instead of trying to strike an elusive "balance" between private piety and the social gospel, we must go to the heart of prophetic religion itself in which a personal God demands public justice as an act of worship.

(Jim Wallis)

Prophetic faith sees justice as central, not ancillary, to salvation. . . . To the degree that we embody justice, God takes form within us.

(William Sloane Coffin)

Jesus never suggested that the task of God's people was to impose its talk, its creeds, or its teaching on the populace. . . . Jesus' call was rather to point to the realm of God, to invite people to enter that realm as members in order to bear a corporate witness to the values of justice that define that realm.

(John Shelby Spong)

We must cry out against injustice or by our silence consent to it.

(Dorothy Day)

> God [is] the Force in the universe that makes possible transformation from a world based on pain and cruelty to a world based on love and generosity ... the Force that makes possible a world of nonviolence, peace, and social justice.
>
> (Michael Lerner)

Depicting public policy as a great barbecue in the late nineteenth century, Vernon Louis Parrington highlighted the unjust inequalities that prevailed in the "gilded age." Government bestowed subsidies, low taxes, land, and other economic benefits on the business elite, but provided few "goodies" to low-income folks:

> A huge barbecue was spread to which all presumably were invited. Not quite all, to be sure; inconspicuous persons, those who were at home on the farm or at work in the mills and offices, were overlooked.... But all the important persons, leading bankers and promoters and business men, received invitations. There wasn't room for everybody and these were presumed to represent the whole.
>
> (Parrington 1930:3:23)

Elitist corporate practices clashed with populist rhetoric. Rather than pursuing a common good that transcended the private interests of the business class, government officials implemented public policies that magnified economic inequalities. The gilded age barbecue hardly resembled the inclusive meals attended by Jesus, who urged his host to invite the marginals: "When you give a banquet, invite the poor, the crippled, the lame, and the blind. And you will be blessed, because they cannot repay you, for you will be repaid at the resurrection of the righteous" (Luke 14:13–14). According to Jesus, justice (righteousness) in the coming Messianic banquet would reflect egalitarian conditions where the outcasts would eat the bread of life. For him, the realm of God brought dramatic role reversals.

Although the Social Gospel as a historical movement peaked from 1890 to 1914, the views on justice originally formulated by Walter Rauschenbusch influenced post-World War II theologians. These included Protestants Jim Wallis, William Sloane Coffin, and John Shelby Spong as well as Catholic Dorothy Day and Rabbi Michael Lerner. For these five, elitist beliefs remain subordinate to values that affirm equal treatment under the law, equal respect for all people as human beings, enhanced sharing of economic resources, and equal opportunities for diverse individuals to develop their potentialities. A nonhierarchical view of justice rests on an individualist foundation upholding civil liberties. Political activism supersedes a fatalistic belief in religious dogma. Rather than urge individuals to concentrate only on private piety and personal salvation, the modern Social Gospelers encourage active participation in the public arena to realize social justice.

Protestant Activists

Adopting slightly different theological views, Jim Wallis, William Sloane Coffin, and John Shelby Spong share similar perspectives about justice. For them, prophetic political discourse contrasts the ethical standards of justice with the unjust conditions that prevail today, especially poverty, global pollution, political oppression, and unequal treatment of marginals. They affirm the virtues of justice (righteousness), truth, compassion, hope, and care for others' well-being over injustice, ignorance, hatred, despair, and self-indulgence. Playing several roles as minister, lecturer, and author, they focus on the need for individuals to become active participants in the public sphere. Nonviolent conflict with established authorities becomes a strategy for mobilizing people against the status quo.

Social activism occurs in a Northeast urban setting. Jim Wallis works to reduce poverty in Washington, DC. William Sloane Coffin served as Yale chaplain in New Haven, Connecticut from 1958 to 1975 and as senior minister at New York City's Riverside Church from 1977 through 1987. For nearly twenty-five years (1976–2000), John Shelby Spong was the Episcopal bishop of Newark, New Jersey. These cities reinforced the liberal Protestant stress on economic equality, world peace, nonpunitive policies, and women's rights.

As they grew older, the three Protestant ministers underwent role reversals that transformed their religious discourse. The father of Jim Wallis acted as a lay minister in the Plymouth Brethren Church, a Pietist denomination that in the immediate postwar generation showed little enthusiasm for political activism. "Let go and let God" assumed priority over mobilizing the faithful behind the cause of income equality, poverty reduction, or world peace. Wallis attended Trinity Evangelical Divinity School, which stressed an inerrant Bible and the second coming of Jesus Christ. Although Wallis retains his evangelical outlook, he now links it to issues of social justice, not merely personal piety. William Coffin grew up in a wealthy New York family, served as a soldier in World War II (1943–47), and during the Korean War joined the CIA as a linguistic specialist fluent in Russian and French. Even if he continued serving as chaplain and minister at upper-status universities and churches, his original aggressiveness was transformed into a nonviolent battle for racial integration, world peace, and nuclear disarmament. Along with Benjamin Spock, he helped lead draft resistance movements against the U.S. involvement in the Vietnamese war. In later life he became an active supporter of gender equality and homosexual rights. Born in 1931 in Charlotte, North Carolina, John Shelby Spong grew up in a racially segregated environment where women played a subordinate role to male patriarchs. Rigid sexual standards gave limited choices to women. Patriotic sentiments generated support for national government wars against foreign oppressors. Yet as Newark bishop, John Spong engineered profound changes in the church, leading the movement for women's ordination as Episcopal priests and for homosexuals' right to become ordained. Support for racial integration and for multilateral approaches to world peace also consumed extensive time. More than Wallis or Coffin, Bishop Spong departed from the orthodox beliefs of the Apostles' and Nicene creeds. Instead, he formulated a new theology adapted to scientific understandings about the Bible and conditions of the twenty-first century.

Although appealing mainly to mainline Protestants, the three Social Gospelers try to win support from an inclusive, ecumenical audience. Even if Episcopalians, Presbyterians, Methodists, Congregationalists, and Unitarians give the strongest support, nontraditional Catholics and reform Jews also participate in the ecumenical movement for social justice. Disdaining partisan and ideological polarization, Wallis strives to unite theologically conservative evangelicals who emphasize personal piety with liberals concerned about social justice, especially ethnic equality, civil liberties, ecology, economic equality, and world peace. Coffin and Spong show less hesitation about identifying with the left. Yet they too encourage participation of Catholics, Jews, and other religions in the struggle for social justice.

Jim Wallis

Of the three modern Social Gospel ministers, Jim Wallis holds the most orthodox theological views about God, the individual, and society. As a self-styled "evangelical," he affirms the Apostles' Creed, the importance of the Bible as the guide to faith and behavior, and the role of Jesus as Lord and Savior—the way to personal salvation (Wakefield 2006:189). Wallis perceives God as a personal God, not an impersonal force, who actively cares for each individual and for the whole society. An active creator, God inspires people to struggle for the common good and social justice, especially for the poor, marginals, and outcasts. Through grace and the teachings of Jesus Christ, God motivates individual conversion, which leads to repentance—a behavior change from evil to goodness. Even if individuals act in an evil way, God made them in the divine image. According to Wallis, sin stems not only from individual abuses but also from collective structures that impose political oppression, economic exploitation, and cultural humiliation on the vulnerable. Given the collective sins, individuals must become closely integrated with the community, so that the pursuit of the common good supersedes competition for private interests. Through both individual and community action, God works to redeem the world to make it like an inclusive family (Wallis 2005a:43–78; 2005b:31–40; Wallis and Gutenson 2006:1–9).

Wallis' interpretations of the interactions among the church, individual, and government flow from his theological perspectives about God. For him, moral-spiritual activism takes priority over a focus on creeds and doctrines, particularly those stressed by fundamentalists. Following the prophetic message of Jesus, the church has the responsibility to realize the Kingdom of God on earth, not merely to achieve a person's salvation. In its pastoral role, it comforts people, converts them, and renews their lives. Performing a prophetic function, the church critiques the status quo, sketches a vision of a transformed society, reconciles antagonistic groups, and struggles for social justice based on compassion. To maximize religious diversity, government and church must remain separate institutions. Although churches should influence public policies, they must refrain from establishing theocratic control. Like religious associations, government agencies have an obligation to promote justice, peace, the common good, and virtuous behavior. Ideally, they need to work as partners to achieve these ethical goals.

More than William Coffin or Bishop Spong, Jim Wallis highlights the redeeming role of Jesus Christ. He perceives Jesus as "God made poor," the son of God, and the Lord and Savior who wields absolute authority over political rulers. As the suffering servant who died for human sins, he brings salvation to all. His resurrection symbolizes the victory of life over death. Along with the Hebrew prophets, his life embodied the commandments to love mercy, practice justice, and show humility toward God (Wallis 2005a:29, 54–63, 87–93, 111–44, 368; Wallis and Gutenson 2006:5–9).

The outlook on social justice taken by Wallis reflects the Protestant views of Walter Rauschenbusch. Wallis asserts a nonhierarchical attitude toward established ecclesiastical and political authority. Opposed to oppressive government bureaucracies like the one that crucified Jesus, he asserts the priority of service and humility over domination and elitist pride. In economic decisionmaking, decentralized, democratic structures should curb the abuse of power and wealth (Wallis 2005a:14; 2005b:5).

The egalitarian stance toward justice reflects Wallis' inclusive perspective. For him, all types of equality—gender, economic, ethnic, national—need strengthening. Opposed to patriarchy, he perceives that women suffer from domestic abuse and subordinate status. Following the message of Jesus to the poor and outcast, the early Christian community led a simple, modest life and redistributed wealth to the poor. Today Christians must lead a similar movement to reduce poverty. Ethnic groups like African Americans, Latinos, and Native Americans are overrepresented among the poor. Hence, Wallis supports a partnership between private associations and government organizations to end segregation, discrimination, and unjust treatment. Echoing Paul's injunction in Romans 8:38–39, Wallis believes that loyalty to God's love as expressed in Christ Jesus supersedes loyalty to the nation-state. National self-righteousness must yield to visions of national equality, under which all governments cooperate for world peace with justice. Created in the divine image, humans need multilateral actions to guarantee their individual rights to dignity, respect, and equality (Wallis 1994:31–125).

Justice rests on a foundation that links the individual to the community. Wallis seeks to blend private individualism with collective action, so that the values of the extended family and the wider, more inclusive spiritual community take priority over cruel, selfish individualism and concern for only the nuclear family. As an inclusive community based on love, the people of God must resemble the "suffering servant community" established by Jesus. Yet more than just religious activities should help transform society. Public policies led by an activist government also have a crucial role to play (Wallis 2005a:69, 115, 147–49; 2005b:340; Wallis and Gutenson 2006:99–112).

Wallis takes a nonfatalistic stand toward justice. Despite the evils of racism, sexism, and imperialism that he sees in the contemporary world, he counsels hope and faith in the possibilities for social justice. Individuals retain choices about their beliefs and actions. Despair, hopelessness, cynicism, apathy, indifference, and resignation reinforce the status quo. Instead, Christians need to recall the crucifixion and resurrection of Jesus, who demonstrated the triumph of life over the death imposed by Roman political authorities. When led by the spirit of God, activists in organized communities can achieve the personal and political efficacy that motivates altruism. Through empowering the individual and community, the grace of God inspires just public policies (Wallis 2005a:171–73; Wallis and Gutenson 2006:113–23).

The public policy preferences of Jim Wallis reflect his attempt to achieve a bipartisan, nonideological movement that reconciles Democrats and Republicans, liberals and conservatives, evangelicals and mainstream Christians, and even members of all religious faiths. He rejects the approaches of religious fundamentalists like Pat Robertson and Frank Dobson, as well as "secular fundamentalists," which he links with the American Civil Liberties Union and the Americans United for Separation of Church and State. According to Wallis, religious fundamentalists adopt a too dogmatic, oppressive, theocratic stance toward public affairs. "Secular fundamentalists seek to remove faith and spiritual values from influence over public policies" (Wallis 2005b:66–71). Whereas the Christian Right has become closely attached to the Republican Party, the secularists lean toward the Democrats. Rather than accepting polarization, Wallis seeks to link the conservative stress on "sexual integrity," personal responsibility, and family values with the liberal affirmation of social justice, racial integration, world peace, and income equality (Wallis 2005b:73–80).

Wallis places the greatest emphasis on distributive justice in his "Covenant for a New America," which aims to overcome poverty through blending "religious commitment" with "political leadership." Unlike Walter Rauschenbusch, who advocated socialist policies as a way to lessen income inequality, Wallis rejects socialism. Instead, spiritual consciousness must supersede class consciousness. He also opposes "unregulated, unrestrained capitalism" that places self-interest and profit above pursuit of the common good. Although upholding the need for narrowing the gap that separates rich from poor, he gives priority to equal economic opportunities over egalitarian outcomes (Wallis 2005a:46; Wallis and Gutenson 2006:33–63, 107). His proposals to reduce poverty share more similarities with liberal Democratic programs than with those supported by conservative Republicans. The Covenant for a New America calls for increased federal government expenditures on education, nutrition, health care, child care, housing, job training, and community development. It wants expanded tax credits for income-earners, dependents, and children. For Wallis, the ideal organizational arrangements for implementing these policies revolve around partnerships between government agencies and faith-based groups (Sojourners/Call to Renewal 2006).

Policies for procedural justice focus on nonpunitive programs that further civil liberties, peace, reconciliation, and the sanctity of life. Democracy involves widespread participation, dissent, and civil liberties as Christians wage a spiritual battle against "false values" and affirm the spiritual values of justice and mercy. Internationally, Wallis urges a commitment to peaceful, multilateral conflict resolution through international law, a stronger United Nations, an international criminal court, and an international police force that would mitigate violence throughout the world. Elaborating on the historical interpretations of a just war, he hardly perceives the United States' military intervention in Iraq as justified by these criteria. Neither capital punishment nor the retribution imposed in prisons warrants Wallis' approval. Instead, he asserts the need for restorative justice. Along with the late Cardinal Bernardin of Chicago, Wallis wants policies for family life and sexual behavior to uphold the sanctity of life. Just as the cardinal rejected capital punishment, he also opposed abortion. Rather than strive to make abortion illegal, Wallis supports measures that will reduce its prevalence. These policies include adoption, expanded child care, economic assistance to low-income women, and greater access to health care. He also backs public programs that offer sex education to teenagers, provide counseling about pregnancies, and make contraceptives more widely available. Even if he rejects gay marriage, he supports expanded rights for homosexuals to a job, civil unions, and active participation in church activities. Like Walter Rauschenbusch, Wallis attacks the "casual sex" portrayed in the corporate media. He feels that pornography, domestic violence, and divorce hinder stable marriages. Unlike the fundamentalist right, however, Wallis expands family values to include not only the nuclear family but also the extended neighborhood, community, and church families. Respect for life will occur only when just policies encompass the wider community (Wallis 2005b: 321–40; 2005c; Wallis and Gutenson 2006:15–30, 65–77, 99–112).

What activities does Wallis recommend to achieve these public policies? He mainly emphasizes education as well as letters to the editor, contacts with legislators, and nonviolent demonstrations. From his standpoint, churches should first concentrate on changing cultural values and public opinion that will then motivate political leaders to enact policy reforms. Main organizational efforts involve the magazine *Sojourners* and the Call to Renewal movement that seeks to overcome poverty. In 2006 these two structures merged to forge the renewal of individual persons, congregations, and the domestic and world society (Wallis 2007:341–46; Wallis and Gutenson 2006:129–51).

Although Jim Wallis seeks an inclusive audience for his prophetic message of social justice, he mainly appeals to mainline Protestants and a few progressive evangelicals such as Tony Campolo and Brian McLaren. The churches that endorsed "A Covenant for New America" comprise mainline Protestant ones: United Methodist, Presbyterian (USA), Evangelical Lutheran, Society of Friends, and Disciples of Christ. Wallis' Protestant background and stress on decentralized religious institutions limit his appeal to Roman Catholics, despite the focus on strong family values. His evangelical theological outlook on the central role of Jesus Christ as the only way to salvation and as the "absolute authority" for all areas of life (Wallis 2005a:19, 29) hinders support from reformist Jews, even if Rabbi Michael Lerner has become a close ally on most public policy issues about economic justice, war, peace, capital punishment, and the environment. Many evangelicals affirm his theological views but reject his liberal social programs, including legal rights for gays. Whereas conservative Republicans generally reject both his economic and cultural policies, liberal Democrats agree with most of his policy preferences yet show little enthusiasm for the evangelical creed. For them, a stress on individual choice and secular government programs overrides public funds for "faith-based initiatives" (Lynn 2005; Sojourners/Call to Renewal 2006; Wakefield 2006:159–90).

William Sloane Coffin

For over 80 years (1924–2006), William Sloane Coffin led a life of action. He boxed as a boy. The U.S. military drafted him into the army at age eighteen. Trained as an infantry soldier, he served in Europe as an intelligence officer fluent in French and Russian. From 1950 to 1953 he worked for the Central Intelligence Agency in Germany, where he recruited and trained Soviet emigrés. As a Yale divinity student, he careened through the streets of New Haven on a motorcycle, with a trembling faculty member on the back of his bike. During the early 1960s he helped train Peace Corps volunteers and became a "freedom rider" who campaigned against racial segregation in the South. Later that decade, Chaplain Coffin at Yale led a draft resistance movement that opposed participation in the escalating Vietnam War. As senior minister at New York City's Riverside Church (1977–87), he encouraged the church to offer sanctuary to Central American refugees, mainly those from Guatemala. After retirement from the ministry, he became president in 1998 of SANE/FREEZE, which campaigned for nuclear disarmament (Coffin 1977; Goldstein 2004:12–87, 103–224, 301).

As Yale chaplain (1968–75) and later as minister at the Riverside Church, Coffin had the freedom to articulate his activist, liberal views on social justice. University chaplains endure fewer restraints than do church ministers about methods for expressing their political stands. Hence, he gained the opportunity to protest racial segregation and militaristic policies at a prestigious university like Yale, where his father had attended. Graduating from the Yale Divinity School in 1956, he learned not only about human possibilities but also about the collective evils that bring hell on earth for the oppressed—teachings stressed by Professor H. Richard Niebuhr.

Established by philanthropist John D. Rockefeller, Jr. in 1930, the Riverside Church soon gained renown for its liberal activist programs.

As its first senior minister, Harry Emerson Fosdick, who served from 1930 to 1946, rejected dogmatic, exclusivist perspectives on nationalism and opposed U.S. engagement in World War II. Although preaching about Jesus' appeal to humble, poor outcasts, he gave less attention to the poverty that plagued New York City during the Great Depression of the 1930s. Yet the Riverside Church became famous for its inclusive, tolerant, ecumenical approach to religion. Appealing to northern Baptists, Methodists, Presbyterians, Episcopalians, and Congregationalists, the Church viewed itself as "international, interracial, and interdenominational." Fosdick's modernist approach to theology challenged fundamentalist beliefs. Upholding a scientific viewpoint, he affirmed a symbolic, metaphorical perspective on the Bible, the precedence of good deeds (service to humans) over dogmatic creeds, and the need to establish the Kingdom of God on earth, not postpone it until the apocalypse. After World War II the Riverside Church took the lead in challenging the status quo as it campaigned actively for social justice: civil liberties, racial integration, world peace, gender equality, and sexual freedom for gays and lesbians. Until the 1990s, the congregation focused less attention on economic equality, perhaps because most members had incomes that exceeded $50,000 in 2000 (Hudnut-Beumler 2004; Mamiya 2004; Tisdale 2004). Given this supportive context, William Sloane Coffin had the opportunity to work actively for his liberal interpretation of political justice.

Coffin placed less emphasis on theology than on actions. According to him, "To know God is to do justice. To recognize this implacable moral imperative of the faith represents the kind of good religion that mixes well with politics" (Coffin 2004:51). From his perspective, new experiences will likely produce greater changes in beliefs than will abstract theories create new ways of acting. Opposed to dogmatic creeds, he remained open to new experiences about wisdom. Doubt and intellectual uncertainty invigorate, rather than impede, wise social actions. For Coffin, God represented an active creative agent in life, a loving, strong father and mother. With his commitment to love, justice, and service, Jesus merged creed with deed. He demonstrated divine love for the weak, vulnerable, and marginalized who needed healing. Rather than worshiping Jesus, Christians should follow his example. Not only for Wallis but for Coffin, the resurrection symbolized victory over defeat, "powerless love" over "loveless power," eternal life over death, and loyalty to God over allegiance to the imperial power wielded by an oppressive state. The disciples of Jesus experienced the resurrection as a visionary experience inspired by the Holy Spirit, which Coffin identified with the living, enduring Christ Spirit (Coffin 1977:216–17; 2004:12–13, 140, 145; 2005:41–42, 158–80).

Coffin's outlook on the interactions among the church, individual, and government showed the same activist impulse that shaped his perceptions of God, Jesus, and the Holy Spirit. Like Rauschenbusch, he saw churches' major task as interpreting and helping to realize the Kingdom of God on earth. Rather than refraining from political participation, church members should become actively involved in "a politically engaged spirituality" (Coffin 2005:126, 149). The need for a separation of churches from government hardly implies a refusal to influence the public policy process. The church has the responsibility to challenge government actions that further injustice. Similarly, individuals must stage protests against unjust political decisions, such as laws justifying racial segregation, preemptive war, and nuclear armament. Like Reinhold Niebuhr and his brother H. Richard Niebuhr, Coffin recognized the prevalence of evil. Perceiving sin as the abuse of human freedom, he perceived that evil arises not merely from personal deficiencies but primarily from collective sources, such as political repression, economic exploitation, and cultural disregard for individuals' shared humanity. Rather than stemming from the vengeance of God who acts to punish evil-doers, evil results from voluntary human choices. According to Coffin, "The magnitude of human malpractice notwithstanding, there is more mercy in God than sin in us" (Coffin 2005:43). By motivating individuals to repent, the church can inspire individuals to work actively for changes in government decisions. Influenced by a belief in human possibilities, activists need to remember that politics is "the art of making possible tomorrow what seems impossible today" (Coffin 2004:70; see too 137–59; 2005:81, 87, 136).

Interpretations of social justice flowed from Coffin's liberal activist stance toward life. He adopted a nondeferential attitude toward all forms of authority: governmental, ecclesiastical, academic, corporate, familial, even biblical. Affirming a scientific, historical view of the Bible, he scarcely regarded scripture as literal or inerrant. Even fundamentalists select particular passages for priority. Personal experiences shape each individual's interpretation of biblical teachings. As a talented pianist, Coffin compared the interpretation of a Beethoven sonata to the search for meaning in the Bible. Playing the piano and living the Gospel become crucial for finding meaning. Given the diverse experiences, no single interpretation will ever secure everyone's consent. Just as Coffin rejected dogmatic biblical authority, so he opposed domination by an established state church. Within universities the purity of theories often took precedence over the relevance of these theories for practical issues of social justice. Within families Coffin valued the independence and freedom of children and women to assert their rights against patriarchal authority. Likewise, he never assumed that obedience to government officials and their demand for order should quell popular protests against unjust policies. He denounced plutocratic governments that enact tax cuts for the wealthy elite but spending cuts for the powerless (Coffin 1999:41–51; 2004:13, 40, 53, 65, 82, 144–59; 2005:63–64, 70).

Coffin took an egalitarian stance toward justice. Affirming the equal dignity of every individual and Jesus' commitment to empower the powerless, he stressed the need to organize the poor. Yet unlike Walter Rauschenbusch, who advocated a socialist conception of economic equality, Coffin upheld the right to private property in a market economy. For him, the use of wealth matters more than its ownership. The rich have a special obligation to use their wealth for the common good and social justice. Confirming Parrington's depiction of the great barbecue, he sought to narrow the gap splitting rich from poor: "Surely Christians would agree that it is better to multiply the loaves and fishes for all than to make a larger, tastier dinner for the few" (Coffin 1993:43). Even if socialism posed insightful questions, Coffin perceived that its policy recommendations seem less relevant for capitalist America during the twenty-first century. Instead, liberal Christians should support policies that regulate the capitalist market, ensure generous social service benefits, and implement progressive taxes (Coffin 1993:36–43; 1999:9; 2004:53–73). These measures would help attain a more egalitarian, just society. First encountering racial segregation as a soldier at Camp Wheeler, Georgia in 1943, Coffin later devoted his career to working for civil rights and ethnic equality. His perspective on gender equality came later in life. His first two marriages ended in divorce; his wives played a subordinate role to his dominant concern for public activism. Only after his third loving, successful marriage to Randy Wilson did he fully acknowledge the need for women's equality with men. Describing himself as a "recovering chauvinist," he stated: "The woman most in need of liberation was the woman in every man just as the man most in need of liberation was the man in every woman" (Coffin 2005:30). Individual liberation was thus congruent with gender equality (Coffin 1977:35–37; Goldstein 2004:311–12).

Coffin's orientation toward the ties between the individual and community reflected his activist position. Although valuing personal freedom and autonomy, he asserted the need for individuals to become interdependent with the community. Churches must link personal conversion to community service. Rather than content to change personal beliefs, they should transform social attitudes, so that public justice takes priority over private charity. Whereas charity deals with the effects of injustice, public policies have greater power to transform its causes. Hence, religious institutions should embrace an activist position on policy change (Coffin 2004:55–67).

Asserting his belief in political efficacy, Coffin never yielded to fatalism, passivity, complacency, indifference, and apathy. Compared with Jim Wallis, he asserted a more confrontational attitude toward the promotion of justice. Dedicated to power maintenance, many government officials implement policies that uphold unjust social arrangements. Throughout his ministerial career, Coffin confronted political leaders who refused to enact laws for ethnic equality, civil liberties, world peace, homosexual rights, universal health care, and housing for the poor (Coffin 2004:62–73, 148). Upholding merciful justice, he felt that "compassion without confrontation is hopelessly sentimental" (Coffin 2005:168).

Whereas Walter Rauschenbusch and Jim Wallis devoted greatest attention to distributive justice, with its focus on poverty and income equality, Coffin gave precedence to procedural justice. For him, civil liberties assumed priority, as revealed in his outlook on civil disobedience. Since absolute truth remains obscure, tolerance for new understandings of truths justifies participation in movements for expanding civil liberties. During the 1960s Coffin joined civil rights protests and draft resistance movements against U.S. military actions in Vietnam. Although he regarded civil disobedience as a "last resort," he perceived it as an ethical way to promote justice. Government officials often enact laws that violate civil liberties; by so doing, they engage in civil disobedience. According to him, unjust laws often protect the powerful elite, rather than secure justice for the powerless, such as African Americans who suffered from centuries of slavery, segregation, and discrimination. Under these unjust conditions, individual rights and well-being must take precedence over institutional rules and order imposed by coercion. For Coffin, the main role of government centered not on promoting obedience and order but on realizing personal responsibility, self-respect, individual conscience, and independent decisionmaking. Following the examples of Mahatma Gandhi and Martin Luther King, Jr., Coffin urged the use of nonviolent tactics to attain these ethical criteria of justice. By ensuring the civil liberties of others and accepting the consequences of law violations, protest movements can invalidate unjust laws (Coffin and Leibman 1972).

The concern for individual rights, freedom, and choice shaped Coffin's views on sexual behavior and women's equality. Unlike Jim Wallis, he supported legal abortion and homosexual rights, including same-sex marriage. Even though regarding abortion as "a mournful undertaking," he affirmed women's reproductive freedom, especially during the early stages of pregnancy. To avoid abortion, public policies should increase access to contraceptives, family planning methods, child care, and parental leave. Criminalizing abortion punishes doctors and women but not men who consummated a pregnancy. Coffin's dedication to gay rights, including the rights to marry and become ordained ministers, stemmed from his belief that the inner worth of individuals and their loving personal relationships with others matter more than specific sexual practices, whether before marriage or between same-sex couples. He also backed gender equality, including expanded opportunities for women to become clergy. If gender equality became more widespread in churches, he foresaw that cooperation, love, warmth, and equality would supersede the stress on competition, power, impersonalism, and elitism (Coffin 1993:60–74; 1999:27–40; 2004:39–41; Rose 2006).

Coffin's nonpunitive outlook on public policies influenced his stands toward war, peace, prison reform, and capital punishment. Hardly a pacifist like Harry Emerson Fosdick, he nevertheless campaigned after World War II and the Korean War for policies that would reconcile, not polarize, conflicts. According to him, U.S. leaders used national self-righteousness to justify military invasions in Vietnam and Iraq. An exclusivist U.S. nationalism failed to recognize an inclusive loyalty to God and the human race. Love of God and the well-being of humanity should transcend allegiance to the nation-state. Opposing the arms race and nuclear weapons, Coffin worked for disarmament, an international police force to deter violent conflicts, and multilateral institutions like the International Court of Justice that would bring just procedures to the world. Within the United States, Coffin rejected capital punishment and sought prison reforms focused on rehabilitation and restorative justice. Just as Jesus upheld the rights of the outcasts and proclaimed "release for prisoners" (Luke 4:18), so Coffin defended prisoners' rights to justice (Coffin 1999:53–67, 75–76; 2004:79–105).

Although the same inclusive perspective that influenced Coffin's ideas about procedural justice also shaped his positions on distributive justice, he devoted less attention to policies for increasing economic equality. Perhaps his upper-class background deterred his efforts to secure a more egalitarian income distribution. Born into a wealthy Manhattan family, he graduated from Phillips Academy (Andover), a private elite secondary school, Yale College, and Yale Divinity School. Later he served as chaplain at Williams College and Yale's Battell Chapel, after which he became senior minister at New York City's Riverside Church, attended mainly by wealthy, highly educated parishioners. Whereas Walter Rauschenbusch proclaimed a Christian socialism and sought to ally liberal intellectuals with working-class unionists, Coffin focused his activities on civil liberties, ethnic equality, disarmament, world peace, and individual rights for homosexuals. Unlike Jim Wallis, whose organized actions stress poverty reduction, Coffin as senior minister of the Riverside Church showed greater concern for civil liberties and world peace than for Riverside programs that supplied shelter to the homeless or food to the poor. Nevertheless, along with Wallis, he did support similar egalitarian public policies for a democratized market economy. These included more progressive income and estate taxes, reduced expenditures for armaments and the military, and higher spending on public housing, food stamps, job training, universal health care, and child care. In his view, multinational corporations should pay higher taxes. Even if he regarded class cleavages as difficult to alleviate, the egalitarian measures advocated by him would lessen income inequalities (Coffin 1993: 42–43; 1999, 76–80; 2004:148; Goldstein 2004:28–31, 301; Weisenfeld 2004:216–18).

How much influence did Coffin have on public policymakers? He achieved the greatest policy successes during the early 1960s, when the Kennedy and Johnson administrations remained open to his actions against racial segregation in the South. Later that decade his protests against the Vietnam War rallied support for negotiation over military assaults as a better way to end the war. With the coming to power of the Republican Reagan, Bush I, and Bush II administrations, Coffin's influence waned. These Republican presidents all preferred inegalitarian tax and spending policies, reliance on the military for national security, and culturally conservative approaches to abortion, gay rights, and prayer in schools. The alignment of fundamentalist Christians, such as the Southern Baptists, with the Republican Party reinforced these policies opposed by Coffin. His larger impact occurred among liberal clergy, especially from denominations like the United Methodist, Presbyterian, Episcopal, Congregational, and Unitarian as well as reform Judaism. His ecumenical approach appealed to liberals of all religious affiliations. Although connected with the United Church of Christ and the American Baptist Churches (U.S.A.), the Riverside Church has always attracted members from several mainstream denominations. A liberal Jew, Cora Weiss, organized the church's disarmament program in the 1980s. A man of action, Coffin preferred to preach about the battles that the Hebrews waged against their oppressors and about Jesus' parables that included the outcasts in the Kingdom of God, rather than deliver theological sermons about the esoteric passages of Paul. An articulate, assertive, confrontational activist who became angry at injustice, William Sloane Coffin probably represented the foremost exponent of the modern Social Gospel during the post-World War II era (Goldstein 2004:284–333; Wakefield 2006:164–65).

John Shelby Spong

A prolific author, lecturer, university professor, and Episcopal bishop (1976–2000), John Shelby Spong perceives himself as a pilgrim on a long journey to seek new interpretations of Christian theological beliefs and liturgies. In a self-imposed exile from the U.S. Episcopal Church and the worldwide Anglican communion, he reformulates the meaning of biblical passages and the symbols of such sacraments as baptism and the Eucharist. Opposed to fundamentalist Protestants for their scriptural literalism and to traditionalist Roman Catholics for their commitment to papal infallibility, he rejects the Apostles' and Nicene creeds, including the concepts of heaven and hell as physical places, a personal God who rewards and punishes, a personal Devil, and the virgin birth, blood atonement, and physical resurrection of Jesus. Denouncing liberals and especially conservatives in the Christian churches, he rejects the dogmatic intolerance of conservatives and the tendency for "liberal" Episcopal/Anglican bishops to place promises above a willingness to take actions that will revitalize the church. From his perspective, liberal bishops have compromised with spiritual principles, thereby failing to thwart more traditionalist church hierarchs who remain dedicated to their orthodox interpretations of scripture, particularly on issues of family life and sexual behavior. As a former bishop, Spong has shown greater concern with the organization of the church than with political organization or public policies. Few specific policy preferences have emerged from his writings, particularly about matters of economic equality and distributive justice. Instead, procedural justice linked to sexual freedom takes priority, mainly as applied to church teachings and actions (Spong 1996:334; 1998:83–98; 1999:101–38, 199–203; 2000:305, 417–54; 2005:213–29).

As a modern-day John Bunyan, Bishop Spong leads his readers along paths toward the Celestial City—the promised land of enhanced meaning of the scriptures. On this pilgrimage, Spong seeks to "liberate" the scripture from fundamentalist notions about its literal, inerrant, and infallible meanings. Taking a historical critical view of the Bible, he assumes that it expresses eternal, not factual or literal, truths. Composed of poetry, symbols, myths, and metaphors, it has significance that derives from scientific evolution, historical investigation, education, reason, and church traditions. Besides highlighting historical inaccuracies, Spong specifies passages he views as morally objectionable: justifications of war, genocide, patriarchy, polygamy, homophobia, and physical punishment of children. However inaccurate its historical narratives, the Bible documents the evolutionary development of human life, especially the meanings that its writers attribute to contextual changes. Spong emphasizes the Jewish heritage of the New Testament. Jesus' teachings flowed from messages of the Torah and the prophets, mainly Joshua, Isaiah, Ezekiel, Amos, Micah, Zechariah, and Malachi, who perceived God as the Ultimate One who blended justice with mercy (Spong 1991, 1993, 1996, 2005). According to Spong, God represents Ultimate Reality—the source of life, love, and wholeness (holiness) of being. When individuals reflect these ultimate, transcendent qualities, they show in their behavior eternal life, unconditional love, and holiness; hence, the God consciousness becomes immanent. Spong regards sin as the destructive, cruel search for survival and as self-absorption, the failure to transcend the self and realize one's full humanity. Rather than inherent in human nature, sin stems from collective sources, including political oppression, economic exploitation, and cultural humiliation based on sexism, homophobia, racism, exclusivist nationalism, and anti-Semitism. Jesus, who empowers individuals with divine consciousness and sketches the vision of a new humanity, can lead people away from these sins on a journey toward the realm of God. On this pilgrimage, individuals must become interdependent as they cooperate for a more humane world society (Spong 1998:160–61; 1999:148–49, 207–21; 2001:119, 148–70; 2005:267–98; 2007:239–75).

Spong's interpretation of the interactions among the church, individual, and government rests on his notion of life as a pilgrimage. Acting in a consensual, persuasive way, religious institutions must not impose their prescriptions on either the individual or government. Instead, they should lead the journey on the best paths that will bring people to the meaning of life and enlightenment about the most ethical decisions. Rather than impose its will, the church ought to influence public officials and the laity. Spong sees the church fulfilling a universal, inclusive, reforming role dedicated to service. Rather than becoming too institutionalized and committed to maintaining its power, wealth, and privileges, the church needs to embody Jesus' vision: love others, heal the sick, teach the truth, and redeem the outcasts. These loving actions should take precedence over conformity to dogmatic creeds. As an adaptable institution, the church must remain open to new experiences, especially the inclusion of all people, not just a chosen few. As the organic body of Christ, the church promotes fellowship among the participants. When individuals consume food in the Eucharist, this communal sacrament symbolizes the sharing of resources. Inspired by Jesus, religious institutions have an obligation to redeem not only the individual but also the world. Spong wants individuals to become active participants in their efforts to influence the government, so that they can challenge unjust public policies and political oppression. Churches have a similar prophetic role to play as they proclaim public programs that will help realize the realm of God on earth. Performing this role, churches must give primacy to the search for meaning about the link between justice and mercy. Particularly when based on exclusivist ties that split insiders from outsiders, social solidarity hinders the search for meaning. Spong regards reassurance against threats as the least important church activity. From his perspective, religious institutions have concentrated too great concern for helping people with their personal insecurities but have neglected the collective implications of love and justice (Spong 1977:11–12; 1993:155–60; 1994:249–93; 1998:195, 224; 1999:126, 141, 221–33; 2001:212–17; 2005:216–18, 298).

The concept of justice stems from Spong's reading of the scriptures. He takes an ambivalent outlook toward hierarchy. Whereas Jim Wallis and William Sloane Coffin led decentralized, autonomous religious institutions, Spong for over 25 years served as Newark bishop in the more bureaucratic Episcopal Church. On the one hand, he favored a national, centralized church and strong leadership among bishops, who in his view showed excessive willingness to compromise when faced with conservative local demands for enhanced responsiveness. On the other hand, he opposed ecclesiastical authority that sought to impose its dogmatic edicts on subordinates. As a Protestant reformer who challenges hierarchical authority, he upholds neither episcopal nor papal infallibility. His critique of hierarchy particularly focuses on the Vatican Curia, which has supported a male priesthood, opposed birth control, abortion, and gay rights, and repressed intellectual dissent from such theologians as Hans Küng, Charles Curran, Leonardo Boff, and Matthew Fox. Roman Catholic claims about the church's authority to determine theological orthodoxy and to punish "heresy" reveal an intolerance of ambiguity, dissent, and individual freedom. Unwilling to show deference toward ecclesiastical authority, Spong seeks to reconstitute the Episcopal Church from the "bottom up." He also sees dangers from the Protestant fundamentalists, despite their decentralized structure. When they justify the power of the ruling political elites, hierarchical authority at the national government level becomes more oppressive (Spong 1998:226; 1999:103, 128–33, 186–87; 2000:304–6).

Spong assumes an inclusive stand on egalitarian justice. Raised in North Carolina when African Americans, women, Catholics, and Jews held subordinate status, he affirms the basic equality of all human beings, whatever their ethnicity, race, gender, sexual orientation, religion, and economic class: "The Word of God in Scripture confronts me with the revelation that all human beings are created in God's image and reflect God's holiness" (Spong 1991:248). This inclusiveness not only comprises men and women, homosexuals and heterosexuals, Christians and Jews, rich and poor but children and parents as well as members of all religious groups. He perceives all religions as complementary, not competitive. Despite the differences on specific theological issues, they all share a general commitment to love of God and neighbor, ethical service, and the need to share resources with the needy. Like other adherents of the Social Gospel, Spong asserts an ecumenical vision for the church, a vision of Christian humanism that includes everyone (Spong 2005:229, 241–44, 290–98).

Along with Jim Wallis and William Sloane Coffin, Spong believes in the merger of individual freedoms with collective responsibilities. Churches must not only stress personal well-being but also play a public role in working to transform society. From his perspective, the private good can thrive only when people also pursue the common good. Like Jesus and Paul, Spong rejects pursuit of self-interest as the supreme value. The self-centered search for material goods or survival hinders the evolutionary development of growth toward the public good. According to him, Jesus never imposed his collective vision of God's realm on others. Instead, "He called people into purposeful community. The Christian message had to be communal not individual, public not private" (Spong 2001:226). From this standpoint, Spong criticizes both conservative and liberal Christians for their failure to recognize the links between individual freedom and collective responsibility. Protestant fundamentalists and orthodox Catholics try to impose their doctrines on dissenters. Liberal Christians focus excessive attention on either self-help counseling or on social action, but neglect the spiritual beliefs about God that shape both individual and collective action (Spong 2001:224–26, 240).

Upholding the need for action, Spong rejects a fatalistic perspective in favor of high personal efficacy. Even if his writings concentrate on reinterpreting historic Christian beliefs and the meaning of the liturgy, he gives primacy to action over creeds. Rejecting notions about original sin, human depravity, and the fall from initial spiritual perfection, Spong assumes that all people, whatever their social background, have the potential to realize the divine qualities revealed in Jesus. He recognizes the evil conditions that faced Jesus and still prevail today.

Nevertheless, he perceives Christ not merely as an example to follow but as "a source of godly empowerment." However divergent their religious faith, individuals with access to God-conscious qualities can achieve the power to transform the world (Spong 2001:145–48, 228).

The specific policy preferences affirmed by Spong derive from this efficacious, egalitarian, communal, and nonhierarchical interpretation of justice. For him, procedural justice takes priority over distributive justice. He gives greater attention to issues of civil liberties and rules about sexual behavior than to economic equality. Even though Spong conceives of God as Ultimate Truth, he views knowledge about truth as uncertain and ambiguous, not as certain and clear. Rather than claiming to monopolize the truth and imposing their doctrine on others, churches should accept the pluralist diversity of alternative truths, remain adaptable to changing ideas, and avoid blind obedience to hierarchical authority. Similarly, in the political sphere, Spong warned against the attempts of Senator Joseph McCarthy and his followers to repress civil liberties under the pretense of ensuring national security against communists. Within government, the church, and university, evolutionary learning requires the right to dissent against established, conventional truths (Spong 1999:80, 130–33, 156–58; 2001:162; 2005:213–37).

Given Spong's commitment to civil liberties, he naturally supports the expansion of sexual freedom. Few issues have generated so much controversy and hostility among conservative Episcopalians, fundamentalist Protestants, and traditionalist Roman Catholics as his stands on sexual behavior and family life. Unlike them, he has upheld the rights to abortion, same-sex marriage, divorce, and sexual relations before marriage. Taking a nonpunitive position, he prefers birth control, sex education, and family planning as the best ways to control overpopulation. Yet he recognizes that under certain specific conditions—rape, incest, dangers of bearing a deformed, retarded child—pregnant women should have the right to gain a legal abortion. Accordingly, he rejects any constitutional amendment that would ban abortion or penalize doctors performing abortions. Spong wants heterosexuals and homosexuals to enjoy the same rights. God has created all people, whatever their sexual orientation, in the divine image. Everyone deserves divine love. So long as gays and lesbians show a monogamous, faithful, loving relationship with their partners, they should have the freedom to marry. Divorce becomes a legitimate option when married couples cannot peacefully settle irreconcilable conflicts. Spong accepts sexual interactions before marriage but only when specified conditions prevail. The partners are adults. Rather than enjoying many sexual encounters with diverse people at the same time, they maintain an exclusive, long-term relationship. Spong also prefers that the interaction remain private, not public. For him, sexual behavior should aim primarily to enhance human life, love, and being, not merely to procreate more children in an overpopulated world (Spong 1988; 1999:113–42, 166–68, 177–84; 2005:297–98).

Spong's affirmation of gender equality parallels his belief in sexual freedom. Recalling his alcoholic father and Pietist, sacrificial mother, he wants women to enjoy full equality with men, whether in the family, workplace, church, or political world. Within the family, Spong perceives women as autonomous, egalitarian partners with men. As Newark bishop, he supported the ordination of women priests and their consecration as bishops. According to him, affirmative action policies in government and the private sector have brought greater equity to American society, not just to women and African Americans (Spong 1991:221–24; 1999:19–23, 104–08, 185–88; 2000:22–23; 2005:71–109).

Opposition to punitive policies stems from Spong's conception of God as the source of love. Procedural justice requires that nations develop peaceful rules for settling conflicts. Having experienced militaristic attitudes in the South, he rejects preemptive wars and defense strategies that rely on military force. Instead, multilateral institutions should rely on negotiation, diplomacy, and persuasion as the primary routes to world peace. When people identify themselves as members of an inclusive world community, not adhere to an exclusivist nationalism, peaceful policies will gain greater acceptance. Within the domestic sphere, Spong sees the need for police and prison guards to pursue actions that avoid torture and other types of physical punishment. Rather than labeled as stigmatized "outcasts," prisoners deserve respect as human beings capable of rehabilitation. For Spong, restorative justice takes priority over retribution based on corporal and capital punishment (Spong 1999:81, 84, 141; 2001:154; 2005:12–13, 152–60).

Denouncing policies that intensify class warfare and exacerbate economic inequality, Spong seeks greater distributive justice from the government. Unlike Jim Wallis, however, he does not outline specific antipoverty programs. Instead, he opposes tax cuts for the wealthy and spending reductions for the poor. Programs for expanding universal health care, especially for the poor and children, as well as policies that increase housing for low-income persons, deserve support from public officials. From his vantage point, these policies will enhance the general well-being of the community (Spong 1994:285; 1999:87, 96, 177, 227).

Not only Wallis and Coffin but also Bishop Spong have achieved greater influence in universities, seminaries, and liberal churches than in government agencies. Given Spong's reformulation of theological beliefs, fundamentalist Protestants, traditionalist Roman Catholics, and conservative Episcopalians show little enthusiasm for his interpretations of the Bible or his public policy stands. Instead, he draws main support from liberal clergy in the United Methodist, Presbyterian, Episcopal, Congregational, Lutheran, and Unitarian Universalist churches. Liberal Catholics, reform Jews, and Buddhists, if not Muslims, also find that his teachings give meaning to their lives (Spong 2001:xxiii). Over government policy Spong's influence remains limited. Unlike Jim Wallis and William Sloane Coffin, Spong has never combined a broadly-based organization with detailed policy proposals linked to issues of social justice, especially poverty, economic inequality, and peace. Now that he no longer serves as Newark bishop in the Episcopal Church, his activities concentrate on teaching, lecturing, and writing. He has established no movements like Wallis' Call to Renewal that pressure political leaders to enact programs seeking world peace, reduced poverty, enhanced civil liberties, and environmental ecology. Hence, Spong's reformation of theology and reinterpretation of the liturgy yield minimal impact on government policies for increasing social justice.

DOROTHY DAY: THE CATHOLIC WORKER MOVEMENT

Although liberal Protestants have dominated the Social Gospel movement, Dorothy Day mobilized Catholics for greater justice. Founded in 1933 by Dorothy Day (1897–1980) and Peter Maurin (1877–1949), the Catholic Worker movement combined a radical program for social justice with orthodox Catholic theological beliefs. It started as a newspaper during the first days of the New Deal, then established several "houses of hospitality" that ministered to the poor, and also organized a few communal farms dedicated to a "green revolution" favored by

Maurin. Day's ideas about spiritual values and justice came from several different sources: Jesus, the Hebrew prophets, St. Francis, St. Thérèse of Lisieux, Thomas Merton, Jacques Maritain, Charles Dickens, Fyodor Dostoyevsky, Leo N. Tolstoy, Upton Sinclair, and Jack London. Her early contacts with socialists, anarchists, syndicalists, and communists and her later experiences with Catholic clergy also influenced her interpretations about the primacy of justice. She not only criticized communist party regimes for their coercive practices but also denounced both capitalism and communism for giving precedence to material interests over spiritual ends.

Throughout her long career as a radical journalist and social activist, Dorothy Day struggled against injustice. For her, the Roman Catholic Church should become the Church of the Poor and the Church of Peace. Justice meant Catholic assistance to the poor, the oppressed, and the marginals as well as powerful opposition to all wars, including World War I, World War II, the Korean War, and the Vietnam War. Social protests by Catholic Workers represented the major means to resist U.S. government policies. She participated in hunger strikes, labor strikes, boycotts, pickets, draft resistance activities, and civil rights demonstrations. However extensive these protests from 1917 through the late 1970s, she devoted less attention to influencing public legislation. Opposed to bureaucratic statism, she doubted the efficacy of government policies to transform society. According to her, charitable assistance rendered by decentralized Catholic Worker communities would achieve greater long-term success than more centralized government programs passed by representatives and implemented by state bureaucrats.

Like Bishop Spong, Dorothy Day took an ambivalent attitude toward hierarchy. On the one hand, as a self-styled "libertarian" and "philosophical anarchist," she supported personal responsibility, decentralization, spontaneity, and subsidiarity—the Catholic doctrine that individuals, families, neighborhoods, churches, and voluntary associations must realize social justice free from centralized, bureaucratic state coercion (Pontifical Council for Justice and Peace 2004: 81–83). Committed to this principle, Day renounced centralized domination by all bureaucracies, especially national governments, labor unions, and private business corporations. From her perspective, capitalism represented "a cancer on the social body" (Day 2005:334), because capitalist corporations like banks, insurance companies, and advertising agencies placed private profit above the common good. Whatever the group opposing centralized authority, she upheld its right to dissent. Rejecting violence and coercion, she condemned all government efforts to restrict civil liberties, including those of draft resisters, war protesters, Communist Party members, strikers, immigrant workers, and prisoners who suffered brutal treatment.

On the other hand, whereas Bishop Spong showed scant regard for either orthodox Roman Catholic theology or for the Vatican Curia, Dorothy Day accepted Catholic doctrines, liturgy, and sacraments. Even if she disagreed with many U.S. cardinals and bishops who supported war, opposed labor unions, and did not identify with the poor, she viewed the church as a divine institution. For her, the church brought meaning to life, social solidarity with her fellows, and reassurance against suffering that threatens the innocents. Its rituals and sacraments supply order to life in contrast to the disorder she perceived in her own experiences, even in the Catholic Worker movement. Hence, she upheld voluntary obedience to the Holy Mother Church, the "mystical body of Christ," and to its teachings. She once queried: "As to the Church, where else shall we go, except to the Bride of Christ, one flesh with Christ? Though she is a harlot at times, she is our Mother" (Day 2005:339). According to Day, Jesus the exemplar embodied both human and divine qualities. God represents goodness, love, and truth. Through the incarnation, "God became man that man might become God" (Day 1997:204). In the sacrament of the Eucharist, Catholics receive bread and wine—food for the life of the soul. Accepting the doctrine of transubstantiation, she believed that the Holy Spirit converts the bread and wine into the body and blood of Christ, so that the man Jesus becomes present in the food served the laity: "Jesus is there as Man. He is there, Flesh and Blood, Soul and Divinity. He is our leader Who is always with us" (Day 2006:167). She not only identified Christ as God but also affirmed orthodox Catholic teachings about the virgin birth, the resurrection of Jesus, and the immaculate conception of Mary, the mother of Jesus (Day 1997:62–65, 86, 139–41; 2005:8–9, 63, 69, 77, 170–73, 243–44, 271–73, 333–35; 2006:17, 71–75, 149–50, 154, 167–68). The Vatican Curia thus granted Day greater freedom of dissent than it allowed such liberation theologians as Ernesto Cardenal and Leonardo Boff.

Along with adherents of the Social Gospel, Dorothy Day believed in the equality of all people. Despite recognizing their evil tendencies, which she perceived resulted from the fall and the free will given by God, she held that God created humans in the divine image and likeness. Whatever their gender, class, religion, ethnicity, or nationality, they have the potential to realize the spirit of God in their behavior. Equality meant not mainly equal opportunities to gain social mobility but equal treatment as persons all loved by God. She wanted to expand economic equality through firms owned jointly by workers and entrepreneurs. Cooperatives, mutual credit unions, and farm communes, where both private and communal ownership prevailed, also deserved support. From her outlook, even if the Catholic Worker movement did not abolish classes, it would help mitigate class warfare. Although willing to defer to the male priests in the church, she upheld the need for greater gender equality in society. During her later life she even came to accept the gradual ordination of married priests and women priests. As a Catholic activist, she affirmed an egalitarian relationship between priests and laity. As a pacifist, she never equated the nation with God. For her, war denied the basic teaching of Jesus who blessed the peacemakers, resisted violence, and urged his followers to return good for evil. Even though regarding the Roman Catholic Church as the "one true Church," she adopted an ecumenical attitude toward other religions. Several Catholic Worker communities contain individuals of many faiths. Raised a Methodist and Episcopalian, Day throughout her life maintained cordial, egalitarian relations with individuals of diverse religious affiliations, including Jews, lapsed Catholics, and even atheists (Day 1997:139; 2005:8, 301; 2006:17, 151).

Like Social Gospelers, Day combined collectivism with individualism. Viewing the church and the Catholic Worker movement as a fellowship of believers united by God's love for humans and their love for each other, she wanted both to promote the personal dignity of individuals and also to perform works of mercy: feed the hungry, visit the prisoners, enlighten the ignorant, and redeem the world from injustice. Although proclaiming the need for individual freedom, dissent, and personalism (respect for the human dignity of each person), she rejected the views on sexual behavior and family life held by William Sloane Coffin and John Shelby Spong. Instead, she accepted the more orthodox doctrines proclaimed by the Roman Catholic

Church, Walter Rauschenbusch, and Jim Wallis. During her early life (1919–27), Day's relationship with journalist Lionel Moise resulted in an unwanted pregnancy terminated by an abortion. She also underwent a "common-law marriage" to anarchist Forster Batterham and raised a daughter born from that union. Even though Day never emphasized sexual behavior issues in her writings, she revered the sacrament of marriage, rejected divorce, and opposed contraceptives, abortion, premarital sex, and same-sex marriage. Nevertheless, she welcomed gays, lesbians, and divorced people into local Catholic Worker communities. Because Forster Batterham believed in neither marriage nor God, she separated from him after four years—a loss that contributed to her loneliness (Day 1997:113, 120, 134–46, 285–86; 2006:131, 145; Ellsberg 2005:xvii–xliii; Riegle 2003:28–30, 97).

Even though her personal sufferings brought despair about injustice, Day never abandoned a feeling of personal efficacy. Rejecting futility, apathy, and indifference, she, like the Social Gospelers, perceived the cross as a "folly of Christ" that led from defeat to victory over death. Opposed to moderation and prudence, she downplayed the obsession with fear and security. Only faith in God's grace can bring true security. Emboldened by their divine potential, people have the obligation to realize heaven on earth, no matter how incremental or long that task. For her, the transformed social order would arrive not by centralized public policies but through the localized activities of Catholic Worker communities. Disenchanted with state bureaucracies, Day assumed that public policy implementation would secure excessive coercion, corruption, administrative costs, and insensitivity to local needs. Although Day accepted policies that secured social security and unemployment benefits to individuals and government aid to hospitals, she felt that dependence on the "impersonal mother" state would erode personal efficacy, particularly feelings of responsibility (Day 1988; 1997:45, 180–81, 216, 222; 2005:69, 84, 87, 175, 243, 273–76, 286, 333, 352; 2006:153, 171–73). Yet as William Sloane Coffin and Michael Harrington pointed out, local Catholic charity hardly serves as a substitute for national justice programs. Without strong political efficacy, a vision for achieving a redeemed social order, and centralized policies that coordinate regional organizations, activists will face difficulties achieving a more just, egalitarian society (Hennessy 2005; Riegle 2003:58–59).

Dorothy Day died in 1980, yet her influence persists. The same injustices that she denounced—war, poverty, economic inequality, capitalist exploitation, racism, religious intolerance, torture, brutal prison treatment, violations of civil liberties—still confront the United States. Today over 180 Catholic Worker communities work in 36 states, Mexico, Canada, Australia, New Zealand, and several Northern European countries to alleviate these problems. Independent, decentralized communities minister to the marginals: the poor, immigrant workers, refugees, asylum seekers, AIDS patients, drug addicts, prostitutes, and the homeless. Houses of Hospitality provide food, housing and syringes; a few even offer condoms. To the Catholic workers, who take a vow of voluntary poverty, the sharing of resources promotes solidarity and brings meaning to their lives. Helping the outcasts provides reassurance that they not feel threatened by stigmatized marginals. Active participation in an inclusive religious structure gives them hope of achieving incremental success in the struggle for greater social justice (Spickard 2005).

Rabbi Michael Lerner: the Network of Spiritual Progressives

The Network of Spiritual Progressives represents a more recent organization that hopes to attain justice. Unlike the Catholic Worker movement, however, it tries to combine a national organization with local groups that focus not mainly on charity but on influence over national government policies. Organized by Rabbi Michael Lerner in 2005, the Network of Spiritual Progressives affirms the prophetic beliefs of the Jewish renewal movement. Influenced by Rabbi Abraham Joshua Heschel, he proposes a "spiritual covenant with America" based on the Torah and the prophets. Whereas Dorothy Day combined an orthodox theology with radical protest activities, Lerner wants to transcend the distinctions between liberals and conservatives. His comprehensive policy recommendations on distributive and procedural justice resemble European social democratic programs as well as the policies supported by Walter Rauschenbusch 100 years ago. Some liberal Protestants even view Michael Lerner as the major successor to William Sloane Coffin (Wakefield 2006:165).

The theological beliefs of Michael Lerner share similarities with those expressed by John Shelby Spong and New Thought disciples. All hold a similar conception of God, the individual, and society. In Exodus 3:14–15 appears the name of God *Ehyeh* (YHVH). Translated as Yahweh or Lord, this name reveals God as the one who brings things into being: I AM AS I AM, I WILL BE WITH YOU. Blending past, present, and future into a coherent whole, God represents an impersonal source of Being, Becoming, Love, Truth, sacred Energy, and Justice—what Lerner (2007:83) calls the "force of healing and transformation (*tikkun*)." God as Ultimate Reality signifies the transcendent qualities of holy oneness. Within each unique individual, God becomes immanent as a loving, forgiving, creative, healing presence (the I AM) that revitalizes life. Although individuals have divine potential, they also display imperfections or sins that miss the spiritual mark. The covenants with Noah, Abraham, Moses, and David direct individuals to practice righteous behavior—not only personal but also societal transformation. Free will gives people the choice to turn from evil and make good choices that serve both God and other human beings. Lerner believes that rather than waiting for God to overcome evil, individuals should actively uphold the transcendent standards of justice, renewal, and compassion inspired by the spirit of God (Lerner 1994:178–79, 267, 416). As the prophet Micah (6:9) declared, service involves just actions, compassion, and humility before God. The Torah and the prophets specified the need to obey God's will by serving the poor, widows, orphans, strangers, and the oppressed. Links between the individual and society rest on a communal basis that upholds interdependence, cooperation, partnership, and merciful justice. Following the spiritual covenant secures the blessings of peace and well-being. Violations lead to evil consequences—the absence of goodness (Aaron 2004; Lerner 2007:28, 82–83; McNamara 2005; Ochs 2005; Shapiro 2004; Spong and Spiro 1999:42–50, 61–74).

These theological assumptions shape Rabbi Lerner's concept of the interactions among religious institutions, the individual, and government. Like Rauschenbusch, he believes that churches, temples, synagogues, and mosques should provide meaning to individual lives. Toward government they must remain separate but seek to influence government public policies so that programs express greater generosity, kindness, justice, and humility, but reduced expenditures for faith-based institutions. Individuals have the responsibility to participate actively in political affairs, challenging government authorities when they neglect *tikkun*—the repair, reformation, and transformation of social imperfections (Lerner 2007:152, 211–12, 238).

Lerner's attitude toward justice derives from his distinction between the left and right hand of God. According to his interpretation, the right hand exemplifies a patriarchal, punitive, vengeful warrior God who demands obedience and condemns individuals for their evil deeds. By contrast, the left hand of God symbolizes a nurturant, loving presence that inspires hope, devotion, and performance of peaceful, just, and compassionate actions (Lerner 2007:24–29).

Interpretations of justice as nonhierarchical, egalitarian, efficacious, and individual/communal resemble the concepts elaborated by Walter Rauschenbusch, modern Protestant Social Gospelers, and Dorothy Day. Opposition to hierarchical authority stems from Lerner's concept of God as the embodiment of persuasive authority, not coercive power or domination. Hence, he supports extensive political and economic participation. Populist movements that emerge from the base should influence the political agenda. These movements must challenge the authority wielded by elitist institutions, such as the national government institutions and the two major political parties that try to centralize control in their national headquarters. Lerner sees the need for enhanced worker participation in private economic management, including election of directors, supervisors, and boards of directors (Lerner 2007:211, 253). Multinational corporations should demonstrate greater sensitivity to local cultural differences and to the health needs of people in developing nations.

Along with opposition to hierarchy goes an egalitarian perspective on justice. Lerner urges that divine nurturance take expression in equal treatment for all people, whatever their ethnicity, gender, sexual orientation, or economic class. Redistribution of wealth for poor people and equal rights for women, homosexuals, and immigrant workers assume primary importance (Lerner 2007:242–87).

Like Dorothy Day and Protestant leaders of the Social Gospel, Lerner desires a union of individual freedom with responsibility to the community. Opposed to an individualism that focuses exclusively on material self-interest and personal choice, he sees individual well-being connected with a cooperative, interdependent, healthy community. For him, spiritual perfection means wholeness (holiness)—becoming more closely connected with the whole community that extends to all humanity. Exclusivist loyalty to one nation-state, even the United States or Israel, negates the universalist aspects of the highest spiritual consciousness (Lerner 2007:268, 321–40).

Rejecting despair, fatalism, cynicism, and passivity, Lerner assumes that justice will emerge only if people feel high personal and political efficacy. As the force of transformation, God inspires activists to affirm a normative spiritual vision of a renewed society that will change the status quo. Despite the prevalence of cruelty, exploitation, and injustice, individuals have the potential goodness to help achieve the prophetic ideals of a more just, compassionate, and humble world. Through his books, articles, lectures, classes, the magazine *Tikkun*, and the Network of Spiritual Progressives (NSP), Rabbi Lerner communicates the need for political efficacy. To realize the prophetic vision, he recommends widespread activities: political education, letters to the editor, messages to other media, demonstrations, discussions at workplaces, and appeals to political parties, especially liberal Democrats and the Greens (Lerner 2005; 2007:82–86, 110, 365–82).

The specific, comprehensive public policy proposals highlighted by the Network of Spiritual Progressives flow from the prophetic vision. Lerner elaborates a complex agenda about procedural and distributive justice. As a Free Speech, antiwar activist in Berkeley during the 1960s, Lerner mobilized others to uphold civil liberties. After becoming a rabbi, he continues to support nonviolent dissent, pluralist diversity, and civil liberties—stands that derive from his concepts about the nurturant essence of God and the partial, uncertain knowledge of the divine. Belief in a nonpunitive God motivates his opposition to torture, capital punishment, and brutal prison conditions. The commitment to procedural justice inspires his policy preferences for international law, multilateral institutions, nuclear disarmament, and less dependence on conventional weapons. The examples of Jesus, Gandhi, and Martin Luther King, Jr. lead him to back nonviolent procedures for reconciling conflicts. More than other modern Social Gospelers, Rabbi Lerner affirms the need for international human rights for Palestinians. The Network of Spiritual Progressives has elaborated comprehensive recommendations for negotiating a peaceful settlement between Israelis and Palestinians. The settlement would involve the establishment of a Palestinian state around the pre-1967 borders, with negotiated adjustments for some areas. The NSP proposes an international consortium providing reparations for Palestinians and an international peace force ensuring security for Israelis and Palestinians against violent attacks by militarists. Rejecting Bush administration and Israeli government policies toward the Middle East, the NSP seeks an end to all violence in the area, an embargo on weapons shipments to all Middle East states, and an international conference that will offer secure borders between Lebanon and Israel. For Lerner, all human beings share sacred qualities. Hence, Iran, Syria, Hezbollah, Hamas, and the Israeli military should end all violent attacks against others viewed as "enemies" (Lerner 2007:67, 237, 349: *New York Times* 2006).

Procedural justice also encompasses policies on gender equality and sexual behavior. Opposed to patriarchy, Lerner affirms the need for women and men to become equal partners in all areas of life, including the family, economy, political sphere, and religious institutions. His commitment to loving, caring, and nurturant human interactions shapes his attitudes toward sexual behavior. According to him, individuals must avoid sexual exploitation, abuse, and domination of others. In contrast to Jim Wallis and Dorothy Day, he supports the stands taken by Bishop Spong and William Sloane Coffin on homosexuality and legal abortion. Rejecting laws that ban same-sex marriage, Rabbi Lerner has officiated at several marriages between homosexuals. From his perspective, whereas religious institutions should sanctify marriages, government must authorize civil unions between two adults and extend the same rights to homosexuals as to heterosexuals. Lerner also opposes government policies that make abortion illegal, particularly during the first six months of pregnancy. To uphold loving, stable family lives, he feels that public programs for family planning, contraceptives, sex education, child care, paid parental leave, increased health care services, full employment, and greater income equality will help ensure stronger family values. Even if he denounces the sexual imagery found in the capitalist mass media, his dedication to civil liberties leads him to reject censorship of the more salacious images depicted by advertisements, movies, television, and the Internet (Lerner 2007:258–76).

Policies on distributive justice reflect Lerner's social democratic preferences that stress generosity, compassion, empathy, and corporate responsibility. Domestically, the Spiritual Covenant with America calls for a universal, publicly-financed, single-payer health system, expanded child and elder care programs, jobs for the unemployed, housing for the homeless, higher wages for workers, and public education that gives priority to creativity, tolerance, compassion, cooperation, and reverence for the natural environment. Internationally, the Network for Spiritual Progressives proposes a "Global Marshall Plan" under which governments from the eight most industrialized countries will contribute 1–2 percent of their GDPs to finance programs that help alleviate poverty, homelessness, deficient health care, low-quality education, and pollution. The NSP urges multinational corporations to show greater responsibility by promoting a healthy environment, safe working conditions for their employees, and accountability to the public for the negative effects of managerial decisions. Through these domestic and international policies, Lerner and the NSP hope to achieve greater distributive justice (Lerner 2007:104, 222–37, 274–319).

The Network of Spiritual Progressives has achieved greater success with its ecumenical appeals than with its influence over political parties. Liberal Protestants, Catholics, Jews, Buddhists, Unitarians, Universalists, and New Thought groups like the Unity School of Christianity and the United Church of Religious Science have shown the greatest support. Progressives from mainline Protestant churches—United Methodist, Episcopal, Presbyterian, Lutheran, United Church of Christ, Disciples of Christ—most actively participate in the NSP. Whereas Lerner works closely with progressive evangelicals like Jim Wallis and Tony Campolo, his attacks on Protestant fundamentalists for their intolerance, dogmatism, polarization, apocalypticism, and opposition to science, gender equality, and homosexual rights scarcely generate any enthusiasm from Pat Robertson, James Dobson, or Tim LaHaye. Friendlier relations occur with liberal Catholics. Joan Chittister, member of the Benedictine Sisters of Erie, Pennsylvania, has served with Lerner as cochair of the NSP. Like Lerner, she upholds pluralism, gender equality, female empowerment, ecumenism, nonviolence, world peace, egalitarian redistribution measures, and the nature of God as Spirit, Life, and Being (Chittister 2004, 2005). Unity and Religious Science adherents share these spiritual values and policy preferences. As a rabbi, Lerner has encountered intense opposition from conservative Jews who denounce his condemnation of the Israeli government's militaristic policies toward the West Bank, Gaza, Lebanon, and Syria. His belief that the universalist values of justice, compassion, peace, and freedom for the oppressed should take priority over loyalty to the specific policies of a nation-state like Israel arouses anger among Jews who focus mainly on the national security of the Israeli state, not on the human rights of Palestinians.

Conservative Republicans assert an opposite interpretation of political justice to that of Michael Lerner. They seek to reduce government regulation of private businesses but to expand it over sexual behavior, especially abortion and homosexual relationships. On these issues, he gains stronger support from liberal Democrats and Greens (Lerner 2007:1–36, 95–212, 335–40). New Thought adherents who identify with the Democratic Party also favor the NSP stand on most public policies, particularly those concerning procedural justice, as the next chapter will show.

Conclusion

Along with the Social Gospel, New Thought highlights human equality, decentralized authority, personal efficacy, and the need to blend individual freedom with service to the general community. Both movements perceive God as transcendent spiritual principle and as a divine potential—the spark of divinity—within each person. Social Gospel activists, however, place greater emphasis on the need for individuals to participate in collective action as a way to influence public policy and secure transformative change. For them, evil stems from a reciprocal interaction between personal sins and structural sources: political oppression, economic exploitation, cultural humiliation. Churches have the responsibility to become actively involved in political organizations to secure public policies that will change empirical reality. By contrast, Religious Science and the Unity School of Christianity focus more attention on changing individuals' conceptions of reality, rather than social structures. Prayer, meditation, and education take priority over political protests or lobbying activities. Harmony among diverse groups becomes more important than conflict with antagonists. As a healer and teacher, Jesus serves as the ideal exemplar of the way to secure justice, compassion, personal well-being, and world peace.

5
NEW THOUGHT AND THE POWER OF THE INDIVIDUAL MIND

The child of true Humanity exists within you. Follow it! . . . A person sees neither with the soul nor with the spirit. The mind, which is between the two, sees the vision.

(The Gospel of Mary)

The guiding star to the arrangement and use of facts is in your leading thought. You will have come to the perception that justice satisfies everybody and justice alone.

(Ralph Waldo Emerson)

Jesus Christ taught that we may uplift our life by uplifting our thoughts. Jesus Christ taught that the only uplifting thoughts are the thoughts of God.

(Emma Curtis Hopkins)

Because God is infinite justice, you can always change the causes you set into operation, and so change the results.

(Myrtle Fillmore)

> Mind is the realm of causes. Conditions are in the realm of effects. Effects flow from causes and not from themselves. Thought is the instrument of Mind. New thoughts create new conditions.
>
> (Ernest Holmes)

In his play *Man and Superman*, George Bernard Shaw imagines a dialogue between Don Juan and the Devil about knowledge of reality. For the Devil, hell represents the dominance of thoughts that stress such earthly pleasures as love, beauty, music, and the amusements Shaw associated with the theater. Satisfied with the status quo, people in hell act in a conventional, conformist, bored way. Social isolation imprisons their minds, making them hostile to philosophical speculation. By contrast, the opposite mental conditions prevail in heaven. Philosophy becomes a guide to action. Differentiating present conditions from new thoughts, high aspirations, and just ideals, the heavenly inhabitants seek to improve conditions. Innovation, creativity, and cooperation supersede isolation and conventional ways of thinking. Rather than pursuing earthly pleasures, they adhere to a higher purpose—the Life Force—that transcends the self. In answer to the Devil's question, "What is the use of knowing?", Don Juan replies:

> Why, to be able to choose the line of greatest advantage. . . . Does a ship sail to its destination no better than a log drifts nowhither? The philosopher is Nature's pilot. And there you have the difference: to be in Hell is to drift; to be in Heaven is to steer.
>
> The Devil: On the rocks most likely.
> Don Juan: Pooh! which ship goes oftenest on the rocks or to the bottom? the drifting ship or the ship with a pilot on board?
>
> (Shaw 1946:169)

Propelled by high self-consciousness, understanding, and hope, the philosophical pilot overcomes the storms of self-indulgence, ignorance, and despair. Mastery of reality assumes primacy over the pretenses that Shaw observed in theatrical productions (McDowell 1987). Social solidarity supplants personal selfishness and isolation. Justice means social solidarity, personal efficacy, and a commitment to spiritual ideals.

Man and Superman illustrates the divergent approaches to reality that contrast idealism with materialism. Metaphysicians inquire about whether reality rests primarily on a materialist or idealistic foundation. Materialists assume that the material world exists independently of the mind. Composed of energy and matter—atoms, molecules, quarks, neurons, cells, electrons—it also includes economic conditions, political power, and cultural interactions. We know reality through reason, empirical investigations of conditions, and intersubjective agreement about observers' experiences. To change empirical conditions, individuals scarcely have complete free will. Instead, socialization, education, material well-being, and one's position in the social stratification system constrain aspirations to change society and even the self. Idealists, however, take a more optimistic position toward reality. They assume that knowledge of the world depends on minds that create political and spiritual reality. Impressions of reality based on empirical observation often rest on appearances, illusions, and delusions. True knowledge derives not only from reason and the senses but also from meditation, prayer, contemplation, revelation, and intuition. Commitment to free will leads idealists to assume that different ways of thinking produce different concepts of reality, which then cause actions that change both the self and the world.

Divergent ethical stands toward justice stem from materialism and idealism. Taking an instrumentalist position, materialists equate justice with desirable outcomes on the self and society. Whereas actions that lead to benign effects—material well-being, education, health, equality, political participation, cultural respect for others—are good (just), malign outcomes are evil (unjust). Idealists suggest that justice means a congruence with spiritual ideals, teleological purposes, and intrinsic ends. As Immanuel Kant proclaimed, the highest ethical principle emerges when individuals, groups, and governments treat people as ends, not means (Thagard 2000:87–164).

Plato elaborated one of the most idealistic perspectives on justice. He identified ultimate reality with ideal patterns or "forms" of Goodness. Unlike opinions, which derive from observations that may be true or false, knowledge of forms rests on an invisible, eternal, and unchanging foundation. Forms of goodness, justice, courage, and self-discipline take primacy. Justice entails an adherence to the Idea of the Good. In *The Republic*, Plato makes an analogy between the human soul and the ideal political system—"a pattern in heaven." Just as reason should control ambition and the bodily passions, so the philosophers—the lovers of wisdom, truth, goodness, knowledge, justice—must guide the political community. Making an analogy between the navigator and the philosopher-ruler, Plato asserts that the pilot has the expertise to guide the ship's crew to a safe port; so too does the philosopher possess the wisdom, knowledge, and expertise about governance to guide the political community to civic virtue, the common good, and justice. Justice emerges through lengthy periods of philosophical contemplation, education, and training. Even if Plato doubted that the ideal republic would ever become feasible on earth, it remained the normative standard for evaluating actual political systems. According to him, functional role differentiation will best achieve ethical ideals. Philosophers rule through reason. Soldiers, police, and administrators who demonstrate courage, honor, and self-assertion ensure security. Moneymakers—farmers, merchants, artisans, laborers—seeking economic gain remain subordinate to the other two higher classes. Injustice arises when the appetites (bodily desires) for food, drink, and sex dominate reason. Political leaders lust after money and wealth. Soldiers dedicated to victory claim superiority over rulers who love wisdom, reason, and knowledge. In this unjust nonhierarchical system, conflict, disorder, and disharmony prevail. No one truth unites the fragmented society. Asserting the purity of philosophic truth over the messy, faction-riven political world, Plato expressed his bias against politics. Even if the philosopher-rulers have the duty to descend from the heavenly sunlight into the dark political cave where shadows of ignorance obscure spiritual wisdom, they risk contaminating their knowledge of the Good (Brooks 2006; Plato 2003; Rosen 2005).

Although New Thought adherents disclaim the hierarchical, elitist stand toward justice taken by Plato, they uphold idealist concepts about the supremacy of the mind and spiritual values. Unity and Religious Science give primacy to spiritual reality over material conditions. Whereas Spirit signifies an eternal, permanent, changeless reality, the material world represents appearances and illusions that change with the historical context. Although the Athenians during Plato's time recognized several personal gods, he viewed God as the impersonal Idea of Goodness. Similarly, New Thought students perceive God as the impersonal Spirit of Goodness, Truth, Light, and Love. Through contemplation, prayer, and meditation, individuals can achieve harmony with the Infinite. As Plato assumed, education becomes a primary way to gain knowledge of spiritual principles. New Thought students focus on reading books and attending lectures as key methods for changing one's conception of reality. As Schleiermacher also emphasized, consciousness-raising or what Plato (2003:246) called the ascent "to the vision of the good" represents the ideal procedure for gaining "the highest form of knowledge." Resulting wisdom will thereby change thoughts, personal behavior, and even social conditions. Unlike material goods, spiritual values when shared with others never become exhausted. Service to other people hence promotes the common good—a key Platonic value.

Despite these similarities with Plato's interpretations, New Thought disciples adopt a different approach to justice. Unlike Plato, they affirm an optimistic view of human equality. God has created all people in the divine image and likeness. Rather than ruled by their insatiable passions, most individuals have the potential to change their thoughts, attain wisdom, and revise their behavior according to spiritual ideals. This egalitarian strain leads to a nonhierarchical concept of justice. Instead of role differentiation, role diffuseness characterizes New Thought organizations, which feature extensive decentralization, widespread participation, and multiple centers of authority. Individualism takes precedence over the communalism, uniformity, and order stressed by Plato. Each individual has the freedom to express her views about the Bible, faith, and spiritual reality. Whereas Plato doubted the feasibility of ever realizing the ideal republic on earth, New Thought students voice high personal efficacy about achieving heavenly conditions in this world, especially because heaven represents an elevated state of consciousness, not a place where people go after death.

If New Thought disagrees with several Platonic tenets, how does it diverge from the "old thought" proclaimed by the Roman Catholic hierarchy, Calvinism, and U.S. fundamentalist Protestantism? Although these three "orthodoxies" scarcely agree on every doctrine, they believe in a personal God who rewards the faithful and punishes sinners. Individuals have the potential for both good and evil. Communal order can help restrain the evil impulses and nourish goodness. The church becomes an important structure for teaching the faith, upholding discipline, and spreading the gospel. Roman Catholics and Calvinists feel a keen obligation to influence government so that it can implement public policies congruent with their moral-spiritual values and material interests. Fundamentalist Protestant leaders such as Pat Robertson and James Dobson share this same inclination for active political participation. By contrast, New Thought theologians perceive God as an impersonal spiritual principle that neither rewards nor punishes. Instead, individuals need to attain harmony with infinite spiritual values of life, light, and love. Reflecting the divine image, they have high potential for good behavior. Instead of depending on intermediary ecclesiastical institutions or charismatic clerics for salvation, individuals should commune directly with God to change their thoughts about spiritual reality. Rather than a highly organized church, Unity and Religious Science are more decentralized movements that spend little time on staging political protests or trying to influence government policymakers.

New Thought and old thought also express divergent approaches to justice. Calvinists, pre-Vatican II Roman Catholics, and most Protestant evangelical leaders take a hierarchical view of authority. A patriarchal elite makes the key decisions. Collectivism unites church members in an organic harmony. Although persons have some free will to determine their fate, the orthodox hierarchs, particularly Calvinists, affirm the sovereignty of God, who ultimately decides on those who shall gain entrance to heaven. Committed to a metaphysical, allegorical, symbolic interpretation of the Bible, New Thought rejects these orthodox assumptions of justice. Its nonhierarchical, egalitarian approach emphasizes equality for women. Individual freedom gives individuals the right to dissent and change their views. No notion of heresy constrains dissenters. Neither views about human depravity nor opinions about predestination limit personal efficacy. Unconstrained by a personal sovereign God, the Devil, or environmental conditions, individuals can effectively change their thoughts, if not all the structural conditions in their personal environment. Influenced by Gnosticism and Ralph Waldo Emerson, the Unity and Religious Science movements reject orthodox interpretations in the Apostles' and especially the Nicene creeds.

THE HERITAGE OF NEW THOUGHT

Several texts influenced the development of New Thought. These include the writings of Mary's Gospel, Ralph Waldo Emerson, and

Emma Curtis Hopkins. They all affirm the power of thought to transform empirical reality. As source of ideas that govern the individual, the "Divine Mind" assumes political dimensions. It has the potential power to control not only the person's mind and body but also societal conditions. Education provides the idealism, knowledge, and wisdom needed for overcoming obstacles.

Early Christian Gnosticism: the Gospel of Mary

Influenced by Plato's beliefs about the dominance of spiritual ideals over the material world, early Christian Gnostic groups expressed interpretations that shaped New Thought during the twentieth century. Rather than a single, uniform, cohesive movement, Gnosticism featured several diverse, conflicting strands within early Christianity. Just as today, during the first and second centuries CE divergent interpretations about the role of Jesus, the most important elements of the faith, the connections that linked the body with the soul, relations with the political order, and future prospects after death produced controversy. Not until the Nicene Creed in 325 did a formal Christian creed emerge. By then a more bureaucratic, hierarchical, centralized church had gained power in Rome. Male bishops wielded dominant authority. For them, the epistles of Paul became the foundations of the Roman Catholic faith. Early church fathers like Irenaeus (115–202) and Tertullian (160–240) regarded several Gnostic texts as "heresies" that contradicted church "orthodoxy." In Greek, whereas "orthodox" means "straight thinking," heresy refers to self-chosen interpretations denying the basic creeds, biblical regulations, and canon law. Several texts about Jesus, including the books of Mary, Philip, Thomas, John, James, and Baruch fell under the heresy stigma. Even if voicing divergent interpretations of spiritual reality, they all held that *gnosis* (knowledge), wisdom, and enlightenment paved the way to salvation (Edwards 2001:313–16; King 2003:155–90; Meyer 2005:vii–xxvii). Of all these early Christian Gnostic writings, the Gospel of Mary offers the most relevant insights into New Thought. Written during the early second century, probably around 120 CE, the Gospel of Mary attracted a Gentile audience that knew Greek and Coptic. Only fragments of the gospel exist today. Missing passages and the brief text limit our ability to comprehend its message.

The basic themes of Mary's Gospel depart from Paul's epistles, the Apostles' Creed, and the Nicene Creed. Whereas they emphasize the resurrection of the body and Jesus as the suffering Christ who died to save the world from sin, the Gospel of Mary focuses on the soul's immortality—the ascent of the soul to God—and the life of Jesus as a teacher of wisdom. Taking an optimistic, egalitarian perception of human potential, Mary's gospel assumes that knowledge comes from visions, intuition, revelations, and personal inspirations, not mainly from Judaic regulations, church creeds, canonical teachings, or patriarchal hierarchs. Gender equality in a decentralized, spontaneous community assumes foremost attention (King 2003:3–12, 69–90, 119–27; 2006:191–214).

The gospel's theological interpretations about God, the individual, and salvation reflect the primacy of idealism. God signifies not only transcendent goodness but also an indwelling child of true humanity. Created in the image of God, individuals are spiritual beings. Through mystical knowledge, the individual attains salvation. Jesus functions as savior, the teacher and revealer of wisdom. Sin arises from ignorance, self-deception, and failure to follow Jesus' teachings as well as imitate his life. When people give lower priority to spiritual values than to material matters like the bodily passions, then evil (impurity) emerges. Only when persons adhere to eternal spiritual realities—the source of perfect goodness—will peace, health, and inspiration result. Under this condition of high spiritual consciousness, the mind operates as the intermediary between the spirit and the soul—the eternal aspect of the self. Harmony and cohesion prevail in society when the soul destroys all evil powers, including darkness, desire, ignorance, and violence.

Concepts about the Christian community, individual, and government flow from notions that affirm the priority of spiritual ideals over material reality. Rather than a centralized, bureaucratic ecclesiastical church, the Gospel of Mary prefers a decentralized spiritual community lacking oppressive laws and creedal regulations. Its teachers heal the sick, preach the gospel, and reveal the spiritual teachings of Jesus. To governments, like that of the Roman empire that ruled during the second century, the Christian community should articulate an alternative vision: one based on enlightenment, life, peace, equality, restorative justice, hope, and love for all, not on ignorance, death, violence, inequality, punitive justice, fear, and hatred of enemies. Yet overt expression of these Christian spiritual values often provoked persecution by the oppressive Roman rulers. Hence, the Gospel of Mary implied a strategy of more covert, adaptable resistance to Roman domination. By communicating spiritual values to its members, the Christian community could delegitimize the empire's political authority (King 2003:13–81).

Interpretations of justice rest on a spiritual base. Rejecting the domination of external authority, especially oppressive regulations, the Gospel of Mary supports widespread participation, education, and dialogue about spiritual realities. Opposition to hierarchy is congruent with egalitarianism. Just as God reflects impersonal spiritual goodness, not a male or female body, so gender equality must thrive in the Christian community. Rather than based on male gender or apostolic patriarchal status, true authority should derive from spiritual maturity, mental power, moral purity, and comprehension of Jesus' teachings. Social institutions create sexual differentiation, which embodies illusions about the primacy of the passions. As a spiritual being, the individual has the freedom to liberate the self from bodily passions, attain wisdom, and thereby secure spiritual transformation. Seeking the indwelling God, people have the divine potential to find healing and inner peace but not the power to redeem the material world from its impurities, corruption, and violence (King 2003: 29–34).

Transcendentalism: the Influence of Ralph Waldo Emerson

Living in the United States during the nineteenth century, Ralph Waldo Emerson (1803–82) and other Transcendentalists had greater freedom to communicate their views about sociopolitical change than did the writer of Mary's Gospel. Opposed to hierarchical institutions, religious dogma, and conventional norms, the Transcendentalists believed that an individual's spiritual consciousness can transcend empirical realities, supersede traditions, and thereby realize egalitarian social reforms. Particularly for George Ripley, the Unitarian founder of Brook Farm, Schleiermacher's ideas about language motivated enlightened individuals to communicate the thoughts that led to political action, such as movements against slavery, women's inequality, and maltreatment of prisoners. Relying on Schleiermacher's analyses of Plato and Luke's Gospel, Emerson also affirmed the importance of discourse as a primary medium for political change (Gura 2007: 66–67, 80–83, 143–44; Richardson 1995:249–50, 290).

A minister, lecturer, teacher, and prolific writer, Emerson based his concept of justice on an idealistic foundation. Influenced by Plato, his essay on "The Transcendentalist" contrasted materialism with idealism. Whereas the materialist perspective on knowledge gives priority to empirical conditions and observable facts, the idealist focuses major attention on thought, consciousness, will, moral sentiments, and other subjective variables. For Emerson, idealism takes precedence over materialism (Emerson 1981:92–110). As he stated in a later essay: "Spiritual is stronger than any material force . . . thoughts rule the world" (Emerson 1929:8:229). The cognitive dissonance between the ideals of justice and the empirical conditions of injustice energizes social change. Committed to ethical ideals, spiritual values, and moral character, Emerson launched a critique against the injustices that plagued nineteenth-century America: slavery, women's inequality, government corruption, materialism, economic exploitation, censorship, cruel treatment of blacks and native Americans.

Emerson's theological views about God, the individual, and society reflected the emergent Unitarianism gaining influence in Boston over Calvinism. Rather than perceiving God as a supernatural person who sent sinners to hell and the righteous to heaven, he perceived God as impersonal, transcendent spirit that also dwelled within each individual. For him, the term "God" signified Unity, Universal Being, Universal Mind, Omniscience, the Over-Soul, First Cause, the Eternal One, infinite Beauty, and the Source of Enlightenment that illuminated individual consciousness. Instead of accepting the Calvinist notions of human depravity, Emerson assumed that Supreme Wisdom became individualized within each person's soul, which can gain awareness of reason and justice: "In the soul of man there is a justice whose retributions are instant and entire. . . . If a man is at heart just, then in so far is he God; the safety of God, the immortality of God, the majesty of God do enter into that man with justice" (Emerson 1981:74). Emerson regarded Jesus not as a demigod but as a prophet who incarnated God and understood the indwelling divine nature of all individuals. Service to him comes by thinking his holy thoughts. Emerson recognized the tendencies for humans to ignore spiritual thoughts but to act in lazy, conformist, ignoble ways. He nevertheless saw in them a high potential to avoid evil, which he termed a "nonentity," and to embrace the reality of benevolence. Evil stems not only from an unholy will but from unjust structural conditions such as slavery, prejudice, intolerance, deficient education, oppressive laws, and cruel prison treatment. To reform these conditions, individuals need to transcend their self-centered isolation and show empathy, compassion, and altruism toward others. God inspires the individual, who then translates faith into virtuous actions that heal a diseased social body (Emerson 1981:72–91, 209–27, 383–94; 1983:383–86; Robinson 2003).

The interaction between God as infinite spirit and the individual as a spiritual being with divine potential shaped Emerson's outlook toward the church and government. His service as a minister to the First and Second Churches of Boston lasted only a brief period from 1827 to 1832. He resigned from the First Church because of his view that the Eucharist symbolized a purely spiritual experience of union with the Christ presence; therefore, the administration of material wine and bread denigrated the symbolic ideals—a position similar to that taken by the Society of Friends (Richardson 1995:78–127). This clash illustrated a more general rejection of the institutionalized church as too ritualistic, formalistic, dogmatic, and imprisoned by outmoded ideas. For him, churches possessed only partial, incomplete knowledge. Even the Bible needed modern revelations that may not agree with the creeds, canons, and teachings of the church fathers. Perceiving the spiritual temple as dwelling in a person's soul, Emerson accorded only limited influence to hierarchical ecclesiastical institutions. No intermediary should limit an individual soul's direct communion with God.

Emerson wanted individuals to play a highly participatory role in politics. Even if elected government leaders should serve the public good, they often came under the undue influence of corrupt businesses and political parties. Electing legislators to representative institutions did not suffice to ensure promotion of the common good. Instead, he favored widespread participation through voluntary associations, churches, rallies, demonstrations, protests, and town meetings. Whatever their ethnicity, religious affiliation, gender, and regional residence, individuals could communicate their diverse ideals. By conversing with others, they could try to persuade others, gain acceptance for their positions, and even revise their own views. Emerson hoped that free speech and assembly would promote the common good at the local, if not at the national, level. Deliberation, debate, and reasonable argumentation would supersede dogmatism, orthodoxy, and traditional thoughts. As active public players, individuals had a duty to disobey unjust laws enacted by the government and favored by elites or even majority opinion. From Emerson's perspective, changes in society would hence occur only through individual transformation. Ethical government involves "right obedience to the powers of the human soul" (Emerson 1929:8:297). Public sector participation should motivate individuals to transcend their private interests and gain an awareness of a more general, universal public good that assures the well-being of all humanity (Emerson 1981:389–94; 2004:131–34, 175; Esquith 2001; von Rautenfeld 2005).

Rejecting hierarchical authority, Emerson equated justice with equality. No institution, whether government, church, or university, possesses complete knowledge. No political leader, especially one proclaiming a populist rhetoric, deserves unqualified veneration. Committed to personal freedom, individuals and social groups need to oppose government oppression, such as prevailed during slavery. All people share a basic equality with others: "As a man is equal to the church and equal to the state, so he is equal to every other man. The disparities of power in men are superficial" (Emerson 2004: 87). Conversations by men and women reveal a similar ability to express their opinions about public issues. Even if each one has different talents and has yet to achieve self-reliance, all persons possess the potential to fulfill their ethical, spiritual qualities (Emerson 2004:118–19; Esquith 2001).

Although Emerson advocated self-reliance, he never regarded the individual as an isolated atom independent of social interaction. Instead, he urged that Americans link their individual freedom to a cooperative spirit that superseded a "solitary imprisonment." Through public conversations, Emerson expected that people would secure greater empathy, altruism, and efficacy to improve social conditions. Apathy, complacency, indifference, and despair hinder action against such injustices as oppression of blacks, violence against native Americans, and economic exploitation of the poor. From spiritual faith in people's divine potential comes idealism. From the contradiction between this idealism and unjust conditions arises the political will for mobilizing collective actions that will alleviate these injustices. Whatever the limiting influence of inherited habits, national history, and present status, efficacy can overcome personal fatalism when individuals acquire the wisdom of a virtuous education (Emerson 1981:387–94; 1983:262–85, 382–83, 439–48; 2004:134–36).

Emerson's position on procedural justice reflected his commitment to personal freedom, equal rights, and compassion. Opposed to government coercion, he strongly supported free speech, dissent against injustice, and free association. Because no external authority or institution has complete knowledge, these civil liberties promote intellectual inquiry, new ideas, and revision of traditional viewpoints. Opposition to repression of the black slaves and native Americans, especially the Cherokee, highlighted his perception that this oppression violated justice, human rights, and freedom for all people to develop their talents. Freedom and equality extended to women as well. Especially after 1860, his enthusiasm for full women's rights grew stronger. Influenced by Margaret Fuller, he backed their rights to vote, hold political office, own and inherit property, gain a university education, achieve secure employment in the professions, and enjoy financial independence. Emerson saw that women had played a key role in the abolitionist movement as agitators for freedom, and in the Civil War as teachers and health personnel. This experience demonstrated their rights to full political equality, financial autonomy, and independence with men. According to him, women, not men, should determine the actual degree of female participation in society and government (Emerson 1929:8:231; 2004:29–32, 118–57, 204–05; Gilbert 2001; Gougeon 1998; Richardson 1995:395–99, 532–34).

Even though Emerson regarded government's primary task as the wise person's education, he still supported activist, egalitarian policies for distributive justice. According to him, moral character took precedence over wealth. Dedication to moral-spiritual values entailed modest living, temperance, hard work, avoidance of debt, and generosity to others. Government leaders had the responsibility to demonstrate similar ideals by enacting compassionate programs for the marginalized: equal rights to financial autonomy for poor women, education for children, assistance to the sick and disabled, high wages for Southern freed slaves and poor whites, as well as prison reform for criminals. Extremes of wealth and the resulting poverty not only demoralized the poor but exacerbated injustice. Hence Emerson favored expanding equal opportunities to gain income. Rejecting the materialism of both capitalism and socialism, he took an ambivalent stand toward both. To the extent that they elevated selfishness and coercion above altruism and freedom, neither gained his approval. Although backing free trade and productive investment by merchants, he denounced their tendency to place private economic self-interest over pursuit of the ethical common good. Capitalist monopolies interfered with everyone's right to equal opportunity. Emerson also showed little enthusiasm for the agrarian socialism that disciples of Robert Owen and Charles Fourier had established in nineteenth-century America. Communal farms gave primacy to a conformist collectivism that hindered individual freedom. Instead, Emerson backed state and local public ownership of schools, libraries, museums, and such scientific equipment as telescopes. According to Emerson, these public goods would provide the culture, education, and science needed for inspiring the citizen to develop an ethical life (Emerson 1929:6:85–127; 1983:358–67; 2004:49, 174–75; Richardson 1995:394, 535; Robinson 2001). Emerson's spiritual idealism inspired Emma Curtis Hopkins and other New Thought teachers during the late nineteenth century. Guided by Emerson's and Fuller's interpretations, they strove to achieve a more spiritual society that blended individualism with egalitarianism. Women's rights, tolerance, prison reform, education, and expanded economic opportunities for the poor assumed priority (Gura 2007:209–39).

The Teacher of New Thought: Emma Curtis Hopkins

The most influential New Thought teacher from 1886 to 1925, Emma Curtis Hopkins (1853–1925) ordained ministers who founded several churches. These included the Homes of Truth, Divine Science, Religious Science, and the Unity School of Christianity. Her eclectic, pluralist ideas stemmed from several sources: the Hebrew Bible, the Greek New Testament, Hinduism, Buddhism, Taoism, Islam, Zoroastrianism, Plato, Spinoza, Swedenborg, and Hegel. Nineteenth-century individuals who shaped her interpretations were Ralph Waldo Emerson and Mary Baker Eddy, the founder of Christian Science. Like Eddy, Hopkins viewed God as impersonal spiritual Principle, regarded the individual as created in the divine image, denied the metaphysical reality of evil, and saw the ideal community as a harmonious fellowship of individuals.

A student of Eddy for a brief time at her Massachusetts Metaphysical College during late 1883 and early 1884, Hopkins quickly became a significant disciple. Eddy appointed her an assistant editor of the *Journal of Christian Science* in April 1884. From the September 1884 through March 1885 issues, she served as editor. Afterwards, she once again became an assistant editor until October 1885, when Eddy dismissed her.

After moving to Chicago, Hopkins in 1886 founded the Emma Curtis Hopkins College of Christian Science, later renamed the Christian Science Theological Seminary that operated until 1895. The Hopkins Metaphysical Association established branches in several cities from Maine across the United States to California. She held classes not only in Chicago but also in urban centers like New York, Milwaukee, Kansas City, and San Francisco. All these educational activities increased her impact on the emerging New Thought movement, which stressed gender equality, women's rights, spiritual knowledge, and the power of idealistic thoughts to transform an individual's personal conditions (Harley 2002:7–91).

Hopkins took a pluralist orientation toward religion. Although stressing the importance of the Christian Bible, especially its New Testament, she synthesized elements from Asian religions, Transcendentalism, Christianity, and several philosophies. As early as April 1884 while an assistant editor of the *Journal of Christian Science*, she linked God's omnipresence to "Truth in every religious system of the world" (Hopkins 1884). Unlike Eddy, she never headed a church. Instead, she ordained ministers in several diverse, decentralized New Thought movements, such as Divine Science, Religious Science, and Unity.

Focusing on individualist concepts of justice, Hopkins assumed that true knowledge comes from the indwelling Spirit. Christians should not perceive the human Jesus as a divine hero but instead venerate the indwelling Christ principle and presence of God. By understanding his teaching as well as emulating the Christ Mind, his followers will gain successful outcomes: health, prosperity, happiness. Even if Hopkins applied her ideas mainly to the individual, her concept of justice as making right judgments also involves the sociopolitical world. From her viewpoint, political justice emerges when government leaders achieve peace, nonviolence, limited crime, and economic equality, rather than allow war, violence, high crime rates, and poverty to continue (Hopkins 1888:55–56, 91; 1891b:3–12; 1891c:14; 1891e:4–5; 1891i:9–10; 1893b:5; 1901:19–24; 1925:112–25, 135–41, 155–58, 181; 1928:34; 2003b:30–71, 195, 232–34; 2005a:8; 2005c:6–28, 43–44).

Hopkins' individualist approach to justice rejected deference to authority, whether in government, the church, or family. Urging individuals to worship the spiritual principles of goodness and right judgment, she opposed loyalty to persons, laws, and creeds. Just as citizens must assert their freedom against a punitive, repressive government ruled by immoral statesmen, so laity should secure freedom from church officials who earn high salaries, demand mindless obedience, but show limited knowledge of God. From her perspective, Jesus freed his followers from orthodox rituals, outdated ecclesiastical creeds, and preconceived doctrines. Each person needs to gain knowledge not from an external authority but from the indwelling Christ Spirit. The freedom of Spirit extends to children as well as adults. Rejecting notions about a punitive God, Hopkins wanted parents to give their children the freedom to learn on their own, rather than taking orders form adult "superiors." Nurturant child-rearing reflected her theological assumptions about nondeferential justice (Hopkins 1888:132, 180, 209; 1891f:8–18; 1891g:3–4, 13; 1891h:18–19; 1891i:15–16; 1892a10–11; 1892b:10–13; 1892d:5; 1893a:2; 1901:4, 68; 1925:206, 347; 1928:89; 2003b:109; 2005b:38–39; 2005c:59).

Egalitarian notions of justice blended with a strong commitment to personal efficacy. Hopkins assumed that individuals' thoughts create society; they need to reject societal pressures for treating people as unequals. She wrote: "Society should not dictate to you that there is any difference among the sons and daughters of God. You should ignore such errors and transcend society with the words of truth" (Hopkins 1892a:7). This egalitarian position stemmed from the example of Jesus who "said all were equal in God. He spoke of the sure goodness of children. He called the despised women daughters of God" (Hopkins 1891f:15). Because God shows impartiality to all people, whatever their social status, Christians should do likewise. All persons have within them the spark of divinity, the indwelling Christ Presence, even if some have attained greater manifestation of their spiritual potential than others. By renewing their human minds with the mind of Christ Jesus, as Paul urged in his letter to the Philippians (2:5), people can achieve freer, more egalitarian lives. Opposed to fatalism, resignation, and despair about failure, Hopkins assumed that their divine potential gives individuals high personal efficacy. They determine their own destiny by transforming thoughts of evil and failure into thoughts that give supremacy to goodness and success. Through verbal denials and affirmations, individuals can attain not only personal healing, prosperity, and happiness but also a more spiritual society (Hopkins 1891d:7; 1891e:14; 1891f:8; 1894b:10; 1925:124; 1928:93; 2003b:87, 102–07, 185–87, 203, 243, 256).

Even if Hopkins focused mainly on individual perceptions and behavior, rather than on politics, her theological assumptions shaped her position regarding public policies. Her belief in individual freedom led to a strong commitment to procedural justice, especially to civil liberties and nonpunitive government programs. Christians must practice tolerance for all people, whatever their religious affiliation or political views. Nonviolent strategies for securing change will most effectively realize spiritual goals. Along with war, high military expenditures contradict an affirmation of God as the only defense: "If there is any nation or globe in the spaces that is preparing to molest the peace of its neighbors, it is out of step with the heavenly legions, visible and invisible, and cannot win its iron-charioted way, even though all its munitions and plannings have risen to the Nth power of antagonism" (Hopkins 1925:348). War thus violates the heavenly conditions of harmony. Commitment to nonviolent, nonpunitive policies also extends to prison reforms that should treat convicts as individuals with divine ideals, not as depraved sinners deserving retributive justice (Hopkins 1891c:14; 1891f:16–17; 1891h:15; 1892c:12–13, 17; 1892e:13; 1893a:1; 1894a:47; 1925:285–86; 2003b:93, 110, 235).

On issues of marriage and sexual behavior, Hopkins asserted the dominance of spiritual values over the bodily appetites. Her notion of spiritual law denied that people remained enslaved to their "lustful passions" and "sensual appetites" (Hopkins 1901:118). According to her, marriage rested on three types of relationships: material, mental, spiritual. Material marriage unites the bodies of a man and woman. Mental marriage joins two people with congenial minds. The spiritual form constitutes the highest type. Theologically, Hopkins believed that the Holy Spirit signifies the Mother of God serving the Father's ministry. Among humans, spiritual marriage results when the individual mind fuses with the indwelling God, the Christ Presence, in loving communion (Hopkins 1891a; 2003a; 2005c:43–44).

Hopkins' stance on gender and economic equality reflected her preference not only for procedural justice but also for distributive justice that provided benefits to all people, whether rich or poor, man or woman. For her, the spiritual attributes of God apply impartially to everyone. All deserve equal treatment, similar opportunities, and even a more egalitarian distribution of possessions. Rejecting conflict between labor and capital, Hopkins sought equal rights for workers, including those in the Woman's Federal Labor Union in Chicago. Women probably comprised around 90 percent of ministers ordained by her. Politically, she backed the vote for women and for greater female representation in government offices. Her enthusiasm for economic equality stemmed from her perception of a loving, compassionate, nurturant, impartial God that never neglects the poor and unemployed but "makes them equals with kings and princes in possessions and opportunities" (Hopkins 2005b:3). Just as God eliminates poor people's feelings of inferiority, so political leaders must demonstrate a compassionate empathy for the needs of others. Through the "right reasoning" of those in power, society will attain greater abundance and prosperity for all (Hopkins 1891c:14–15; 1891f5, 15; 1892a:7; 1893c: 2–3).

Without a powerful church institution, Hopkins indirectly affected the public agenda through those who heard her lectures, read her books, became her students, and ministered to churches. Beginning in the 1890s, her followers organized coalitions, the International Divine Science Association (1892) and the International Metaphysical League (1900). In 1914 New Thought adherents established the International New Thought Alliance. During 1918 it elected Hopkins as its honorary president, even though she never played a leading role in the INTA. Instead, she continued a mystical, individualist, secluded life centered around private consultations in New York City. Today her influence over New Thought continues through Religious Science and the Unity School of Christianity, especially the texts of her students Myrtle Fillmore, Charles Fillmore, H. Emilie Cady, and Ernest Holmes (Harley 2002:50–55, 67–141; Larson 1985:291–94).

The Unity School of Christianity

Of all contemporary New Thought movements, the Unity School of Christianity has attracted the greatest following. Myrtle and Charles Fillmore founded Unity during the late 1880s. Influenced by Christian Science dissidents such as Joseph Adams, E. B. Weeks, and especially Emma Curtis Hopkins, they affirmed everyone's divine heritage and the need to express the health that flows from God. Hopkins ordained both Fillmores as ministers in December 1890. After she moved to New York City in 1895, Myrtle continued corresponding with her teacher until Hopkins died in 1925. The Fillmores praised her compassion, vast knowledge, and understanding of spiritual truth (Vahle 1996:6, 215–21, 247–59; Witherspoon 2000:37–40). Like Hopkins, they wanted the Unity School to stress individuals' spiritual receptivity to "the good in all sects and systems" (Mosley 2006:10). First published in 1891, *Unity* magazine originally printed articles about Eddy's Christian Science, theosophy, Quaker beliefs, spiritualism, and Hinduism. By the mid-1890s, however, *Unity* focused mainly on the Christian Bible, particularly the New Testament.

H. Emilie Cady (1881–1941), a homeopathic physician who studied with Emma Curtis Hopkins in New York City, became a leading writer on scriptural passages and their relevance to modern concerns such as healing, prosperity, and personal relationships. She wrote the basic Unity textbook, *Lessons in Truth*, modeled after the twelve lessons taught by Hopkins. Today this book forms the key introduction to Unity teachings. Even though appropriating the most significant concepts from Hopkins, Cady placed greater emphasis on the Christian heritage, with most citations derived from Psalms, the Hebrew prophets, the four Gospels, and St. Paul as well as from philosophers such as Ralph Waldo Emerson. Cady emphasized enlightened spiritual individualism, with a focus on the individual as a potential expression of God. With her individualist perspective on spiritual equality and personal efficacy, she gave little attention to political power, public policies, or the ways that government actions could improve people's lives. Unlike the Social Gospelers, she underestimated the collective sources of goodness and evil, especially the influence of such structures as capitalism and government (Cady 1995).

Charles Fillmore shared with Cady an individualist orientation that elevated the individual over churches and governments. He rejected all external church structures. For him, the "true church" comprises all those individuals who hold similar spiritual ideas and who have attained a similar consciousness of truth. As these spiritual perceptions gradually become manifest through an organic evolutionary process, the Kingdom of God becomes more manifest on earth. Until then, established religious institutions that rely on imposed traditions hinder spiritual change:

> Whoever formulates a creed or writes a book, claiming it to be an infallible guide for mankind; whoever organizes a church in which it is attempted, by rules and tenets, to save men from their evil ways; whoever attempts to offer, in any way, a substitute for the one omnipresent Spirit of God dwelling in each of us, is an obstructor of the soul's progress.
>
> (Fillmore 1989:104–05)

Fillmore's skepticism about ecclesiastical institutions extended to Unity's membership in the International New Thought Alliance (INTA). In 1922 he decided that the Unity School of Christianity should withdraw from the INTA because it downplayed the distinctive message taught by Jesus. Yet today the Association of Unity Churches International and specific Unity ministers actively participate in the INTA (Vahle 2002:383–97).

Charles Fillmore placed little reliance on government and political decisions to achieve personal well-being. From his viewpoint, people should demonstrate primary loyalty to the indwelling God, the personalized I AM. The individual mind assumed political aspects: "Every man is a king ruling his own subjects. These subjects are the ideas existing in his mind, the 'subjects' of his thought. . . . They can all be brought into subjection and made to obey through the I AM power that is the ruler of the kingdom" (Fillmore 1999a:277–78). According to him, personal mental reforms based on "the activity of the almighty Mind" will more effectively secure justice than any human legislation (Fillmore 1967:180–81). Like most individualistic Americans, Fillmore remained disenchanted with governments, political decisionmaking, and party activities because he associated them with conflict, rather than with the unity and harmony perceived by him as necessary for a just society. Yet this apolitical stance scarcely diminished his dedication to individual freedom. Obedience to the universal spirit of justice took precedence over obedience to unjust, repressive government laws

(Fillmore 1967:280; 1998a:110; 1998b:184; 1999a:370; 1999b:67; 2005:126–28).

His dedication to individual freedom led Fillmore to show strong support for procedural justice. Rejecting punishment by God, parents, and governments, he wanted justice to merge with spiritual compassion. Spiritual laws must take priority over human procedures intended to secure justice. The Christ teachings should guide all government decisions. Opposed to an oppressive, exclusivist nationalism and to personal dictators who claim to rule by divine right, Fillmore urged the formation of a world federation that unites all humanity through universal ties. Both Myrtle and Charles Fillmore attacked war and high military expenditures, believing that they stemmed from selfishness and greed. Instead, the spiritual principles of the Christ need to shape political leaders' actions as they seek peaceful ways to resolve conflicts. Procedural justice should also influence prison reforms. Rather than punishment, ethical education is the most effective way to attain restorative justice (Fillmore 1998a:110–11; 1998b:97; 2005:123–24; Witherspoon 2000:223).

As cofounder of Unity, Myrtle Fillmore emphasized equal nights for women. In one of her "healing letters" (M. Fillmore 1988:85), she wrote about the divine potential in all individuals: "Think of all men, all women, all children as abiding in God's presence and expressing God's qualities." Denying the basic differences between men and women, she affirmed: "Though personal to each one of us, God is IT, neither male nor female, but *Principle*. . . . God is All-Intelligence; there is but the one Mind and in reality there are no separate men and women" (M. Fillmore 2006:25). Charles Fillmore concurred with his wife's assessment of gender equality. According to him, rather than inborn essential attributes of the human species, male and female represent divine ideas present in all individuals. When life and intelligence unite with love and imagination, a complementary equilibrium will result. Under this condition, marriages will become liberated from male compulsion of wives and harmony will ensue (Fillmore 1999b:53, 166).

Viewing humans as spiritual beings, neither Fillmore regarded sexual behavior as the preeminent goal that superseded all other purposes in life. According to Charles, "carnal thoughts" of lust derive from ignorance of spiritual knowledge and lead to perversion. If divine ideas overcome the bodily passions, then purity will emerge: "So long as your eye sees sex and the indulgence thereof, on any of its planes, you are not pure. You must become so mentally translucent that you see men and women as sexless beings–which they are in the spiritual consciousness" (Fillmore 1999b:167). For Myrtle Fillmore, the most elevated marital relationships occur when people appreciate each other's spiritual qualities and share them with their partner. In this ideal arrangement, love reinforces the divine law (M. Fillmore 1988:151–52).

Even if Charles Fillmore devoted less attention to distributive justice than to spiritual procedures, his concept of prosperity affirmed the need for a more equal distribution of resources than prevailed during his lifetime, which extended from the late nineteenth century, through the booming 1920s, into the 1930s depression, and until the conclusion of World War II. Unlike Walter Rauschenbusch, he refrained from endorsing socialism and labor unions as effective ways to attain economic prosperity. No inversionary discourse proclaimed the need for a socialist transformation. During the 1924 and 1928 elections Myrtle Fillmore supported Republican candidates Calvin Coolidge and Herbert Hoover for president because she perceived them as expressing the ethical character and optimism needed for effective leadership (Witherspoon 2000:220–23). Yet unlike contemporary libertarians, neither Fillmore regarded the accumulation of private property as the highest priority. For both, service to others took precedence. According to Myrtle Fillmore:

> All undue accumulations of money or power by individuals are in direct violation of the divine law. Just to the extent that man tries to claim anything as his personal property, so does he wander away from God the Principle of goodness, equity, love, truth, justice, health, and harmony.
>
> (M. Fillmore 2006:25)

Similarly, Charles Fillmore preferred a humane capitalist economy based on service, not on the pursuit of money and high profits. For him, prosperity will result when persons cease thinking thoughts of lack or limitation but focus their thoughts on God's abundant supply. In contrast to neoclassical economists who equate economics with scarce resources, Fillmore perceived that the ideal economy rests on abundance, not on a zero-sum game that the rich win but the poor lose. He assumed that individuals achieve prosperity when they declare the reality of abundant support that emerges from making the demand. Although upholding self-reliance, Fillmore rejected notions about the self-made man. Instead, God supplies all human needs. Even if he proclaimed the desirability of serving others, he looked askance at charity if it bred economic dependence. His enthusiasm for reducing the gap that split rich from poor did not weaken a belief that higher economic rewards should go to those who demonstrate greater effort. For him, the most just economic distribution will occur when individuals place spiritual ideas about the constructive use of money above the greedy pursuit of material gain (Fillmore 1967:185–224; 1998b: 147–52).

The individualist ideals of Charles Fillmore retain relevance for the contemporary Unity movement, which relies on the actions of decentralized churches and their specific members to advance its public agenda for justice. Education and prayer, rather than public policy campaigns, represent Unity's key activities. It publishes three journals—*Daily Word, La Palabra Diaria,* and *Unity Magazine*—and several books that express its basic teachings. Spiritual retreats at Unity Village, Missouri and online classes promote the educational mission. The Society of Silent Unity receives over two million prayer requests each year. The Unity School also distributes free literature to prisons, hospitals, public libraries, and retirement homes. At the local level, Unity churches focus on issues related to ecology, gender equality, and community service activities that benefit low-income individuals. These programs aim to feed the hungry, house the homeless, and educate children. Basing their local projects on Unity's spiritual principles, churches provide ethical education to local prisoners, teach nonviolence, sponsor community credit unions, and beautify neighborhoods. They also contribute money to nonprofit service organizations, assist those who suffer from disastrous hurricanes, and campaign for a federal government Department of Peace. Individual Unity members such as Virginia Swain have organized a Reconciliation Leadership Training Program that trains individuals as peacemakers at the United Nations as well as in other institutions. She also established the Center for Global Community and World Law (V. Swain 2006). All these activities reflect Unity's commitment to demonstrate the spirit of a loving, nurturant, indwelling God to those needing greater peace, justice, beauty, and compassion in their lives.

Although Unity and Unitarian leaders emphasize their differences, they share several similarities, such as a focus on compassionate social service supported by the Social Gospel. Despite the Unity preference for intuition and revelation as sources of knowledge and the Unitarians' greater belief in reason, both affirm Enlightenment values: universal equality, individual freedom, evolutionary progress, optimism, science, a just society based on law, humanitarian reforms, criticism of biblical orthodoxy, and a denunciation of repressive churches and government bureaucracies. Members from both denominations participate in the Jesus Seminars sponsored by the Westar Institute, which takes liberal attitudes toward both theology and politics. Rather than idolizing the scriptures, Unity and Unitarian adherents rely on nonliteral, allegorical, symbolic interpretations of the Bible. Both affirm concepts formulated by Ralph Waldo Emerson and more contemporary Buddhists. Even if the Unitarian Universalist denomination contains more agnostics, its Christian members, like Unity students, perceive of God as a spiritual principle, a divine presence in the world, not as a judgmental person in the heavenly skies. A human being, Jesus expressed the divine qualities present in all persons.

Structurally, Unity and Unitarianism maintain highly decentralized, pluralistic churches that give laity extensive opportunities for participation. Women play key ministerial and leadership roles. Placing priority not only on gender equality but also on rights for gays and lesbians, both denominations support the ordination of homosexual ministers and promote the formation of church groups comprising lesbians, gays, bisexuals, and transgender persons. High tolerance of diversity motivates an ecumenical spirit that seeks enhanced cooperation with other faiths (Taussig 2006:7–52). Combined with a liberal interpretation of the Bible, the stress on tolerance leads both Unity students and Unitarians to uphold public policies for domestic nonviolence, world peace, a healthy environment, and a pluralist state free from theocratic influences. Whereas Unity focuses more on education and prayer as ways to attain social justice, Unitarian leaders devote greater attention to influencing government officials to enact just public policies.

Religious Science

Like the Fillmores, Ernest Holmes (1887–1960), the founder of the Religious Science movement, gained insights from Emma Curtis Hopkins. Born in Maine and raised a Congregationalist, when he was 18 he moved to Boston. There he studied Christian Science and other metaphysical philosophies. In 1912 he left for California and helped his brother Fenwicke who served as a Congregational minister in Venice, a Los Angeles suburb. Over a decade later he took a week's lessons from Hopkins, whom he regarded as a mystical healer with a high "Cosmic Consciousness" (Holmes 1991:61). After his sessions with Hopkins, he later recorded his impression of her:

> She turned out to be very witty, cheerful and lovable. At one time she told me of a convention she held in Chicago, and there was a student, an Absolutist who began screaming, "I am God," and she said, "There, there, George, it is all right for you to play you are God, but don't be so noisy about it."
>
> (F. Holmes 1970:197)

Along with Ralph Waldo Emerson, Hopkins influenced the biblical interpretations formulated by Ernest Holmes.

Unlike the Unity School, Religious Science accords greater prominence to its founder. H. Emilie Cady, not Charles or Myrtle Fillmore, wrote the basic Unity textbook *Lessons in Truth*. Neither *Daily Word* nor *Unity Magazine* carries many citations from Charles Fillmore's writings. In the Religious Science movement, however, Holmes occupies a preeminent position. First published in 1926, his book *The Science of Mind* serves as the key text that introduces Religious Science ideas to students. Each issue of the monthly magazine *Science of Mind* features an article by Holmes; daily readings cite a passage from the basic textbook. As early as 1932 Holmes insisted that local branches use *The Science of Mind* as their official text. Even though Holmes initially resisted the establishment of a church, plans for a Founder's Church of Religious Science took form after 1940. Its completion occurred in 1960 shortly before his death.

During the immediate post-World War II years, the rapid growth in Religious Science churches, combined with Holmes' desire to maintain centralized coordination, provoked a split in the movement. Structural disputes over authority, not theological issues, caused the division.

Affirming his belief in the oneness of God and the need to maintain consistent, pure teachings against rival interpretations, he tried to exercise dominant central leadership over the highly pluralist, decentralized Religious Science organization. Yet local churches sought greater autonomy from the Board of Trustees that governed the Institute of Religious Science and Philosophy. In 1947 Holmes agreed to the establishment of the International Association of Religious Science Churches (IARSC). The two organizations never effectively coordinated their overlapping responsibilities. After the Institute became the Church of Religious Science in 1953, Holmes and its Board of Trustees formulated a plan for a more centrally controlled institution. Under this plan, Holmes would serve as Permanent Trustee of the Board, which would assume most activities performed by the decentralized IARSC. Supporters of that association objected to this centralized transfer of authority. Holmes refused to compromise. The Religious Science movement in 1954 split into two organizations. Ministerial supporters of the IARSC created the Religious Science International. Its magazine *Creative Thought* accepts the basic teachings of Ernest Holmes but gives less attention to his prolific writings than does *Science of Mind* magazine. The United Church of Religious Science, the larger organization, retained support from most local branches and publishes *Science of Mind*. Both the United Church of Religious Science/United Centers for Spiritual Living and Religious Science International actively participate as members of the International New Thought Alliance (Armor 1999; Holmes 2002:240–41; Larson 1985:358–94; Leo 2006: 42–45, 116–20; Mosley 2006:138–39; Vahle 1993:111–30).

Holmes' interpretation of Religious Science synthesized diverse strands from religion, philosophy, psychology, medicine, and natural science. Taking a pragmatic utilitarian approach that stressed effective results, he aimed to reconcile the perfect spiritual world with the imperfect material world in his applied teachings. Although emphasizing Christianity, Holmes reformulated orthodox beliefs to focus on the similar values that unite all religions: Judaism, Islam, Buddhism, Hinduism, Taoism, Confucianism. Like other New Thought adherents, he distinguished between Jesus the human being and the Christ Principle (Spirit of Truth) that indwells all individuals, whatever their religious affiliation. God signifies both transcendent universal, eternal, infinite standards—love, life, truth, health, abundance—as well as a personalized father-mother incarnated within every individual, whom Holmes considered a spiritual being.

Philosophically, Holmes relied on an idealistic, not a materialist, outlook to explain the impact of mind, ideas, and perceptions on environmental outcomes. Changes in human behavior stem from changes in spiritual consciousness. He perceived Jesus as a "practical idealist." The philosophers Plato, Kant, and especially Emerson influenced his thought. From metaphysicians such as Phineas Quimby, Ralph Waldo Trine, and particularly Thomas Troward came concepts about the importance of mental ideas that produce healing, prosperity, and peace among individuals.

A commitment to spiritual idealism reinforced Holmes' interest in psychological developments, especially those in psychoanalysis and psychiatry. Influenced by Carl Jung, he stressed the need for psychological treatments to stress the spiritual dimensions of life. Holmes viewed the Christ or Cosmic Consciousness as the Infinite Spirit individualized within the finite human mind. To achieve the healthiest personal conditions, he assumed that the spiritual consciousness should dominate conscious thoughts, which then will have a positive impact on subconscious memories, thoughts, and emotions.

Holmes accepted the fact, if not the spiritual reality, of illness, and worked closely with medical professionals to further spiritual mind healing. Reiterating the importance of spiritual values in healing the individual's mind and body, he perceived that physicians and surgeons complemented the activities of metaphysicians. Rather than remain antagonistic, they should cooperate with each other.

The priority placed on spiritual reality scarcely weakened Holmes' commitment to a scientific view of the world. For him, science involves universal laws, systematic knowledge, and impersonal criteria that link causes to specific effects. He assumed that individual thoughts produce external conditions, whether personal actions or environmental circumstances. Thoughts of God cause goodness. Ignorant, selfish, deluded thoughts lead to destructive results, such as ill health, poverty, unhappiness, and world wars. Evolution accounts for change in the individual and society. As people gain more knowledge and comprehension of the world, their ideas evolve. Progress toward a more just society results (Holmes 1988:29–31, 73–74, 90–97, 114–26, 321, 341; 1991:69–82, 252–65; 2005; 2006:81; Vahle 1993:51–52).

Ernest Holmes based his interpretation of justice on law. Individualism shaped his belief in personal efficacy, equality, and disdain for hierarchy. The indwelling Divine Mind—Spirit, conscious intelligence—guides, directs, and inspires the inner law, which executes the outcomes derived from personal actions. Individuals can use or abuse this law of cause and effect. When constructive use prevails, freedom results. Ignorant use that focuses on lack, failure, and evil, rather than on thoughts of God, produces bondage. Liberation from bondage requires not changes in law but changes in its use so that personal actions adhere to the incarnated perfect law. Since the law operates impersonally and applies equally to all individuals, whatever their social status, they deserve equal treatment. Because the Divine Person dwells in everyone, people should respect others as brothers and sisters who share a divine inheritance. Opposed to dominant personalities or dogmatic creeds that intervene between the individual and divine law, Holmes rejected hierarchical authority. Ideally, all should have direct access to God. Personal efficacy took priority over fatalism, despair, and doubts about positive outcomes. Rather than predetermined by God, a personal Devil, or even external circumstances, individuals enjoy free will. They can choose their thoughts about ways to use or abuse the law. From his optimistic perspective, Holmes felt that constructive thoughts about success would transcend beliefs in failure (Holmes 1970:24–37; 1991:118–21, 171–72, 196–212, 395; 1999a:118, 122, 213; 1999b:84–85, 170–71; 2002:180).

Formulating his concepts about the interactions between the individual and government, Holmes politicized the individual mind. His alienation from government and political parties reflected a commitment to maintain the individual's independence from external control by governments, parties, and churches. Like Emerson, he supported self-reliance, personal initiative, and individual responsibility for the consequences of one's behavior. Justice prevails when individuals recognize their dependence on divine law. God governs individuals' thoughts; hence, they should devote full attention to normative ideals, not to apparent conditions: "We are living in a Spiritual Universe whose sole government is one of Harmony. . . . The use of right ideas is the enforcement of its Law. . . . The government of Good is enforced through the Law of man's own Divinity" (Holmes 1991:1, 220). Holmes urged Religious Scientists to apply these teachings not only to their personal lives but also to issues facing society, such as civil liberties, world peace, gender relations, and poverty (Holmes 1988:315–16; 1999a:9; 2002:116–18, 171–81).

Even if Holmes accorded the individual the greatest significance in his religious interpretations, he recognized the need for collective action to establish the Kingdom of God on earth. As a New Thought teacher, he regarded heaven as a harmonious state of spiritual consciousness. Through a gradual evolutionary process, Holmes expected that numerous social groups—aggregates of individuals—would realize that heaven already prevails in their human minds. Inspired by a common purpose, a "group consciousness," they would take active steps to cooperate for the attainment of the spiritual ideals linked to the "Divine government of Good" (Holmes 1991:434). Given his emphasis on divine law as the foundation of justice, he gave priority to procedural, not distributive, justice.

Civil liberty formed a key aspect of Holmes' outlook on justice. According to him, the law of God led to liberty, which involved more than passive tolerance but an active recognition of individuals' divine potential, an understanding of other people's needs, and a respect for their unique qualities. Committed to individual freedom, he rejected coercion and protests as ways to enhance social liberty. Since heaven signified harmony, groups should rely on nonviolent means to secure world peace, which begins with individuals' mental peace. They must liberate their conscious minds from delusions about fear, insecurity, lack, and discord. Holmes saw the need for legal principles to supersede precedents about the inevitability of war. For him, democracy involved shared powers. His support for the United Nations stemmed from a belief that it should rest on similar legal principles that shape the U.S. federal system, such as shared powers between the federal and the state governments. By maintaining the United Nations as a legal institution that balances autonomous nation-states with cooperative activities at the international level, national leaders can help attain a world law that deters aggression, strengthens individual freedom, and secures peace with justice (Holmes 1991:215–19; 1999b:169–71; 2002:171–81; 2006:78–79).

Concern for liberty, not license, framed Holmes' ideas about sexual behavior. Both repression and overindulgence create bondage. If married partners dedicate themselves mainly to the pursuit of spiritual love that all can share, greater happiness will result than if they practice only a passionate, possessive love. Viewing individuals primarily as spiritual beings, contemporary Religious Science ministers, like those in Unity, welcome gays, lesbians, and bisexuals into their churches where they often form study groups. This hospitality reflects Holmes' belief in personal freedom, individual choice, self-expression, and openness to new ideas that evolve as knowledge expands (Holmes 2002:116–18).

Gender equality draws widespread support among Religious Scientists. Women play key roles as ministers, teachers, counselors, and church leaders. They edit the two Religious Science publications *Science of Mind* and *Creative Thought*. Holmes affirmed the inclusiveness of Jesus' message intended for all people: "Jesus was the greatest individualist who ever lived, yet, at the same time, he was the greatest inclusionist because he included the individual in the Universal" (Holmes 1999b:176). Like Unity teachers, Holmes stressed the egalitarian spirit of Jesus' gospel: "Anyone who lives in harmony with the Truth automatically becomes the brother, the sister or the mother of all. . . . Jesus was a consciously cosmic soul, who recognized his unity with all. He knew that love must become universal before it can reach its maturity" (Holmes 2002:181).

Holmes' commitment to gender equality took precedence over an egalitarian emphasis on distributive justice. As a spiritual individualist, he affirmed entrepreneurial virtues—reliability, initiative, expertise, skills—that he perceived necessary for financial success. For him, capitalist images describe God, who represents the Great Business Manager, the Supreme Source of Abundant Supply, the Original Banker. Prosperity requires reciprocity between God and the individual, who become partners. According to the indwelling Law of Opulence, thoughts of unlimited spiritual supply create employment offers and successful businesses. God supplies all material goods but only to individuals who link their thoughts to divine will and accumulate love, faith, joy, and peace in their spiritual bank account. As centers not only of accumulation but distribution, they need to provide free services and practical help to others. Receiving depends on giving. Their reciprocal actions will bring benefits to the self as well as to other people. Minimizing the structural impact of economic conditions on personal well-being, Holmes assumed that the individual, not God or the Devil, bears responsibility for economic failure: "Both prosperity and poverty are states of mind. . . . *Poverty is lack of knowledge of God!* If we had a complete realization of the allness of Good and our oneness with God, *we would automatically express abundance*" (Holmes 1936:7). Unlike the Social Gospelers, Holmes refrained from advocating public policies that would protect workers, limit corporate influence over government decisions, and ensure greater income equality. Nevertheless, he did expect that reduced expenditures for military armaments would help eliminate poverty (Holmes 1938:68; 1991:232–37, 340–48, 393–95, 413–17; 1999a:25–33; 2002:174).

Conclusion

The major difference that separates Social Gospelers from New Thought adherents in Unity and Religious Science involves their divergent attitude toward individualist justice. Whereas the Social Gospel links personal freedom to improved sociopolitical conditions, New Thought students give priority to individualist causal attribution. The individual mind, thoughts, and ways of thinking become politicized. Governing the mind assumes greater importance than governing the society. Downplaying collective political action, they stress prayer, education, and voluntary activities as primary ways to achieve a just society. Although Ralph Waldo Trine (1910) recommended socialist ownership, not corporate exploitation, of public service utilities, the Fillmores and Ernest Holmes upheld the entrepreneurial individualist virtues linked to a capitalist market economy. Unlike Trine, few contemporary New Thought followers denounce the unequal distribution of income or campaign for greater union rights—stands taken by Walter Rauschenbusch. As a spiritual religious movement, New Thought denominations lack the structural organization to exercise leverage over the public policy agenda. For most, Jesus assumes greatest significance as a teacher and healer, not as a prophet condemning social injustice.

By contrast, contemporary Social Gospel supporters work through such denominations as the Unitarian Universalist, Congregational, Episcopal, Methodist, and Presbyterian. With their institutionalized power, they can form national organizations that seek influence over government legislation affecting economic distribution, world peace, ecology, immigrant rights, and individual freedom. For them, societal transformation demands conflict with established traditions that violate justice. The Hebrew prophets and Jesus represent examples to follow. Applying their teachings to the modern era, Social Gospelers today emphasize the egalitarian, nonviolent inheritance from the past. Like Walter Rauschenbusch, they seek an implementation of social democratic service policies found among Scandinavian countries. The priority on world peace reflects the Social Gospel focus on environmental conditions influencing individual thoughts and actions.

Rather than attributing war and other evils to false thinking, Social Gospelers stress the structural causes: political oppression, economic exploitation, cultural humiliation. Personal efficacy depends on the openness of sociopolitical structures. People living under repression can more easily control their thoughts than the outcomes they endure. To Jews destined for extermination in the Nazi concentration camp at Auschwitz, thoughts about God's omniscience and omnipresence provided little comfort. As they entered the Nazi gas chambers, no thoughts of a loving God saved them from death. As the Social Gospel message affirms, to redeem the world from evil requires not only a transformation in individual thoughts and leaders' behavior but also changes in sociopolitical structures. These changes involve an open, democratic government, a more egalitarian economic system, and cultural values that highlight individual rights, limits on leaders' authority, inclusiveness, and respect for all humans, whatever their ethnic, religious, or economic status (Oliner and Gunn 2006). Along with Rabbi Michael Lerner, Rabbi Mark L. Winer connects a just political system with *tikkun olam*—the repair of the world so that egalitarian public policies prevail:

> Morality is dependent upon the justice of a system. Thus our *tikkun* must not only transcend unjust situations, but also make the world just for all people. . . . Only when we feed the hungry, clothe the naked, shelter the homeless, heal the sick, and act to make the world more just can we expect to find God, because such action partakes of the eternal.
>
> (Winer 2006:340–41)

As leader in the World Union for Progressive Judaism, Rabbi Winer shares the same beliefs about justice held by Social Gospelers.

Whatever their differences about collectivism vs. individualism, Social Gospel and New Thought followers uphold common beliefs that motivate them to support the policies for social justice mentioned by Rabbi Winer. Justice implies human equality, high personal efficacy, individual freedom, and opposition to hierarchical authority. Both support gender equality, including expanded rights for African American women. Particularly in New Thought churches, black female ministers have gained extensive leadership experience. Influenced by her mother-in-law's membership in an Oakland Unity church, Elouise Oliver, the minister of the East Bay Church of Religious Science, stresses gender equality, gay rights, individualism, personal empowerment, and prayer as effective ways to enhance justice (Martin 2005). Despite housing segregation faced by Johnnie Colemon at the Unity School during the 1950s, she became an ordained Unity minister and president of the Association of Unity Churches. In 1974 she left the Unity denomination to establish the Universal Foundation for Better Living, which belongs to the International New Thought Alliance. Her disciple Mary A. Tumkin serves as president of this Foundation, heads the Universal Truth Center in Florida, and participates as an associate fellow of the Westar Institute that sponsors the Jesus Seminars. Like other members of the seminars, she articulates a liberal, historical, symbolic interpretation of the Bible as well as liberal public policies for social justice. Taking a positive view of human potential, New Thought and the Social Gospel assert high personal efficacy as their churches seek to reform (repair) world conditions. An ecumenical spirit uniting diverse religious faith accompanies extensive church decentralization. Limited ecclesiastical control gives individual laity within local churches opportunity for active participation.

Yet the reluctance of both these liberal religious movements to work through nationally powerful church structures limits their influence over the policy process. Why have religious conservatives gained greater policy influence, especially from 1996 through 2006? Chapter 6 explains that the reasons partly stem from the Protestant evangelicals' more cohesive social networks, tighter organization, greater support for active political participation by clergy, and a more coherent, comprehensive vision. Hence, conservatives allied with the Republican Party develop a stronger commitment to their cause than do religious liberals.

6

THE POLICY INFLUENCE OF RELIGIOUS LIBERALISM

> The politics of Jesus enjoins us to work immediately for justice whenever we encounter injustice.... Jesus sought not only to heal people's pain but also to inspire and empower people to remove the unjust social and political structures that too often were the cause of their pain.
>
> (Obery M. Hendricks, Jr.)

Written by John Galsworthy, the tragic play *Justice* had a deep impact on public policy in early twentieth-century England. First produced at a London theater in 1910, the drama portrayed the contradiction between procedural justice and distributive justice. Falder, a 23-year-old junior clerk in the law office of James and Walter How, forges a check written by his employer Walter How, the son of James. Falder commits the crime because of his love for Ruth Honeywill, married to a violent, drunken husband who tried to strangle her and who beat their two children. Using the money from the forged check, Falder hopes to sail with Ruth to South America, where they and the children can live a happy life free from the abusive husband who refused to grant her a divorce. Despite the pleading of Cokeson, the managing clerk at the How law firm and a Nonconformist (non-Anglican) who attends the same chapel as Falder, the judge refuses leniency, rejects appeals to combine justice with mercy, and sentences him to a three-year period of "penal servitude." In prison Falder has to endure solitary confinement, which prison officials assume will cause repentance. Retributive justice with a stress on deterrence supersedes restorative justice, which focuses on humane treatment, compassion, and training for employable skills. After serving time in prison, Falder bears the stigma of a convict unable to gain secure employment. Malnourished and homeless, he seeks the renewal of his former job at the How law office. James How agrees to grant Falder his old position only if he agrees to two conditions: admit the just treatment received from public authorities and abandon his love for Ruth Honeywill. James How blames Falder for his "weak character," his obsession with his past status as a victim, and his failure to concentrate on the future and gain a steady reputation from the reputable elements of society. Viewing Ruth as a modern Eve, James How also blames Ruth for tempting Falder to steal money from the firm. Unable to accept these two conditions, especially the abandonment of Ruth, and failing to notify the police about his whereabouts, Falder faces arrest by a detective, who will send him back to prison. To escape this tragic fate, Falder jumps out the window, breaks his neck, and dies (Galsworthy 1984). The good intentions of Walter How, Cokeson, the defense lawyer, the judge, and prison chaplain hardly lead to benign consequences for the young felon.

The popular play *Justice* resonated with both the London audience and government policymakers. Motivated by the dramatic themes, Winston Churchill, the Home Secretary, enacted policies that improved prison conditions. He reduced the use of solitary confinement, provided educational lectures to prisoners, and made the leave procedures more flexible (Nightingale 1984:xi–xiv).

The play illustrates several themes about just public policies highlighted by New Thought and especially Social Gospel theologians. Prison treatment involves not only punishment but also employment, education, health care, and housing. The causes of crime stem from immoral behavior as well as from dire economic conditions, unhealthy environments, and unstable, violent family situations. The consequences of imprisonment depend on the personal will of the former convict and on opportunities for gaining a job, health care, and housing after release from prison—opportunities that can flourish only from comprehensive public policies. Unfortunately for Falder, during his brief life he lacked these opportunities. To remedy sociopolitical conditions, John Galsworthy in his novels, plays, and political activities worked to enhance civil liberties, establish women's suffrage, reform divorce laws, improve prison conditions, ensure healthy foods produced in factories, and promote world peace. Impelled by compassion, empathy, and understanding, he articulated the liberal demands of contemporary policy activists. At the end of the play, Cokeson, whose prayers for Falder have scarcely saved him from his tragic fate, assures Ruth: "He's safe with gentle Jesus!" (Galsworthy 1984:116). Perhaps Cokeson recalls Jesus' call when he began his ministry: God's Spirit "has chosen me to tell the good news to the poor. The Lord has sent me to announce freedom for prisoners, to give sight to the blind, to free everyone who suffers" (Luke 4:18).

The prison conditions in England 100 years ago still prevail in the United States today. During the early nineteenth century, prisons originated as religious institutions that sought inmates' repentance. Penitentiaries used solitary confinement as a way to produce penitent prisoners. Alone in the cell, inmates faced regimentation, external discipline, and constant surveillance, which aimed to transform their thoughts. Since the 1970s, the goal of rehabilitation has waned. Few prisoners receive the education, vocational training, and health care needed for their well-being after release from prison. Solitary confinement in the "hole" continues as a widespread punishment, sometimes lasting more than ten years. Most state and federal prisons implement a hierarchical concept of justice that stresses security, order, and discipline. Retributive justice, incapacitation, and deterrence take precedence over restorative justice. Yet such practices as corruption, coercion, violence, and rape bring disorder. Labeled as "security threats," members of the same ethnic group are segregated. Ethnic gangs coerce their opponents. Guards bribe and collude with gang leaders. Prisoners enjoy few civil liberties, such as the rights to form unions, litigate their rights, and file class action suits against prison authorities. Corrections officers suppress conflicts focused on the legitimacy of prison rules and practices. Violations of petty rules—for example, the exchange of library books among inmates—bring punitive treatment, such as solitary confinement. Prisoner unions have only limited rights to conduct meetings and solicit members. Particularly in a private, for-profit prison, convicts suffer the worst conditions. Few opportunities prevail for them to lodge grievances against punitive working conditions, scarce health care services, and denial of family visits. Private prison companies lobby government officials to enact longer sentences, build more prisons, and curtail mandated policies for offenders' opportunities to secure employment after release from prison. Not only in private prisons but also in public ones, low-income persons, African Americans, Latinos, immigrants, and the mentally ill endure the greatest harm from the prison environment. Unlike the situation in Denmark, Finland, Sweden, Canada, and Spain, few states, except Northeastern ones like Maine and Vermont, grant prisoners the right to vote. Most state governments restrict even ex-prisoners' voting rights. In 2005 this restriction affected over 4 million individuals, especially low-income African American young men with less than a high school education (Magnani and Wray 2006; Manza and Uggen 2006:34–94, 235, 247; Santos 2006). Imprisonment and disenfranchisement reflect the current inequalities of American society.

After the terrorist attacks of September 11, 2001, the Bush Republican administration implemented punitive prison policies, both in the United States and overseas. Private security organizations, the armed forces, CIA, National Security Agency, and FBI waged a global war on terror. They sent suspected "enemy combatants" to secret prisons, rarely charged them with an explicit crime, and conducted coercive interrogations. Punitive treatments encompassed handcuffing, sleep deprivation, beatings, mock executions, simulated drownings, and sexual humiliation. Under the policy of "extraordinary rendition," CIA operatives seized alleged terrorists and secretly transferred them to overseas prisons where foreign security agencies used torture. Muslim immigrants and migrant workers suffered harassment, arrests, imprisonment, and deportation. Solitary confinement and refusal to grant defense counsel hindered attempts to secure justice for suspects often held for indefinite periods (Arnold 2006; Fernandes 2007; Johnson 2006:90–136, 143–79; Schwarz and Huq 2007:65–207). Pursuing a hierarchical approach to procedural justice that stressed secrecy and personal loyalty, the Bush administration proclaimed the need for unilateral actions by a unitary executive to thwart dangers to national security. Neither political nor religious liberals had the power to restrain presidential decisions.

Why have religious liberals gained less influence over the policy process than have religious conservatives, particularly the white Protestant evangelicals allied with the Republican Party? The three "i"s—ideas, institutions, individuals—help explain this limited policy influence. The following sections focus on the religious visions, organizational power, and individual support of liberals and conservatives.

THE EXERCISE OF POLITICAL INFLUENCE

When churches seek to influence the policy agenda, four types of ideas become important: cognitive worldviews, normative frameworks, policy frames, and programmatic solutions. Cognitive worldviews explain and interpret social conditions, delineating the crises, problems, and new situations that produce injustice. Causal attributions assign responsibility to structures, cultural values, and individual attitudes and behaviors that have produced perceived injustice. Among the various policy options, which alternative will most likely lead to a desired effect? The most coherent, clear, and comprehensible worldviews offered by religious activists will likely wield the greatest influence.

Normative frameworks delineate the basic values and norms guiding the policy process. Core values comprise general priorities, such as justice, freedom, equality, and efficiency. Norms define meanings, particularly about the customs that shape interactions within a religious group and with other groups. Both shared values and norms promote ingroup solidarity by specifying obligations and rights of members. Whereas accommodative norms stress the need for cooperation with other diverse groups, adversarial norms distinguish between insiders and outcasts, thereby deterring peaceful relations. Conflict with outgroups strengthens ingroup solidarity. Churches that have forged intensive commitments to shared values and norms can potentially gain influence over public policymakers. Even if church members do not agree on the precise meaning of values and norms, recognition of their policy importance strengthens their impact.

Policy frames explicate the key problems perceived as most important for government responsibility. By defining the meaning of such terms as justice, equality, individualism, freedom, liberalism, and conservatism, frames shape the political discourse. Ways of speaking, whether in a bombastic or circumspect manner, influence policymakers. To what extent do they accept the legitimacy of the policy solutions articulated by church leaders? Simple language used in clear frames often enhances legitimacy. Particularly if the discourse appears in narrative forms, such as novels, plays, or motion pictures, government officials can more easily understand the policy frame. To enhance their influence, religious leaders also need to focus on emotions that link general moral-spiritual values to specific policy proposals. In what ways will the proposed policies protect people's lives and improve their well-being? The most persuasive communications not only make rational arguments about expected costs and benefits but also express anger against injustice, reassurance against fear, empathy for individuals' lives, and hope that specific programs will help people resolve their problems.

Programmatic solutions represent precise guidelines for resolving a basic problem pertaining to procedural or distributive justice. For example, what actions should government take regarding abortion and homosexual behavior? How can public authorities best ensure civil liberties when a nation faces terrorist attacks? To what extent should the government, rather than private businesses, churches, nonprofit agencies, and individuals, assume responsibility for delivering social services? How should social service programs be financed? Effective policy proposals clearly identify the most feasible policy options, not only ones that will most effectively realize the desired objective, but alternatives that will help policymakers form needed coalitions with other agencies playing a key role in the policy process (J. L. Campbell 2002, 2004:90–123; Lichterman 2005:51–59, 174–79; Westen 2007).

The exercise of political influence also depends on the individual support that a group can mobilize. Support particularly becomes needed from political activists, who exert greater impact on the policy process than do more passive spectators. Activists formulate the normative frameworks, cognitive worldviews, policy frames, and programmatic solutions that affect government decisionmaking. These ideas need to resonate among supporters so that they become motivated to participate in the political arena. If a religious movement can gain both material benefits and moral-spiritual values from political participation, then its support will grow. Activists try to secure these moral and spiritual benefits from policymakers. In exchange for popular support, government officials offer such concrete benefits as tax credits, subsidies, and financial assistance to churches for performing certain activities, like providing education, health care, and drug treatments to followers. Moral-spiritual values reflect a policymaker's commitment to uphold justice, rectitude, faith, equitable procedures, and compassion.

Policy entrepreneurs perform a dominant role negotiating alliances among key actors: framers, theorists, experts, business elites, religious leaders, policy formulators and implementers. To enhance support for specific programs, entrepreneurs not only reconcile conflicts among allies but also meld disparate values into a coherent whole. They justify new policies by highlighting their continuity with older shared symbols. Entrepreneurial activists show the key links between material interests and moral-spiritual values. Rather than distinct, these twin benefits reveal a close interaction. Protestant evangelical and traditionalist Catholic opposition to abortion reinforces conservative legislators' decision to eliminate public funds for legal abortion. Seeking justice, homosexuals regard the right to legal marriage as less important than their right to obtain the same health-care and retirement benefits as heterosexual married couples. Support for increased government spending on social services may reflect an ethic of care, compassion, empathy, and generosity—spiritual values stressed by the Social Gospel (Andrain and Apter 1995:282–309; J. L. Campbell 2004:69–77, 100–10; Schaffner and Senic 2006).

To maximize its policy influence, a religious group must establish effective institutions that accumulate resources, motivate its followers to use them for political action, and gain effective skills in mobilizing support. Without a powerful organizational base, neither visionary ideas nor popular support will produce intended outcomes. The exercise of political influence requires several types of resources: cultural, economic, and political. Cultural resources include the information, values, legal authority, and educational qualifications that confer high status. As a subset of cultural values, spiritual resources comprise theological values, priorities, faith, commitment, and sacred knowledge. Economic resources entail control over wealth, money, finances, property rights, and usable time. Groups with the greatest cultural and economic resources can gain the political power to shape public policies through both coercion and consensus. The mere possession of resources scarcely generates political influence. Instead, a group needs the motivation to employ their accumulated resources for political ends. Religious vision and strong identification with a spiritual cause often inspire individuals to organize behind a political movement. Anger against injustice and hope for realizing a more just society can motivate supporters to use their resources for policy influence. Effective skills also become crucial. By participating in church associations, members can develop important skills: communication, organizational coordination, expertise, information processing, adaptability, control over emotions, and empathy with other persons' needs.

In a democracy institutional power rests on four foundations: cohesion, coordination, cooperation, and a balance between centralized and decentralized power. Not only do formal organizations like churches, mosques, synagogues, interest groups, political parties, social movements, and the media play a significant role, but the informal networks within each of them generate support for political action. Cohesive organizations composed of dedicated, disciplined members can mobilize supporters and demobilize opponents. Solidarity that forms around intensively-held shared beliefs, especially a commitment to the religious group's cause, provides the sense of togetherness uniting members. When a religious institution seeks influence over the national government, centralized control strengthens access to the policy process. Yet to retain local support, religious leaders often decentralize some authority that responds to the immediate priorities of church members. Decentralized control also allows them a greater voice in political communications directed to local, regional, and national legislators. Given the pluralist structures of democratic governments, effective policy influence requires coordination among all the agencies affecting government policies. To form coalition partners, religious groups have to participate in cooperative relationships with supportive political parties, interest groups, social movements, and the institutions responsible for making and implementing the policies, whether these involve procedural or distributive justice. Through its effective exercise of power, a religious organization can expand its legitimacy among the populace as well as with public policymakers. By transmitting policy preferences and linking them to general spiritual values, the mass media can help organize, educate, inspire, and persuade potential supporters. In turn, citizens supply the energy, popular enthusiasm, and spontaneity needed to mobilize collective action behind the vision of enhanced procedural and distributive justice (Andrain and Apter 1995:125–96; Bourdieu 1986; Deutsch 2006; Jasper 2006:87–118; Pitchford et al. 2001; Stenger 2005).

Religious Vision

Religious liberals have sketched a spiritual vision based on individualist, nonhierarchical, and egalitarian values. They identify God with the spiritual principles of justice, love, and wisdom that all individuals potentially share. Open to change, liberals stress the need for individual conscience to guide ethical decisions. They want individuals to realize greater independence from control by dominant hierarchical institutions. Collective responsibility blends with a focus on enhanced individual rights for women and lower-status groups. Social Gospelers and New Thought students uphold religious pluralism. Several decentralized churches should compete yet also cooperate with each other on common goals. Rather than the government controlling churches or churches wielding dominance over the government, both institutions need to retain independence. Religious groups strive to influence public policies, not exercise tight control over policymakers. According to the liberal vision, universal rights, inclusiveness, equality among people, personal efficacy, and pluralism assume primacy over particularistic standards, exclusivity, elitism, fatalism, and monism.

Public policy preferences flow from this general religious vision. Liberals in the Social Gospel and New Thought camps favor world peace, specifically a reliance on diplomacy and multilateral institutions, not on high military expenditures for preemptive wars. Whereas Social Gospelers want to reduce poverty through public policies such as increased spending on health care, education, housing, and expanded employment opportunities, New Thought adherents place greater emphasis on changing individual attitudes about the abundant supply that God makes available to those who seek righteousness over material accumulation. Supporting ecology, both liberal groups prefer "green" policies that secure harmony with the environment, not its exploitation. On cultural issues, New Thought churches like Unity and Religious Science strongly assert the need for gay rights. Among Social Gospelers, Bishop Spong and Rabbi Lerner take a similar position that differs from the reluctance of Jim Wallis to uphold same-sex marriage.

The pluralist diversity among religious liberals hinders their policy influence. Like John Locke, liberals perceive truth as uncertain, diverse, and changing. Hence, they cannot easily mobilize followers who feel a strong emotional commitment to the liberal cause. Despite adopting a social democratic platform that stresses more equal economic outcomes, not just opportunities, many Social Gospelers avoid close identification with the liberal label. They also hope to secure influence with theological conservatives who view personal piety as more important than establishment of the reign of God on earth. Criticism of the capitalist structures weakens support from those preferring mild changes in market operations. Conflict with established institutions leads to mobilization by religious groups defending the status quo. By contrast, New Thought adherents find conflict unsettling. Favoring cooperation and harmony among diverse groups, they hesitate about becoming actively involved in politics. Their individualist orientation also hinders collective political action. Prayer, meditation, and voluntary religious activities that serve others take primacy over the struggle to influence the policy process. Neither Unity nor Religious Science has formed a lobbying organization like the Friends Committee on National Legislation.

Theological conservatives sketch a more unified, hierarchical, communal, elitist vision than do religious liberals. A literal interpretation of the Bible forms the foundation of the conservative vision. A personal God plays an active role not only in personal affairs but in the public arena. The individual must subordinate the self to hierarchical authority: God, the church, the male head of the family. Communal interdependence strengthens national solidarity; harmony with ingroup friends counterbalances conflict with outgroup enemies. The church has the responsibility not only to save individuals through a personal commitment to Jesus Christ but also to secure control over societal law, education, and the interpretation of moral values. Laws to regulate sexual behavior, marriage, birth control, divorce, and death become crucial decisions for government officials. In this monistic vision, ecumenical movements to establish close ties with other churches, especially liberal mainline institutions, weaken ingroup solidarity. Although most conservative evangelicals and traditionalist Catholics want to gain tighter control over the government, the dominionist movement works for a more theocratic state governed exclusively by Christians. With Calvin's sixteenth-century Geneva as its model, the dominionist vision would deny civil liberties to all its opponents, abolish labor unions, abandon public schools, consign women to the home, and refuse citizenship rights to those judged as non-Christian. Even if this theocratic movement has gained minimal popular support, it has established powerful organizations to propagate its vision, including television networks, religious radio stations, and even some leaders within the Southern Baptist Convention (Hedges 2006).

Whatever the political inclinations of conservative church members, during the 2004 election right-wing Christian activists played a crucial political role. In such organizations as Council for National Policy, Focus on the Family, Family Research Council, the Christian Coalition, and Concerned Women for America, leaders claimed that Christians should participate in politics, focus on political issues, educate citizens about these issues, contact government officials, make campaign contributions, and use their influence to protect traditional moral values. Aligned closely with the Republican Party, these activists supported vouchers for private schools, restrictions on legal abortion, a constitutional amendment to ban same-sex marriage, and the need for judges to interpret laws according to their original intention. Strongly opposed to environmental protection, over half also rejected increased spending for social services (Green et al. 2006). Even if conservative Christian followers failed to agree with all these policy preferences, the powerful organizations established by right-wing Christian activists promoted their influence over the policy process.

Political Organization

The policy influence of Christian conservatives stems from their cohesive, coordinated organizations. Even though they lack the high educational and income resources of liberal Jews, Episcopalians, and Unitarians, their socioeconomic status has risen during the last decades. Financed by wealthy members, conservative congregations feel a strong motivation to use their resources for political action.

Disturbed by the growth of perceived "secular humanism" that accompanied 1960s social changes, conservative churches seek to restore traditionalist values about sexual abstinence, family stability, and heterosexual marriage. A strong commitment to local church teachings and leadership partly derives from the benefits gained from congregational membership. These not only include moral-spiritual values like ethical character, sobriety, and decency but also material goods: access to government grants that finance "faith-based" initiatives for social services. Numerous organizational activities further conservative solidarity. Local churches sponsor Bible study, home schooling, sports clubs, vacation retreats, employment services, and day care centers. National conservative institutions organize a coordinated set of interlocking media: television networks, radio stations, newspapers, magazines, the Internet. These media communicate messages intended to proselytize more followers. Yet the missionary impulse, the high social interactions within conservative churches, and the hostility to religious outgroups produce strong internal cohesion but weak ties to the ecumenical movement dominated by mainline Protestant churches, liberal Catholics, and reform Jews. Loose coalitions, however, have formed with traditionalist Catholics opposed to abortion and same-sex marriage, as well as with Orthodox Jews who fear threats to the Israeli state from Palestinians seeking land occupied by Jewish settlers (Beyerlein and Hipp 2006; Smith and Faris 2005; Stevens 2002).

The major reason for the policy influence of conservative white Christians involves their tight links with wealthy business executives and particularly with the Republican Party. Since the early 1980s, white Protestant evangelicals have grown closer to the Republicans, partly as a reaction against the integrationist stands taken by Democrats and their culturally liberal position on sexual behavior, judicial appointments, and separation of church from state. Despite their divergent priorities, business elites have fused with evangelicals to demand a return to economic and cultural policies implemented before the 1960s. Whereas wealthy businessmen provide the funds that finance both church and Republican activities, the Protestant evangelicals supply the mass base for mobilizing voters. Through voter registration drives, campaign voting guides, and transportation to the polls, they help mobilize higher turnouts for Republican candidates. Evangelical leaders give legislators expertise about family issues, especially those involving abortion and gay rights. In turn, Republican legislators implement restrictions on abortion and same-sex marriage, finance faith-based charities at conservative churches, and approve the appointment of judges and other government officials who will uphold conservative stands on key cultural issues. Although the national Congress has failed to pass constitutional amendments banning abortion and same-sex marriage, in other respects most policies implemented by the Bush II Republican administration fulfilled many policy preferences voiced by conservative Christians, especially highly-educated activists who reject government programs that reduce income inequality, uphold homosexual rights, and legalize abortion (Clifton 2004; Felson and Kindell 2007; Jacobson 2007:239–62; Knuckey 2005; Nossiff 2007; Oldmixon 2005; Sager 2006; Sinclair 2006:36–66, 366–67).

Religious liberals have failed to develop the cohesive, coordinated organizations established by the conservative movement; hence, their policy influence after the 1970s remains limited. Taking a pluralist approach, they focus on establishing ties with diverse groups, both churches and more secular organizations, such as world peace, environmentalist, women's rights, and consumer movements. Several agencies try to rally support behind liberal policies. Among the Social Gospelers, Jim Wallis sponsors the Call to Renewal that coordinates a congregational network of Faith and Justice churches. It supplies guidelines for preparing prophetic sermons and forming small-group discussions about poverty, peace, immigration, and the environment. Led by Rabbi Michael Lerner, the Network of Spiritual Progressives organizes peace demonstrations, conferences, local discussion groups, and mail campaigns to legislators. It seeks to mobilize support from diverse religious groups: Christians, Jews, Muslims, Buddhists, and those who view themselves as "spiritual" but belong to no specific denomination. The International New Thought Alliance and the Association of Global New Thought unite such religious associations as the United Church of Religious Science, Religious Science International, the Association of Unity Churches International, Divine Science, Universal Foundation for Better Living, and Affiliated New Thought Network. Assuming an optimistic, humanistic perspective, the INTA affirms beliefs in the immanence of God as Mind, Spirit, and Ultimate Reality, in the unity of all individuals as spiritual beings, and in the need to establish a democratic, peaceful, harmonious world (International New Thought

Alliance 2006). Liberal mainline Christian churches have also instituted several associations comprised of diverse religious groups: the Interfaith Alliance, Church Women United, the National Coalition on Religion and the Environment, Center for Progressive Christianity, Americans United for Separation of Church and State, the National Council of Churches, and the World Council of Churches. All these ecumenical efforts impede coordination among them all. When these alliances attempt to organize diverse religious groups, support for explicit policy goals weakens among church members, many of whom feel alienated by coalition leaders' universalist orientation. Hence, the liberal religious movement lacks the high cohesion needed to wield effective influence over the national policy process (Beyerlein and Hipp 2006; Stenger 2005; Taussig 2006:145–61).

Although liberal religious movements publish several periodicals, their magazines take less political stands or lack the large audiences reached by the vast conservative media. Unity's *Daily Word* has a circulation in the millions yet its lessons never concentrate on explicit policy position or ideological themes. Instead the daily message conveys optimism, hope, constructive thinking, and practical ways to attain greater health, happiness, abundance, and cooperative relations with others (Albanese 2007:429–34). Appealing to the individual, it downplays the need for collective political actions. Prayers for world peace affirm that each person should abandon "error thoughts," develop a "tranquil mind," show love for others, and perceive the sacred qualities of all people, whatever their ethnicity, nationality, or political orientation (*Daily Word* 2006). This inspirational message appeals to people of all denominations, even to those who belong to no church, synagogue, or temple. Religious Science's *Science of Mind* adopts similar ecumenical themes but with a less Christian emphasis. Compared with *Daily Word*, it focuses greater attention on collective activism to overcome war and poverty. One article praised Dolores Huerta, who with César Chávez founded the United Farm Workers in 1962. Securing collective bargaining rights for California farm workers, the UFW improved their working conditions and health benefits. Today Huerta strives for more egalitarian access to housing, health care, education, and employment for all, especially women and youths. According to her, "When you organize, you're ultimately trying to affect public policy. Democracy is when people get involved and they are able to make their voices heard at the political level" (G. Swain 2007:16). Like Huerta, Religious Scientists assume that individuals need to develop the vision—the high consciousness—that will inspire ways to secure a more egalitarian, peaceful world. The Global Heart Vision promotes individual freedom, gender equality, ecological beauty, and world peace. Cooperating with the Association of Global New Thought, Religious Science leaders in late 2006 participated in the Abraham Path Initiative, a project designed to secure more peaceful interactions with the diverse residents of Palestine, Israel, Jordan, Syria, and Turkey (Hearn 2007; Jennings 2006, 2007).

Social Gospel periodicals like *Sojourners* and *Tikkun* make more explicit political appeals than does *Daily Word*. For example, *Sojourners* repudiates public policies that bring injustice, war, and economic misery. With a similar agenda, *Tikkun* highlights the need for governments to secure peace in the Middle East, more generous government expenditures for social services, and enhanced civil liberties—issues of procedural and distributive justice. Before the November 2006 congressional election, *Tikkun* printed a Network of Spiritual Progressives questionnaire for political candidates that probed their policies on educational priorities, health care, global poverty, global warming, and the war in Iraq. Yet these questionnaires reached far fewer church members than did Christian Coalition voter guides, which clearly indicated support for conservative Republican candidates. Liberal denominations lack access to other media sectors, like radio stations and television networks, which communicate policy preferences to the public and especially to legislators. Hence, religious liberals cannot so easily gain leverage over the public policy agenda.

Unlike religious conservatives, who have established close ties with the Republican Party, business groups, and the right-wing ideological movement, religious liberals maintain looser connections to the Democratic Party, labor unions, and leftist organizations—structures that uphold policies for civil liberties, economic equality, higher spending on social services, and individual choice about sexual behavior. Since the Carter administration (1977–80), the Democratic Party has adopted a more conservative position toward egalitarian economic redistribution. Dependent on the business sector for financial contributions, Presidents Carter and Clinton backed programs that deregulated some industries, consolidated telecommunications, cut capital gains taxes, restricted social service payments, increased defense expenditures, and refused to expand labor unions' power over the workplace. Unlike conservative Republican legislators in the House of Representatives, who in 1996 received substantial contributions from businesses and evangelical churches, liberal Democratic representatives secured only limited contributions from unions, modest funds from business lobbies, and virtually none from the evangelicals. Among denominations, only Jewish associations gave generous campaign donations to the liberal Democrats. Mainline Protestants and Catholics donated to both Republican and Democratic candidates, whatever their ideological orientation. As expected, liberal Democratic legislators showed the strongest commitment to legal abortion, homosexual rights, gender equality, progressive taxes, and government expenditures for social services. Conservative Republicans opposed all these measures. Yet the Republican majority in the House from 1996 through 2006 prevented liberal Democrats from enacting their policy preferences. Aligned with corporate business elites and Protestant evangelicals, the Republican Party had the wealth, centralization, coordination, and cohesion to dominate the policy process, especially during the first six years of the Bush II presidency. It particularly won support in the South, Midwest, and Rocky Mountain states (Brenner 2007; Francia et al. 2005; Hacker and Pierson 2006).

Individual Support

Popular support for liberal policies comes mainly from groups who share similar political identifications and cultural views about the place of religion in public life. As theological orthodoxy and church attendance decline, commitment to liberal policies rises. Believing in an impersonal God of love and interpreting the Bible from an allegorical perspective, religious liberals want churches to remain adaptable to changing conditions and to concentrate on attaining social justice. Individuals who identify with the Democratic Party and view themselves as liberals most strongly support egalitarian policy attitudes. They favor reduced military expenditures, higher government spending on social services, increased taxes on those with incomes above $200,000, legal abortion, homosexual rights, energy conservation, and reliance on the United Nations and multilateral diplomacy. Protecting civil liberties takes precedence over expanding government authority to fight terrorism. Jews, Unitarians, nonaffiliates, modernist Catholics, and liberal mainline Christians such as Episcopalians, Congregationalists, and Presbyterians most enthusiastically prefer these Social Gospel positions (Bader et al. 2006; Green 2003, 2006).

During the 2004–07 period, liberal policy stands on distributive and procedural justice gained fairly widespread support from the general U.S. population. National sample surveys revealed that over 60 percent of Americans favored higher government expenditures for health care, education, energy conservation, job training, employment, and veterans' benefits. Tax increases on the wealthy (persons with greater than $200,000 income) represented the favorite method for financing social service programs. A majority backed reduced spending on transportation, the federal administration of justice, and such weapons as nuclear missiles, destroyers, and bombers. According to survey questions probing issues of procedural justice, 60 percent upheld civil liberties for undocumented immigrants, including their right to stay in the United States, retain their jobs, and apply for citizenship, particularly if they paid a fine, committed no crime, and learned English. Over two-thirds favored a woman's right to an abortion if the pregnancy endangered her health, resulted from rape, or could produce a birth defect in the baby. Even if the majority rejected same-sex marriages, over 60 percent supported equal employment rights for homosexuals and their opportunity to serve in the armed forces. Although more Americans identified themselves as "conservatives" than as "liberals," most still preferred these specific liberal measures for distributive and procedural justice (Greeley and Hout 2006:123; Hook 2007; Kull 2005; Lotke et al. 2007; Toner and Elder 2007).

Despite the public approval for these liberal policies, why did religious liberals achieve little influence securing their enactment during the early 2000s? The success in implementing specific policies largely depends on the parties controlling the Congress and the presidency. From 2001 through 2006, conservative Republicans dominated both houses of Congress and the executive branch. Republican Party leaders promoted high cohesion. Based in the South, which has become a key financial center that experiences low wages, regressive taxes, weak unions, limited social service government expenditures, high income inequality, and the presence of numerous military bases, the Republican Party could mobilize support behind its conservative policy preferences on both economic and cultural issues. Not only in the South but everywhere except the Northeast, white Protestant evangelicals actively worked with conservative business executives to uphold Republican programs. Allied with evangelicals, the National Federation of Independent Business backed corporate tax cuts, subsidies and contracts to private enterprises, government deregulation of business, less union power, and lower spending on social services. Research institutes like the Heritage Foundation and American Enterprise Institute supplied the expertise for Republican government officials. The Christian Coalition led the campaign against reproductive choice and homosexual rights. Many appointees to the Bush administration came from such evangelical Protestant institutions as Jerry Falwell's Liberty University, Regent University led by Pat Robertson, and Patrick Henry College. Committed to conservative Republican viewpoints on national security, crime, abortion, and homosexuality, they upheld President Bush's hierarchical approach to procedural justice.

After losses in the 2006 congressional elections, factional divisions weakened the Republican Party. Ideological identifications split Republican unity on public policy preferences. Whereas "conservative" Republicans rejected legal abortion, immigrants' rights, and environmental regulations, "moderate" and the few "liberal" Republicans more strongly supported these measures. Despite these ideological divisions, the alliance between corporate executives and white Protestant evangelicals strengthened the power of the Bush presidency. The Republican National Committee communicated the conservative Republican agenda and provided finances to local social networks composed of conservative business executives and evangelicals.

Compared with liberal religious groups, conservative evangelicals had stronger incentives and organizational resources to mobilize individual support behind their cause. During the 1996–2006 era, they wanted their clergy to run for elective government offices, establish political movements, and express dissatisfaction with social conditions on television talk programs. Educated evangelical activists particularly viewed religion as a public, not just private, concern. Their extensive religious participation in praying, reading the Bible, attending church services, contributing funds to their local churches, and joining congregational networks reinforced their motivation to participate in politics, especially on behalf of Republican Party candidates. A homogeneous theology affirming a literal interpretation of the Bible, belief in a personal active God, and the importance of religious values to one's personal life further stimulated the mobilization of popular support for the Republican Party.

By contrast, liberal churches faced lower cohesion that weakened their organization of popular support. Except for Unitarian Universalists, Jews, and black Protestants who mainly favored liberal positions on policy issues, Catholics and mainline Protestants refrained from closely allying with either major political party. They remained less committed to the liberal policy agenda preferred by the Democratic Party. Among mainline Protestants, splits occurred between national officers of their denominations and laity, who generally held more conservative attitudes toward procedural and distributive justice.

The Democratic Party faced more ideological disunity than did Republicans. In late 2006 nearly 50 percent of Democrats viewed themselves as "moderates," rather than "liberals." Residing mainly in the Southern states where white Protestant evangelicals dominate, "conservative" Democrats showed a greater tendency than liberals to oppose abortion rights, expanded immigration, and government regulation of business, but to uphold public school library bans on books with "dangerous ideas." By contrast, liberal Democrats expressed a stronger commitment to civil liberties. Feeling less threatened by dangers to national security, they held a skeptical attitude toward government authority, especially after 2002. They asserted the need to challenge that authority when it violated legal freedoms.

Reflecting its ideological disunity, the Democratic Party since the late 1970s has shown lower policy cohesion, rallied less influential interest groups, and mobilized voters through weaker local networks than have the Republicans. Seeking support from the knowledge sector, telecommunications industries, and cosmopolitan financial conglomerates on Wall Street, Democratic leaders have downplayed economic equality but placed higher priority on financial deregulation and free trade agreements. Besides these measures, issues like expanded cultural freedom appeal to a highly-educated professional base that has increasingly voted for Democratic Party candidates in the Northeast and along the Pacific Coast. Liberals in the women's movement, consumer groups, and environmental associations largely represent the interests of educated professionals. Jews, Unitarians, and Episcopalians possess the high income and formal education that give them an active role in Democratic activities. Yet its other group supporters—Latino Catholics, nonaffiliates, urban low-income workers, single women, ex-prisoners—lack the resources, political efficacy, and social group connections to participate actively in campaigns advocating more egalitarian policies favored by a majority of Americans. With the declining power of labor unions, the Democratic Party has lost a mass base for organizing the populace behind a distributive justice agenda (Brenner 2007; Davis 2007; Hacker 2006; Hacker et al. 2005; Hacker and Pierson 2006; Jacobson 2007:19–60, 52–262; Kellstedt et al. 2007; Kohut 2007; Monson and Oliphant 2007; Newport et al. 2006; Olson 2007; Schaller 2006; Sinclair 2006:3–66, 308–43; Smith and Faris 2005).

Conclusion

The same structural conditions explaining the limited policy influence of religious liberalism in the United States account for the enactment of more liberal programs in Canada and Western Europe. Although Western Europe retains a few established churches, today state and church enjoy extensive autonomy. Just as government officials no longer dictate to the clergy, so religious leaders wield less policy influence than before the 1960s. Industrialization, extensive public education, urbanization, and the emergence of mass communications have spread beliefs about the autonomous individual who values change over tradition, reason over mysticism and revelation, and liberal reformism over a conservative attachment to patriarchal authority. Rational enlightenment, individual empowerment, progress, and creative vitality take primacy over superstition, oppression, stagnation, and adherence to ancient rules and rituals. Deference to traditional authority declines. Despite the prosperous economic conditions in the United States, modern values secure more widespread appeal in Western Europe, where citizens hold less orthodox religious beliefs and participate less actively in religious institutions. Particularly in Scandinavia, the Netherlands, Belgium, and Britain, few citizens believe in a personal God, interpret the Bible from a literal perspective, and attend church every week. Even if businesses play the key role in the European market economies and shape public economic policies, labor unions wield greater influence than in the United States. Although close ties between leftist parties and unions have waned, the labor movement still retains an active voice as it expresses its policy preferences to leftist parties. Unlike the U.S. situation, where the Democratic Party has moved to the center and the Republicans uphold more right-wing positions than before the 1980s, left-wing parties—left socialists, social democrats, labor, greens—play an active role in coalition governments. They tend to implement more liberal policies on procedural and distributive justice than favored by both major American party leaders, especially the Republicans (McDonald et al. 2007; Meulemann 2004; Minkenberg 2002; Therborn 2007).

Western European policies, which have produced greater income equality than have U.S. programs, demonstrate a stronger commitment to the Social Gospel view of distributive justice. During the late 1990s in Scandinavia, public policies facilitated comparatively high levels of income equality after taxes and expenditures. Despite high value-added taxes and social security contributions, numerous individuals, whatever their income, benefited from public education, health care, pensions, and child care. Minimal reliance on means-tested programs not only weakened bureaucratic surveillance and citizen fraud but expanded individual autonomy. Neither federalism nor a powerful, independent presidency impeded the enactment of programs that increased social service benefits and reduced income inequalities. No powerful alliance between conservative business executives and evangelical Protestants blocked the egalitarian approach to distributive justice (Iversen and Soskice 2006; Mishel et al. 2007:323–58).

Political leaders in Canada and Western Europe pursue policies for sexual freedom, gender equality, and nonpunitive treatment favored by New Thought and Social Gospel adherents. Unlike the United States, neither Canada nor the Western European nations implement capital punishment. Lower imprisonment rates for every 100,000 persons occur in those countries with a unitary, centralized government, high union density, economic equality, and programs that facilitate economic cooperation among corporate executives, labor leaders, and public authorities (Gylfason 2007:36; Jacobs and Kleban 2003; Sutton 2004). Nonpunitive procedures extend to sexual freedom. Particularly in Scandinavia and the Netherlands, governments impose few restrictions on legal abortion and homosexual rights. Individuals have access to sexual education in public schools, government-financed contraceptives, and free termination of pregnancies. Low teenage birth rates result (Page 2006:79–81). Gender equality obtains procedural justice for women. Whereas in 2007 women comprised over one-third of legislators elected to the lower house of the national parliaments in Scandinavia, the Netherlands, Belgium, and Spain, that share constituted only 16 percent in the United States (Inter-Parliamentary Union 2007). Western European female representation brings tangible economic benefits for both sexes: publicly-financed child care, paid parental leave, universal health care, free public preschool education, four-week paid vacation time, and the right of part-time workers to receive similar income and fringe benefits as do full-time employees (Gornick 2007). Procedural justice thereby reinforces distributive justice. In the United States, however, the New Thought and Social Gospel movements lack the organizational power to elect government leaders who support egalitarian programs for political justice that resemble Western European policies.

Just as liberal policy performance affects public opinion, so voters' policy preferences lead government officials to enact measures that enhance civil liberties, sexual freedom, gender equality, and economic equality. Sample surveys conducted during the early 2000s indicate that a higher proportion of Americans than Canadians, French, Germans, British, Italians, and Spaniards want governments to use some degree of torture against terrorist threats. Western Europeans reject torture because of its immorality and violation of international human rights. White Protestant evangelicals who identify themselves as conservative Republicans most strongly approve policies that justify torture against suspected terrorists. Support for punitive policies, including capital punishment, against criminals ranks higher in the United States, especially among native Southerners who express a conservative ideology and take a harsh, hierarchical view of God (BBC 2006; Green 2007;. Unnever and Cullen 2006). Compared with Canadians and most Western Europeans except the Irish, a larger percentage of Americans regard homosexual sex and abortion as always wrong. High attendance at orthodox, traditionalist Catholic churches, such as in Ireland, leads to restrictive policies on sexual choice. Lower religious participation in Protestant nations, like Scandinavian ones, produces greater support for sexual freedom. Egalitarian attitudes to women's rights also stem from less orthodox religious values. Where ecclesiastical institutions uphold a patriarchal religion that prescribes different roles for men and women, enthusiasm for gender equality declines. This condition most notably applies in Ireland, but not in Scandinavia, especially Sweden and Denmark (Greeley 2004:92; Hoover et al. 2002; Minkenberg 2002; Stopler 2005).

On distributive justice issues, leftist ideology, union membership, and economic status, rather than religious affiliation, influence Western European attitudes toward economic equality. Low-income, unemployed persons who belong to a union, identify with a left-wing ideology, and rarely attend religious services give the highest support to public spending on retirement pensions, health care, and unemployment benefits. Preference for egalitarian government policies occurs mainly among individuals who view the actual degree of inequality as unfair. From their perspective, the rich corporate executives receive too high incomes but poor unskilled workers earn too little. In contrast to most Western Europeans, Americans view the distribution of income as relatively fairer and hence place less reliance on government social service programs that will narrow the income gap (Andrain and Smith 2006:46–52; Brooks and Manza 2007; Lübker 2007; Osberg and Smeeding 2006; Scheve and Stasavage 2006).

As we have seen, the policy influence of religious groups partly depends on the degree of individual support that they can rally behind specific policy positions. Compared with the greater strength of Protestant evangelicals, mainline Protestants, and Catholics, today Social Gospelers and New Thought believers represent minority positions among Christians. Yet their liberal interpretations of justice have attracted some support from Unitarian Universalists, Congregationalists, Disciples of Christ, Episcopalians, Methodists, Presbyterians, Lutherans, Friends, liberal Catholics, and progressive Jews like Rabbis Michael Lerner and Mark Winer. Sample surveys enable us to comprehend the impact of religious values on attitudes toward civil liberties, sexual freedom, gender equality, and economic equality—issues we have explored in previous chapters. The case studies suggested crucial explanatory variables that may account for positions on these four issues. For example, what is the impact of holding a nurturant concept of God, taking a symbolic, nonliteral interpretation of the Bible, affirming the need for high children's autonomy, and expressing an optimistic outlook? How does church affiliation interact with other variables to affect public attitudes? In what ways do the four approaches to justice and the three functions of attitudes explain the American public's stands on specific policy issues? The 1998–2004 U.S. General Social Surveys provide tentative answers to these questions, as Chapter 7 indicates.

7
LIBERAL AND CONSERVATIVE ATTITUDES TOWARD JUSTICE

> The only freedom which deserves the name is that of pursuing our own good in our own way, so long as we do not attempt to deprive others of theirs or impede their efforts to obtain it. . . . In an imperfect state of the human mind the interests of truth require a diversity of opinions. . . . The essence of religion is the strongest and earnest direction of the emotions and desires towards an ideal object, recognized as of the highest excellence, and as rightfully paramount over all selfish objects of desire. This condition is fulfilled by the Religion of Humanity.
>
> (John Stuart Mill)

During the 1920s the Sacco-Vanzetti case highlighted the ideological conflicts that split the United States over issues of political justice. Two Italian immigrants, Nicola Sacco and Bartolomeo Vanzetti, came to the U.S. in 1908, worked as unskilled laborers, participated in strikes, and joined the anarchist movement. Raised as Catholics by their devoted parents, they abandoned their Catholic faith and became anarchists fighting capitalism. In 1920 police officers arrested them for murdering a paymaster and guard near a shoe factory in a Boston suburb. At this time the Red Scare, xenophobia, hostility to Italian immigrants, and perceived dangers from imminent world revolution created fear among Americans, especially conservative Bostonians. Insufficient evidence, conflicting testimonies, and a prejudiced judge marred justice at the trial. When a jury judged them guilty in 1921, conservatives defended the sentence, claiming that the two anarchists formed part of a worldwide terrorist network determined to bring violent revolution to the United States. Taking the opposing side in this "culture war," liberals, radicals, and socialists led protests that accused the jury and Massachusetts officials of discrimination against immigrant anarchists. Despite protests at home and overseas from Western Europe to Latin America, the state government executed Sacco and Vanzetti in 1927. As a result of the trial and execution, numerous poems, songs, novels, and plays emerged. Some writers even portrayed the two as Christ-like martyrs, victims of injustice at the hands of a Massachusetts governor who resembled Pontius Pilate (Temkin 2007; Watson 2007:299–302, 356). Several mourners at the funeral for Sacco and Vanzetti wore red armbands that read, "Remember Justice Crucified, August 22, 1927." Committed to free speech and opposed to government abuse of power, Vanzetti's letters placed civil liberties on the public agenda (Frankfurter and Jackson 1928:esp. 306–07). In a famous jail interview to a newspaper reporter four months before his execution, he linked his sacrifice to ultimate victory: "Now we are not a failure. . . . Never in our full life can we hope to do such work for tolerance, for justice, for man's understanding of man, as we do now by accident. . . . That last moment belongs to us—that agony is our triumph!" (Felix 1965:178).

Influenced by the Sacco-Vanzetti case, James Thurber and Elliott Nugent wrote a play portraying threats to civil liberties at Mid-Western University. First produced in 1940, *The Male Animal* told the story of English professor Thomas Turner. A liberal college senior and editor of *The Literary Magazine* wrote an editorial that announced the intention of Professor Turner to read his students the 1927 interview by Vanzetti. Ed Keller, a wealthy, conservative real estate developer and the most influential member of the university's board of trustees, threatens to engineer the dismissal of Turner if he reads Vanzetti's 1927 interview to his composition class. At first, Turner's wife tries to dissuade him because the trustees have recently fired other professors for behaving like "Reds." After a brief time of indecision, Turner decides to stand up for his convictions, demonstrate his commitment to civil liberties, read the interview, and exemplify "the male animal." Reflecting on Vanzetti's beliefs about tolerance, justice, human emancipation, and civil liberties, Professor Turner proclaims that universities have the obligation to pursue truth, enlighten students, protect free speech, and avoid succumbing to prejudice and authoritarianism. Keller, however, fears that the brief interview will poison students' minds with ideas about socialism. From his business perspective, the university must teach "Americanism," rather than allow "wishy-washy" faculty to indoctrinate students with "red" communism or "pink" socialism (Thurber and Nugent 1941:43–44, 128–30). Unlike Professor Drummond, who asserted his masculinity by moving "south of the slot," Professor Turner expresses his courage by resisting business pressures from trustees like Keller, who cares more about winning football games than about protecting civil liberties in the university.

In several respects, political life resembles a play. The playwright, director, actors, and stage hands produce a performance for an audience. The script presents a plot with heroes and villains. Performers want the play to gain audience appeal. To achieve this goal, resonance with the audience's values becomes crucial. From the metaphorical perspective, a similar process takes place with politics. Political leaders articulate policy positions on important issues that the people regard as relevant to their lives. Through political discourse, government officials, political party activists, and their group allies try to gain popular support for specific policy preferences on civil liberties, gender equality, family life, and economic distribution. By mobilizing activists, recruiting passive individuals to more active status, and demobilizing opponents, political entrepreneurs focus on constructing a cohesive base. Communications clarify the meaning of ambiguous situations. Solidarity mounts behind a visionary cause. Under polarizing conditions, material interests become invested with moral-spiritual values. Defensiveness against threats provokes ingroup battles with outgroups. Fundamentalist crusaders urge the exorcism of demons: secular humanism, ethical relativism, moral decadence. Purification of political life takes precedence over the pragmatic negotiation of material interests (Apter 2006b). Under these conditions, support for civil liberties, sexual freedom, gender equality, and economic equality diminishes.

Threats to civil liberties arise in times of social change and perceived dangers to the established order. These situations upset conventional meanings. Ambiguity about the course of events results. New groups with divergent demands seem to weaken national solidarity. Defensiveness against perceived threats from radicals, immigrants, "free thinkers," and "outside agitators" increases demands for repression. During the Progressive era the Southern Methodists gained control of the Oklahoma State Board of Education and engineered the dismissal in 1908 of several University of Oklahoma faculty, including English professor Vernon Louis Parrington. Accused of immorality for smoking cigarettes and for misleading students, he asserted the injustice of his dismissal. According to him, the Oklahoma land speculators, businessmen, and fundamentalist ministers worshiped materialism but neglected civic morality, personal ethics, honor, and justice (Hall 1994:146–51). Under the Red Scare (1919–20) following World War I, the federal government ordered the deportation of anarchists, socialists, and communists—all those suspected of sympathy with the Soviet Revolution. Not only the national but also state governments repressed leftist movements, political parties, and unions. In 1938 the House of Representatives formed the Committee on Un-American Activities (HUAC). It defined "disloyalty" to include leftist Democrats, communists, and more radical union leaders, especially those in the CIO (Congress of Industrial Organizations). After the war the HUAC continued its investigations into those individuals and organizations that the committee perceived as disloyal "subversives." Numerous dismissals occurred at both the national and state government levels. University professors who refused to sign loyalty oaths lost their jobs. Senator Joseph McCarthy seemed to represent a figure like Ed Keller. Opposed to this hunt for heretics, James Thurber upheld the need for civil liberties during the 1950s, when the repressive adherents of the anticommunist crusade sought to limit activities of unions, racial integrationists, and homosexuals. Intimidated by sponsors and threatened by the play's controversial tone, television executives in 1956 refused to broadcast *The Male Animal* over their networks. After the terrorist attacks of September 11, 2001, Muslims and immigrants became the main targets of coercive government policies (Foner

1998:177–78, 217–18, 249–73; Watson 2007:360). Fearing threats from these groups, public officials regarded the rhetorical pledge to defend freedom as more important than the competent administration of procedural justice.

The Motivational Basis of Attitudes

As Chapter 1 indicated, attitudes express three motivations: the interpretation of meaning, promotion of social solidarity, and defense against perceived threats. For most individuals, attitudes toward public issues show complexity, conflict, and change. Their subjective nature limits comprehension of "objective" reality. Meaning can derive from conflicting sources: religious values, political ideologies, class identifications, nationalist sentiments. Often support for one attitude—enthusiasm for individual freedom—contradicts an urge for solidarity based on homogeneous values. Even though all people hold these motivations, the specific ways that they express them vary among individuals. Whereas some persons seek unity in diversity as the basis of social solidarity, others stress a polarized conflict between the "pure" ingroup vs. stigmatized outgroups. The priority attached to these motivations also differs. When ego-defensive motives take precedence over the search for meaning through enhanced education, support for civil liberties declines (Jervis 2006; Smith et al. 1956).

The framing process becomes especially important as individuals interpret the meaning of an ambiguous political world. George Lakoff (2006a:25) defines frames as "the mental structures that allow human beings to understand reality—and sometimes to create what we take to be reality." Resting on shared, durable, and abstract principles, frames organize information, specify problems (injustice), highlight solutions to popular grievances, identify the causes of the problem, recruit group allies, motivate supporters, and mobilize them to take action. By shaping valued goals, influencing expectations about feasible outcomes, and stimulating emotions, frames lend meaning to political situations. The moral vision of an idealistic cause affirms the desirability of political justice. Emotions provoke the hope, anger, or fear that promote collective action. To rally support behind the political cause, communication of meaning becomes crucial. Church leaders must find the media that will best communicate their principles and specific policy preferences to a sympathetic audience. Credible, comprehensible media messages that resonate among the public help recruit supporters (Gerhards 1995; Noakes and Johnston 2005; Reese 2001).

Political discourse features three connected frames that interpret political conditions: deep frames, issue frames, and slogans. Deep frames express fundamental values, such as hierarchy vs. opposition to authority, individualism vs. collectivism, egalitarianism vs. elitism, and efficacy vs. fatalism. Comparing Social Gospel and New Thought adherents, we have seen that these values influence more specific policy issues, including civil liberties, legal abortion, gender equality, and economic equality. Slogans refer to simplistic labels applied to opponents and policy stands: "limousine liberal," "robber barons," "family values," "cut and run" (Lakoff 2006a:25–48; Nunberg 2006). The most effective communications link deep values, issue preferences, and slogans so that a coherent message resonates among supporters.

Frames affect the ideological preferences taken by liberals and conservatives. Despite the multiple meanings attached to these terms, self-identified ideological positions shape attitudes toward several public issues. Highly-educated political activists hold the most consistent, coherent stands. Unlike passive spectators, they view ideology as an abstract, deductive, systematic set of principles that lend meaning to specific conditions. For them, abstract ideas interpret concrete situations.

Lakoff links ideologies to family models. According to him, conservatives uphold the ideal of a "strict father" who values hierarchical control, order, and patriarchal authority. Punishment and discipline of children lead to their self-discipline. Moral-spiritual values also rest on hierarchy. God represents a strict father who judges, punishes, and disciplines his subordinates. Moral polarization divides the upstanding good people from underhanded evil persons. Whereas the saved ascend to heaven, the damned descend to hell. When self-indulgent individuals cannot control their passions, they fall from grace. Hierarchical conservatives believe that morality stems from religious values. It means obedience to absolute rules and to the personal commands of the male leader. Rules about ethical behavior come from a literal interpretation of the Bible. Although valuing conformity to established authorities, conservatives assert a competitive individualism that requires discipline, hard work, and strong willpower for economic success. Equal opportunity to achieve takes precedence over equal outcomes, which reduce the incentive to produce.

Specific policy preferences flow from the strict father model. Lakoff assumes that conservatives will give support to order above civil liberties for unpopular groups that challenge authority. Opposed to homosexual behavior and abortion, conservatives uphold gendered marriage of husband and wife. For them, abortion means murder of human life and destroys family integrity. Gender equality violates the need for men to play a dominant role in the home, business, and politics. The government provision of social services promotes excessive economic equality. Instead, private businesses, churches, families, and the individual should assume the main responsibility for providing such services as child care, health benefits, and economic assistance.

By contrast, liberals affirm the "nurturant parent" model. They perceive the need for egalitarian parents who express a loving, caring, empathetic attitude toward their children. Instead of stressing obedience, liberals want their children to value independent thinking. Viewing God as the spirit of love and a nurturant father-mother, they deny the depravity of individuals. Created in the divine image, people have the potential for virtuous behavior. Through education and environmental improvements, individuals can change their beliefs and actions. Self-fulfillment assumes priority over self-denial. Morality stems from compassion, empathy, and personal responsibility—values stressed in the liberals' metaphorical, symbolic interpretation of scripture. Rather than based on absolute rules, morality reflects general, flexible guidelines that need adapting to particular situations. A concern for the well-being of others in society motivates the liberal focus on social justice. It rests on a cooperative ethic that reconciles differences, especially the gap that separates rich from poor. Liberal policy attitudes derive from the nurturant parent ideal. Government has the obligation to supply universal social services, including education, health care, day care, elder care, pensions, and employment opportunities. Upholding civil liberties for dissidents, liberals want government to guarantee freedom. Free choices for people to engage in homosexual behavior and for women to gain an abortion during the early stages of pregnancy take precedence over government regulation of private sexual interactions. Religious freedom entails independence of the political from the religious sphere, so that government refrains from controlling churches.

They in turn wield no theocratic dominance over the public policy process. For liberals, freedom extends to women's rights to perform the same roles as do men in the family, business sector, and government (Barker and Tinnick 2006; Grafton and Permaloff 2005; Lakoff 2002, 2004, 2006a, 2006b; Nunberg 2006:121–49; Permaloff and Grafton 2003; Smith 2003).

Americans not only interpret meaning through their ideological lenses but also through political party identifications. Since the New Deal period, Democrats and Republicans have taken divergent stands on economic issues, especially government regulation of private business and government provision of social services. Whereas Democrats support greater regulation and public provision, Republicans prefer business autonomy, deregulation, and privatization. Libertarian Republicans most strongly adhere to these views. During the 1980s cultural issues linked to abortion, gay rights, and prayer in school became a more important aspect of the political discourse. As white evangelical Protestants shifted their votes to the Republican Party, especially in the South, the Republican Party platform placed greater emphasis on opposition to abortion and homosexual behavior. The strongest commitment to the Republican stand on cultural issues occurs among white Protestant evangelicals who most frequently pray, read the Bible, and attend church services. Libertarian businessmen uphold the need for reduced government regulation and greater private provision of social services. Among Democrats an opposite ideological tendency prevails. They gain more support from educated professionals (trial lawyers, university professors, social workers, government employees, information processors), unionized workers, Jews, and people who remain unaffiliated with any church and rarely participate in religious activities. Just as the most actively-involved Republicans express the most coherent, consistent, comprehensive conservative ideology, so activist Democrats most enthusiastically favor the liberal cultural and economic stands taken by their party. For both party's activists, ideology, political party allegiance, and religion congeal to give meaning to specific policy issues, especially those linked to economic equality and abortion. Fewer issue cleavages divide the major parties on civil liberties and gender equality. Passive party supporters show fewer differences on all four issues (Abramowitz 2006; Carsey and Layman 2006; Dionne 2006; Fiorina 2006; Fiorina and Levendusky 2006; Glaeser et al. 2004; Greeley and Hout 2006; Green 2006; Kohut et al. 2000).

As indicated by the influence of churches and political parties on issue preferences, social solidarity motivates attitudes toward various policies. The greatest solidarity (strong feelings about belonging to a group) emerges when members share values, hold similar policy positions, frequently interact with one another, form cohesive social networks, receive clear messages from leaders, and erect barriers for membership and dismissal, so that defections rarely occur. Religious institutions display the features that promote social solidarity. Particularly when their leaders articulate a comprehensive, long-term vision of a just society, the intensely-held cause motivates members to adopt the dominant attitudes. The sacred cause draws no distinction between the public and private, sacred and secular. General theological views influence more specific policy preferences. Scriptural education and catechisms form requirements for membership. Those judged guilty of unethical behavior or heretical beliefs face punitive sanctions: ostracism, dismissal, or excommunication. Although this powerful solidarity strengthens conformity, the dogmatic closure to new ideas weakens individual autonomy. Support for civil liberties declines.

The impact of social solidarity on policy preferences seems strongest in Protestant evangelical churches. Active participants in church activities, laity establish cohesive social networks. Their leaders articulate clear messages about the evils of culturally permissive values asserting the need for legal abortion and gay marriage. Compared with other denominational members, evangelical Protestants regard church teachings as highly important and affirm their desire to follow these teachings. Mainline Protestants, Catholics, Social Gospelers, and New Thought students belong to weaker, less cohesive churches. Given their lower degree of solidarity, they have weaker influence over members' public attitudes (Bader et al. 2006; Cochran et al. 2004; Everton 2005; Greeley and Hout 2006:15–38, 113–35; Mulligan 2006; Weeden and Grusky 2005; Wintrobe 2006).

The conflict between sacred and secular values explains the continuing impact of religious institutions on social solidarity. As Émile Durkheim indicated, the structural differentiation linked to modernization weakens the solidarity formerly experienced in rural village life. As industrialization, urbanization, mass formal education, impersonal communication, and globalization grow, atomization, isolation, alienation, and fragmented identities increase. Tolerance for "deviant" lifestyles rises along with pluralist worldviews and individual autonomy. A bureaucratic nation-state becomes more powerful. Secular rationalization involves a dynamic society that engineers rapid growth and material progress. Through reason, technology, and the physical sciences, individuals can understand and control not only the material world but also the social situation. These modernized conditions prevail in Western Europe, especially Scandinavia, the Netherlands, and Belgium, where church attendance remains lower and orthodox religious beliefs attract less support than in the United States. American Protestant evangelicals who regard the Bible as the source of divine law and traditionalist Catholics who revere Vatican teachings assert the priority of sacred values over secular permissiveness depicted in the mass media. They seek to increase the influence of government regulation over family life and sexual behavior. Their belief in a transcendent God who enunciates universal, objective ethical standards rejects the amorphous religion of humanity favored by John Stuart Mill. When voicing their policy preferences about civil liberties and abortion, these traditionalist Christians seem motivated by defensiveness against perceived threats from liberal relativism, secular humanism, and rationalism (Andrain and Apter 1995:51–53, 60–64; Durkheim 1972:219–49; Rasor 2003).

Based on psychoanalysis, ego-defensive theories of attitudes focus on unconscious thoughts and emotions like fear and anger. People who experience anger against authorities and fear of personal weakness erect defense mechanisms against these threats. Ego-defensive motivations particularly explain opposition to civil liberties and sexual freedom. Such defense mechanisms as rationalization, displacement, projection, and repression become frequently-used strategies. Rationalization occurs when altruistic reasons justify coercive actions. For example, political leaders invoke the need to defend national security when justifying torture. Hostility toward expansive immigration programs often stems from workers who lose their jobs. They displace their anger on low-status immigrants, who get blamed for unemployment. When individuals condemn others for motives they deny in themselves, projection occurs. They stress the need to coerce outgroups labeled as immoral, unclean, and guilty of sexual licentiousness. Vulnerable feelings about their masculinity stimulate some men to launch homophobic attacks. As studies of the authoritarian personality revealed, repression of hostility often occurs. Glorification of parents, especially the father, disguises children's ambivalence toward them. Repressed hatred of punitive family authority becomes displaced on marginal groups. An idolized political autocrat serves as a substitute father figure to love.

Rejection of civil liberties stems from three beliefs: conventionalism, submission to established authority, and aggressiveness toward "deviant" groups. Conventional norms about women's role in society and about ethical patterns of sexual behavior dictate that children obey their parents, wives honor their husband's leadership, and laity follow the official edicts of church hierarchs. Fearing a dangerous world, intolerant individuals urge obedience to parents, government officials, and religious leaders. Aggressive attitudes label unconventional, unpopular groups as repulsive. Corporal punishment, capital punishment, and strictly enforced laws illustrate policies that authoritarian personalities assume will repress deviants and establish social order. When these ego-defensive conditions become the dominant motivation behind public attitudes, individuals perceive high threats from other people. A pessimistic view of the world engenders views of others as unfair, unhelpful, and untrustworthy. High personal dissatisfaction reinforces aversion to civil liberties, sexual choice, and gender equality. Fundamentalist Christians who view God as a punitive judge, regard the Bible as a source of absolutist divine laws, and perceive a world polarized between good and evil adopt these coercive attitudes. An urge for homogeneity, conformity, and clear solutions to ambiguous problems magnifies intolerance (Altemeyer 1996, 2006; Andrain and Apter 1995:239–44; Duckitt 2006; Kam and Kinder 2007; Stenner 2005; Weiler and Hetherington 2006).

Hypotheses about Issue Preferences

Using the 1998–2004 General Social Surveys for relevant questions, I formulate several hypotheses that explain attitudes toward civil liberties, legal abortion, gender equality, and government provision of social services. The Appendix specifies procedures used to measure these attitudes. Civil liberties questions focus on support for allowing atheists, communists, militarists, homosexuals, and racists the rights to speak freely, teach in college, and have their books available in public libraries.

Individuals expressing the least opposition to abortion want public policies to grant the legal right to it if the baby has a defect, pregnancy endangers the woman's health, the pregnancy resulted from rape, a single woman declines marriage, the woman comes from a poor family, or she wants an abortion for any other reason. The gender equality index refers to role similarity. Both men and women should have equal rights to hold political office and to work outside the home as paid employees. Economic equality measures the degree of support for public policies that reduce income differences, improve living standards of low-income people, and increase expenditures on health care, cities, and aid to blacks and the poor.

Derived from general assumptions about justice, specific hypotheses about issue preferences fall under three categories: cultural values, political identifications, and economic dimensions. Cultural values include not only such variables as personal optimism and parental stress on children's autonomy but explicit religious factors: view of the Bible, perception of God, religious affiliation, and religious participation such as prayer and church attendance. Political variables comprise identifications with a political party and with a liberal or conservative ideology. Income and class identification designate two key economic dimensions that may shape public attitudes, especially toward distributive justice. Tables 7.1 and 7.2 specify the hypotheses.

According to previous survey research, the strongest support for civil liberties, legal abortion, and gender equality comes from individuals who adopt a nondeferential, individualistic, optimistic approach to procedural justice. Identifying themselves as "liberals," they rarely attend church, adopt a symbolic interpretation of the Bible, hold an egalitarian view of God, feel few threats from other people, and encourage children's independent thinking. High education and income strengthen their liberal positions. By contrast, self-described "conservatives" take a more hierarchical, elitist orientation toward justice. These persons frequently participate in religious activities, perceive God as a hierarchical personal being, feel threatened by dangerous "others," and promote obedience in their children. Low socioeconomic status reinforces this conservative outlook (Bolzendahl and Myers 2004; Dillon and Wink 2007:148–67; Eisenstein 2006; M. Emerson 1996; Jelen and Wilcox 2003; Moore and Ovadia 2006; Moore and Vanneman 2003; Tuntiya 2005; L. Weber 2003; C. Wilcox 2003).

Table 7.1 Hypotheses about civil liberties, legal abortion, and gender equality

Explanations	Higher support	Lower support
View of Bible	Symbolic, allegorical interpretation	Literal, inerrant interpretation
View of God	Loving, nurturant, egalitarian	Punitive, judgmental, hierarchical
Religious participation (frequency of church attendance and prayer)	Low	High
Religious preference	Jews, nonaffiliates	Evangelical Protestants
Important value taught to children	Autonomous thinking	Obedience
Personal optimism and happiness	High	Low
Party identification	Strong Democrat	Strong Republican
Ideological identification	Liberal	Conservative
Formal education attained	Bachelor's and graduate degrees	Less than high school
Income	High	Low
Class identification	Middle and upper	Working and lower
Age	Young (under 30)	Old (over 60)
Sex	Women	Men

Rather than religious values or participation, political identifications and economic status better explain attitudes toward distributive justice. Most churches devote greater attention to sexual behavior and family integrity than to income distribution. Even though cultural issues have drawn more recent attention from political parties, they still emphasize economic policies, whether tax cuts for business or increased government expenditures for social service programs. Survey research has demonstrated that liberal Democrats, rather than conservative Republicans, express higher enthusiasm for policies intended to reduce income inequalities. Liberal Democrats more likely assume that poverty stems from structural conditions: prejudice, deficient education, few available jobs, and limited opportunities to earn income. Conservative Republicans, however, take a more individualist stance

Table 7.2 Hypotheses about economic equality

Explanations	Higher support	Lower support
View of Bible	Ethical, symbolic interpretation	Literal, inerrant interpretation
View of God	Loving, nurturant, egalitarian	Punitive, judgmental, hierarchical
Religious participation	Low	High
Religious preference	Jews, nonaffiliates	Mainline Protestants
Important value taught to children	Autonomous thinking	Obedience
Personal optimism and happiness	Low	High
Party identification	Strong Democrat	Strong Republican
Ideological identification	Liberal	Conservative
Formal education attained	Less than high school	Bachelor's and graduate degrees
Income	Low	High
Class identification	Working and lower	Middle and upper
Age	Young (under 30)	Old (over 60)
Sex	Women	Men

toward poverty. Drawing a sharp distinction between the "deserving" and "undeserving" poor, they blame low-income people for their failure to work hard, gain needed skills, and demonstrate discipline, self-control, initiative, ambition, and personal responsibility. Allied with the Republican Party, white Protestant evangelical leaders stress this individualist outlook. Hence, they reject public policies that raise spending on health benefits, child care, elderly assistance, family leaves, pensions, and measures for reducing income inequalities. Privatization of these services and government grants to "faith-based" agencies take priority over benefits administered by political authorities. Earning lower incomes than men and assuming greater responsibilities to care for children, the elderly, and the sick, women remain more enthusiastic about these egalitarian public programs. Oriented toward individualism, wealthier persons who take an optimistic perspective on life and who identify with the middle or upper class oppose measures to reduce income disparities. For these optimists, economic success derives from individual merit. Believing that their achievements reflect economic justice, they show little enthusiasm for egalitarian redistributive policies (Bénabou and Tirole 2006; Clydesdale 1999; Curry et al. 2004; Eagly and Diekman 2006; Hetherington 2005; Hunt 2002; Jacoby 2006; Rudolph and Evans 2005; Schneider and Jacoby 2005, 2007:561; Steensland 2006; Street and Cossman 2006).

Even if analysts cannot easily measure notions of justice, they rely on specific survey questions that tentatively reflect such abstract values as egalitarianism, hierarchy, and individualism. They presume that people who stress the need for childhood obedience, rather than independent thinking, take a hierarchical position. So do those viewing God as a patriarchal master judge. Concepts of God as a loving spouse and mother reflect greater egalitarianism. Personal optimism expresses both high individualism and efficacy, not fatalism and dissatisfaction. These individualist, nonhierarchical, egalitarian conceptions strengthen support for civil liberties, gender equality, and legal abortion.

The functional basis of attitudes also helps explain issue stands. If meaning derives mainly from a literal view of the Bible, a conservative ideology, and Republican Party identification, resistance to legal abortion and economic equality results. Solidarity with white Protestant evangelical churches, as measured by frequent participation in church activities, strengthens opposition to civil liberties and abortion. When solidarity emerges from identification with a liberal ideology, the Democratic Party, and the working class, support rises for government social service programs that expand economic equality. Pessimism reveals ego-defensive attitudes that fear a dangerous, threatening world. Perceiving other people as unfair, untrustworthy, and unhelpful, pessimists remain highly dissatisfied with their lives. Hence, they may oppose procedural justice but back measures for enhancing income equality.

To test these hypotheses, the following sections first examine national public opinion and then analyze the public attitudes of specific religious groups, including evangelical Protestants, mainline Protestants, Roman Catholics, Jews, and nonaffiliates. Which hypotheses show the greatest credibility? On what specific issues do the various explanations seem most important? To what extent do the interpretations stressed by Social Gospelers and New Thought adherents account for liberal attitudes toward procedural and substantive justice? In this regard, a symbolic interpretation of the Bible, an egalitarian view of God, personal optimism, advanced education, and parental values stressing high children's autonomy become relevant.

Because the indices and most other variables stem from survey questions with continuous responses, I use Ordinary Least Squares (OLS) regressions after standardizing each variable for comparability. All explanatory variables have minimal multicollinearity, as indicated by tolerance levels near 1. Low standard errors (under one half the unstandardized regression coefficient) and high regression coefficients specify the variables that account for the greatest variance in attitudes toward civil liberties, legal abortion, gender equality, and economic equality. Religious group comparisons rely on mean scores and regression equations to discover if the same variables explain issue preferences of different denominational members.

NATIONAL PUBLIC OPINION

According to Table 7.3, regression equations for the 1998–2004 samples explain a high variance in the attitudes toward procedural justice. Particularly for opinions about civil liberties and abortion, the adjusted R^2s equal .471 and .423 but only .125 for gender equality. To understand the importance of religious values on support for women's rights, I made a separate probe of the 1998 survey data, which contain replies to questions about perceptions of God (see Table 7.4). Do respondents view God as a hierarchical master or as a more egalitarian loving mother? Incorporation of this variable into the regression equation raises the adjusted R^2 for gender equality to .301.

Attitudes toward civil liberties and legal abortion reveal the powerful impact of cultural values about hierarchy and individualism. As belief in the value of children's obedience rises, support for civil liberties and abortion falls. Whereas personal optimists back enhanced liberty for unpopular groups, individuals who take a pessimistic outlook on their own lives and other people resist libertarian policies.

Demographic characteristics interact with solidarity and identity to influence preferences for procedural justice. Less-well-educated persons who find their solidarity in the church and affirm a conservative identity most strongly oppose civil liberties and the legal right to an

Table 7.3 Explanations for attitudes toward civil liberties, legal abortion, gender equality, and economic equality, 1998–2004

Explanatory variables	Civil liberties			Legal abortion			Gender equality			Economic equality		
	B	S.E.	beta	B	S.E.	beta	B	S.E.	beta	B	S.E.	beta
View of Bible (high = symbolic interpretation)	−.200	.008	−.225	−.443	.010	−.430	.073	.009	.098	.039	.005	.059
Religious participation	.320	.010	.300	.245	.012	.198	.071	.009	.100	−.030	.005	−.047
Children's autonomy (high = stress on independent thinking)	.101	.010	.092									
Personal optimism	.057	.007	.074	−.109	.009	−.121				−.091	.005	−.138
Party identification (high = Republican)	−.063	.010	−.058	−.175	.013	−.137	−.093	.008	−.127	−.229	.003	−.489
Ideological identification (high = conservative)	.210	.007	.277	.149	.009	.169	.050	.006	.098	−.201	.005	−.303
Education	.088	.010	.075	.076	.012	.056				.025	.003	.055
Income				.059	.011	.050				−.064	.005	−.090
Class identification	−.201	.008	−.218				−.099	.007	−.161	−.094	.005	−.150
Age				.024	.005	.046	.033	.003	.109	−.037	.004	−.066
Sex (high = female)										.056	.002	.204
Constant	.463	.012		.646	.014		.577	.008		.923	.006	
Number 7,845												
Adjusted R^2	.471			.423			.125			.670		

Note: All variables are standardized from 0 to 1. All regression coefficients are statistically significant at $p < .001$.

Table 7.4 Explanations for attitudes toward civil liberties and gender equality, 1998

	Civil liberties			Gender equality		
Explanatory variables	B	S.E.	beta	B	S.E.	beta
View of Bible	.442	.022	.391	.085	.017	.105
View of God[a]	.113	.028	.076	.176	.021	.167
Children's autonomy	.061	.020	.060			
Personal optimism				.050	.016	.065
Ideological identification	−.072	.020	−.066	−.106	.015	−.137
Education	.178	.016	.208	.083	.013	.136
Income	.087	.023	.069	.050	.018	.056
Age	−.185	.018	−.181	−.230	.015	−.316
Sex				.079	.007	.222
Constant	.457	.025		.532	.019	
Number 2,063						
Adjusted R²	.408			.301		

Note: All variables are standardized from 0 to 1. All regression coefficients are statistically significant at p < .001.
[a] High score for view of God indicates an egalitarian, nurturant perception.

abortion. Support stems primarily from highly-educated individuals who identify themselves as liberals and who rarely participate in religious activities. University education in social sciences, the humanities, and law often generates the cognitive skills linked to an open mind: intellectual flexibility, comprehension of diverse ideas, analysis of complex information, and logical procedures for applying general principles like freedom to specific cases. With the critical, rational, pluralist thought processes emphasized by John Stuart Mill, university graduates show empathy for persons adopting different lifestyles, however nonconformist. These cognitive abilities lead them to uphold procedural justice, particularly the importance of legal guarantees for all citizens (Andrain and Apter 1995:245–51; Crowson et al. 2005; Moore and Ovadia 2006; Ohlander et al. 2005).

Although Republicans show a slight tendency to give greater support to civil liberties than do Democrats, ideology interacts with party identification to shape that support, as Table 7.5 clarifies. Of the two

Table 7.5 Impact of ideological and partisan identifications on policy preferences: mean scores

		Ideological identification		
Policy	Party identification	Liberal	Centrist	Conservative
Civil liberties	Democrat	26.18	25.01	24.72
(Range = 15–30)	Independent	26.13	25.13	24.82
	Republican	25.96	24.95	24.95
Legal abortion	Democrat	12.05	11.16	10.53
(Range = 7–14)	Independent	11.95	11.14	10.47
	Republican	12.05	10.52	10.52
Gender equality	Democrat	10.00	9.93	9.89
(Range = 4–14)	Independent	9.95	9.96	10.00
	Republican	10.05	9.96	9.96
Economic equality	Democrat	22.47	20.29	17.98
(Range = 7–29)	Independent	21.86	19.97	17.89
	Republican	21.80	17.77	17.77

identifications, ideology assumes more importance. Among Democrats, independents, and Republicans, as self-identification moves from liberal to centrist to conservative, enthusiasm for civil liberties weakens. Within each ideological group, fewer differences occur. Whereas liberal Democrats secure the highest mean score, conservative Democrats rank lowest on civil liberties. Compared with conservative Democrats, both conservative and centrist Republicans express a stronger preference for civil liberties—a libertarian position that also extends to market transactions.

Even if party conflicts over abortion appear striking, ideological identification exerts a stronger impact. Along with centrist Republicans, conservatives of all partisan identities express the greatest resistance to legal abortion. Liberals, including Democrats, independents, and Republicans, show the least disapproval. However few in number, liberal Republicans remain disenchanted with the stands taken by the national party headquarters on cultural issues like abortion.

Orientations toward gender equality also reflect the dominance of cultural values. Congruent with the assumptions about God and the Bible affirmed by Social Gospel and New Thought adherents, a nurturant perception of God and a symbolic, allegorical interpretation of the

Bible strengthen this egalitarian perspective. Young, highly-educated liberal women especially believe that women should enjoy equal opportunities in the family, workplace, and government. By contrast, opposition to equal rights for women comes from older men with less formal education. As self-styled "conservatives," they resist modern trends that have expanded egalitarian relationships. Committed to children's obedience, they perceive God as a patriarchal judge, master, and father, not as a loving mother. Their outlook on family interactions and women's rights partly flows from their interpretation of the Bible that upholds a strict father image (Lakoff 2002:245–62).

Although respondents who adopt a symbolic, metaphorical interpretation of the Bible and who value independent thinking in children demonstrate a slight tendency to favor policies for decreasing income equality, party, ideological, and class identifications linked to structural explanations of poverty most strongly influence preferences about distributive justice. (See Table 7.3 for the adjusted R^2 of .62.) Democrats, liberals, and working-class identifiers back measures that expand government provision of social services for health care, cities, the poor, African Americans, and other programs designed to reduce income inequalities. Whereas liberal Democrats most strongly support these policies, conservative and centrist Republicans express the greatest opposition—a stand rejected by Social Gospelers. Unity and Religious Science emphasize an individualist, optimistic ethic that places major responsibility on individuals themselves, rather than government programs, for overcoming poverty. The regressions confirm the New Thought tendency for higher personal optimism to promote lesser enthusiasm for egalitarian public policies. Satisfied with their lives and perceiving other people as helpful, fair, and trustworthy, wealthier optimists resist government actions to mitigate the gap separating rich from poor.

In sum, the 1998–2004 survey results confirm more hypotheses explaining procedural justice than distributive justice. When personal optimism and value of children's autonomy rise, so does support for civil liberties. Frequent religious participation produces opposition to civil liberties and abortion. Political identifications interact with cultural values to shape policy preferences. Ideology matters more than does partisanship, with liberals expressing the strongest commitment to gender equality and legal abortion. Advanced education leads to greater approval of civil liberties and abortion but has a weaker impact on gender equality. Compared with men, women show more enthusiasm for gender equality, as do youths and those 1998 respondents who held an egalitarian concept of God.

Political identifications, economic status, and optimism, not religious variables, primarily explain attitudes toward distributive justice. Individuals who take an optimistic outlook on life, possess greater income, and identify with the middle or upper class resist policies to expand government social services. Unlike income or class identification, education barely affects preference for economic equality. More important, party and ideological identifications shape views about egalitarian policies, with liberal Democrats favoring them and conservative Republicans rejecting these programs. Neither religious values and participation nor belief in the need for children to think independently exerts an important effect on opinions about economic equality. Although Lakoff assumed that a strict father model leads to popular support for promarket policies, this dedication mainly derives not from evangelical laity but from white conservative Protestant leaders like Pat Robertson who have aligned with the Republican Party (Greeley and Hout 2006:84–89; Lakoff 2006a:49–81).

Public Opinion Among Religious Groups

At the 1992 Republican national convention, Pat Buchanan rallied delegates behind the religious war fought for "the soul of America." How polarized are the value conflicts among different religious groups? The "culture war" image has stimulated extensive research about the diverse religious and political attitudes held by evangelical Protestants, mainline Protestants, Roman Catholics, Jews, and nonaffiliates. Even if sample survey studies have uncovered general differences among denominations, polarization occurs mainly when political identifications and socioeconomic variables, especially education, interact with religious beliefs and practices. The greatest cleavage arises over cultural issues such as abortion, gay rights, and civil liberties. Economic policy preferences, which provoke fewer attitudinal divisions among church members, derive primarily from class, party, and ideological identifications (Fiorina 2006). Since 1990 "conservatives" have defended moral traditionalism, sought increases in defense expenditures but decreases for social service spending, and rejected legal abortion. On these issues, "liberal" identifiers have taken opposite positions: support behind the legal right to an abortion, higher government expenditures for social services but lower spending on the military, and enhanced tolerance for newer lifestyles. Unlike liberals, conservatives feel more threatened by secular relativism that endangers social order, especially traditional family ties. Comparison of different religious affiliations reveals that Jews and nonaffiliates hold the most liberal stands on these issues, with evangelical Protestants favoring the most conservative view. Adopting a centrist orientation, mainline Protestants and Roman Catholics share similar policy preferences (Bolzendahl and Brooks 2005; Cohen and Liebman 1997; Davis and Robinson 1996; Ellison et al. 2005; Green 2006; Knuckey 2006; Kohut et al. 2000; Layman and Green 2007; McConkey 2001; Petersen 2001; Roof and McKinney 1987; Steensland et al. 2000). Compared with laity and passive voters, church leaders and political activists more strongly link their specific policy preferences to a general ideological perspective, whether conservative or liberal.

Ideological frames become important for explaining the issue stands assumed by affiliates with a religious denomination. Even vague ideological self-identifications help individuals understand information about procedural and distributive justice. Empirical information about political situations needs interpretation. Liberalism and conservatism can supply this meaning. Ideologies also stimulate emotional evaluations of political conditions. Examples include anger against injustice, fear about threats to family stability, disdain for relativistic values, and approval of programs that reduce income inequalities. Ideologies often motivate political action, such as decisions to vote, contribute money to a cause, campaign for a candidate or party, and stage protests against doctors performing abortions. Among church members, the highest participation rates come from those who express the most intense ideological commitment, possess the most formal education, and have the highest proportion of friends in their congregation. With greater income and formal education, mainline Protestants in the 2000 election voted, contributed money to campaigns, and attended political rallies at slightly higher rates than did evangelical Protestants (Pyle 2006; Smidt 2007).

However great the ideological differences that separate religious denominations, the Protestant, Catholic, and Jewish camp each shows variations. Among all denominations, conservatives contend for influence with liberals. By examining the views of both factions about God, the individual, society, church, and government, we can partly explain their policy preferences for procedural and distributive justice. Liberal Protestants comprise a larger share of mainline churches, including the United Methodist, Evangelical Lutheran Church in America, Presbyterian Church U.S.A., Episcopal, United Church of Christ (Congregationalist), Disciples of Christ, and American Baptist Churches in the U.S.A. Conservatives dominate the evangelical Protestant denominations: Southern Baptist Convention, Lutheran Church–Missouri Synod, Wisconsin Evangelical Lutheran Synod, American Baptist Association, Assembly of God, Pentecostal, Church of Christ, Nazarene, and Seventh Day Adventist. Whereas most other studies distinguish between black and white Protestants, this analysis merges the black evangelicals—Church of God in Christ, Church of God in Christ (Holiness)—with other evangelicals and combines black mainliners (National Baptist Convention of America, National Baptist Convention U.S.A., African Methodist Episcopal, African Methodist Episcopal Zion) with white mainline churches. Even if African Americans hold divergent views about distributive justice, especially the need for government programs that expand social services, blacks in each Protestant camp share with whites similar theological beliefs and attitudes toward procedural justice. Compared with mainline Protestants, evangelicals, whether black or white, more often identify themselves as "Bible-believing Christians," "born-again Christians," and theological conservatives. A larger percentage of mainliners than evangelicals think of themselves as "mainline Christians" and theological liberals (Bader et al. 2006:17). From both a theological and political perspective, conservative Protestants take a more hierarchical outlook on procedural justice. The traditional nuclear family, a strong church, and a powerful government ought to regulate sexual behavior, guarantee order, protect ethical values, and uphold national defense. By contrast, liberals voice a more egalitarian position toward justice that blends the need for inclusive cooperation with individual choice about sexual freedom and political dissent.

Evangelicals' religious values shape their interpretations of life. More than other denominational members, they view God as a punitive father who punishes the faithless sinner. For them, scriptural commandments apply everywhere to all people. Their perception of the Bible as the foundation of all human behavior draws few distinctions between public and private life. Its edicts apply not only to political decisionmaking but also to private family life, science (evolution), and sexual behavior. The holy scriptures—the "word of God"—supply meaning to an ambiguous world.

For evangelical Protestants, solidarity comes from active participation in their church. Among all Christians, they rank highest in weekly church attendance, religious contributions, daily prayer, and Bible reading. Church and family regulate individual behavior. Particularly in the megachurches, some followers call their charismatic ministers "bishops and cardinals" (Gushee and Phillips 2006:33). Laity feel compelled to follow their hierarchical teachings about family interactions, sexual relationships, and policy preferences. Within the family, evangelical men most actively engaged in church activities stress the greatest need for children to obey their parents. Corporal punishment and strict discipline become primary ways to ensure obedience. Believing that the Bible authorizes divergent roles for men and women, male evangelicals want the husband to act as spiritual head of the household, make key decisions, and provide the main family income. Although evangelicals approve more educational opportunities for women, seek equal pay for the same work, and reject domestic violence against women, these Protestants assume that women's primary responsibility involves nurturing children and caring for their husbands, who should treat their wives with affection. Opposed to legal abortion, pornography, and same-sex marriage, evangelical churches want the government to place strict limits on these sexual activities. Fearing threats from the federal courts, the mass media, and liberal feminism, churches have sought to expand their influence over government agencies, if not establish a Christian theocracy. Key issues focus on opposition to abortion, gay rights, contraception, and stem cell research, with abortion and homosexual rights taking priority. Recruited by the Republican Party, evangelical ministers and laity operate well-organized, cohesive churches, a powerful infrastructure, and a comprehensive media, including television, radio, and the Internet.

Feeling threatened by secular liberalism, conservative evangelicals actively participate in voting, campaigning, and contributing money to Republican candidates. Particularly when individuals regard cultural issues like abortion as highly important and recognize the divergent stands that the two major parties have adopted, votes for the Republican Party rise and conservative ideological identifications increase. Opposition to civil liberties, gender equality, and legal abortion results. Resistance to a liberal concept of procedural justice stems from several sources: hierarchical perceptions of family and church authority, belief in the inerrant Bible as the source of all church authority, intolerance of ambiguity, polarization between the good ingroup vs. evil outgroups, and exposure to media that communicate similar messages, especially about the virtues of conservatism and the vices of liberalism (see Alwin et al. 2006; Bader et al. 2006:14–17, 24–37; Beyerlein and Chaves 2003; D. Campbell 2006; J. Evans 2002; Gallagher 2004a, 2004b; Green et al. 2006; Hood and Smith 2002; Layman and Green 2006; Reimer and Park 2001; Scholz 2005; Starks and Robinson 2005; W. B. Wilcox 2004:74–96, 190–212).

Compared with evangelical Protestants, mainliners, especially those in the Episcopal, Presbyterian, and Congregational churches, express more liberal perspectives on theology and public policies. Although conservatives compete for influence, liberal ministers lead the national church headquarters. More liberal than the laity, they communicate beliefs about God, the individual, society, church, and government that correspond with the Social Gospel approach as well as many New Thought insights. Meaning comes from plural sources: the Bible, churches, education, research, the media, prayer, and interaction with others. Solidarity stems from a belief in an ecumenical, inclusive community that finds unity in diversity. Advanced education prepares the individual for defense against real or imagined threats. Mainline liberal Protestants view God in impersonal or nurturant terms as a cosmic force and benevolent being, rather than as a punitive, angry judge. Made in the image of God, individuals have divine potential to improve themselves through education and to secure social justice. Churches should play a crucial role in establishing the reign of God on earth. Reforms in society involve reducing the inequalities created by class, ethnic, and gender disparities. Adopting a tolerant, pluralist view of the Bible, society, and government, liberal mainliners emphasize a symbolic, metaphorical, not a literal, interpretation of scripture. Rather than infallible or absolutist, its truths depend on the historical context. Humans should adopt a humble attitude toward all knowledge, whether from the Bible or empirical investigations. Recognition that knowledge is incomplete motivates tolerance among mainline Protestants for diverse viewpoints. According to them, although the church should influence government policies, it must not dominate the policy agenda. Neither institution should impose its will on individuals, who need autonomy to make their own choices.

These religious beliefs shape liberal Protestants' commitment to an individualist, egalitarian approach to justice. Opposed to institutional hierarchy, they affirm the need for personal autonomy that reinforces responsibility for the community's well-being. Given their high education and income, the reduction of ethnic and gender inequalities takes priority over narrowing the income gap separating rich from poor. Mainline Protestants thus show a more liberal attitude to procedural justice than to distributive justice. Unlike evangelical Protestants, mainliners display greater support for civil liberties, legal abortion, and gender equality but a weaker commitment to public policies that will expand government services and raise economic equality (Bader et al. 2006:11, 25, 30–37; Eisenach 2004; Greeley and Hout 2006:21, 85–87, 98–100, 121–23, 139; Jelen 2005; Williams 1998).

Despite the former cleavages that divided Protestants from Roman Catholics, today greater factional conflicts have emerged within Catholicism. Most mainline Protestants and Catholics share similar theological beliefs about God and the Bible. Even though Catholics express slightly more hostility to legal abortion and give a bit more support to economic equality, their other policy preferences remain nearly identical with those of mainline Protestants. Disputes within Catholicism revolve around the scope of ecclesiastical authority. Unlike most Protestant denominations, the Roman Catholic Church operates a more centralized, bureaucratic, hierarchical institution that ever changes but never changes. Conservative hierarchs who advocate lay obedience to the Vatican Curia compete with liberal egalitarians who seek a more collegial, decentralized, participatory church like that preferred by liberal mainline Protestants. Theological disputes matter less than structural control. Both Catholic factions affirm the importance of the sacraments, the Apostles' and Nicene creeds, and the role of savior played by Jesus Christ. Neither group perceives the Bible as the source of all truth. Instead, the church becomes a key source of ethical teaching and knowledge about spiritual truth. Inspired by the Vatican

II Council (1962–65), egalitarian Catholics want a more decentralized institution under which local bishops, priests, laity, youths, and women enjoy greater authority. For them, the local parish, neighborhood, and Catholic school form the center of social solidarity. The narratives about God's love for all people, whatever their social status, offers meaning to individual lives. Participation in the Eucharist strengthens communal solidarity. Hearing the good news about Jesus' struggle for social justice brings hope to parishioners. As a worldwide institution, the Church should play a universal, inclusive role vis-à-vis national governments. If government officials enact policies that oppress people, limit their rights, and increase economic inequalities, the Church must campaign for liberation, which includes social justice, civil liberties, gender equality, ethnic equality, homosexual rights, and reduction of poverty.

In contrast, the conservative hierarchs show less enthusiasm for the Vatican II reforms. They want to restore the authority exercised by the pope and the Vatican Curia over national churches, its bishops, priests, and local laity. Doctrinal orthodoxy and traditional Catholic teachings reflect the monistic Truth that brings meaning to believers, solidarity to the faithful, and defense against threats from moral relativists. Perceiving the world polarized between good and evil, hierarchs urge the Church to redeem society from modern liberal secularism that legitimates permissive morality. Strongly opposed to legal abortion, homosexual behavior, artificial contraception, premarital sex, prostitution, and divorce, they campaign for laws that will restrict all these activities. Ordination of women priests also comes under attack. For the hierarchs, procedural justice takes precedence over distributive justice. These cultural issues assume greater importance than struggles to reduce social inequalities.

A generational gap has arisen within the Roman Catholic Church over the scope of central ecclesiastical authority. Whereas younger priests affirm a more conservative, hierarchical stance than held by older priests, among the laity the greatest commitment to conservative teachings comes from older Catholics who attend Mass at least once a week. Younger Catholics who rarely attend Mass prefer a more individualist, egalitarian stance that accepts premarital sex, legal abortion, gay rights, and gender equality. The declining number of priests and nuns impedes the Vatican's enforcement power over the sexual behavior of lay youth. Whatever the public messages communicated by Vatican officials, including the pope, the hierarchical strategy thus may yield outcomes deemed undesirable by its advocates (D'Antonio 2005; D'Antonio et al. 2007; Greeley 2004; Greeley and Hout 2006:123, 139; Jelen 2003; Levesque and Siptroth 2005; Sullins 1999).

Even though Jews comprise only around 2 percent of the American population, their high education, income, and professional status enable them to play an influential role in political life. Compared with Christians, they assert a more liberal, nonhierarchical, egalitarian interpretation of both religious values and political attitudes. Most Jews perceive of God as an impersonal cosmic force or take an agnostic view. They regard the Hebrew Bible as mythical stories and ethical teachings about the need to practice justice, mercy, and humility. Doctrine becomes less important than ethical action that links individual freedom to concern for the community's well-being. Compared with Christians, Jews less often attend religious services, except on a few holy days. Solidarity focuses less on the synagogue than on the family. Despite the relative unimportance of synagogue attendance, Jews actively participate in political activities. More than members of any Christian denomination, they perceive political participation as highly important. Most Jews vote for Democratic candidates, identify themselves as "liberals," and favor liberal stands on both procedural and distributive justice. For them, support for civil liberties, legal abortion, gay rights, gender equality, and government provision of social services ranks fairly high—preferences they share with nonaffiliates.

Major divisions among Jews involve conflicts between Orthodox Jews, on the conservative end, and Reformists and Reconstructionists, on the liberal side. As we have seen, Michael Lerner, a Jewish Renewal rabbi, shares the liberal perspective. It finds meaning in the Torah, the prophets, Jesus' message about justice, Jewish theological writings, scientific investigations, historical studies, artistic works, and novels. Solidarity flows from membership in an inclusive, universal community that practices the virtues of justice, compassion, empathy, and generosity. The major threats originate in elites and institutions that implement political oppression, economic exploitations, and cultural humiliation.

Orthodox Jews assert a different interpretation of meaning, solidarity, and defense. Adopting a hierarchical view of justice, they find meaning to daily behavior in the Torah, which they assume God wrote. Its ancient laws apply to contemporary life. Solidarity comes from a strong family headed by the husband, from active participation in synagogue activities dominated by male leaders, and from strong identification with the Israeli nation. Like Protestant evangelicals, Orthodox Jews perceive major threats arising from secular modernism that has caused moral decay and family decline. Anti-Semitic attacks on Jewish leaders, synagogues, and Israeli national security also pose grave threats. Some conservative Jews even attack liberal Jewish rabbis, artists, educators, journalists, and writers who seek greater Palestinian rights than provided by the Israeli government's military policies. Rabbi Michael Lerner has served as one target for Orthodox Jews. Given their traditional outlook on cultural values, they show little enthusiasm for liberal procedural justice. Unlike Reformist, Reconstructionist, Conservative Jews and those unaffiliated with any synagogue, the Orthodox voice less support for civil liberties, legal abortion, homosexual rights, and especially gender equality. Instead of deriving from the egalitarian provision of government social services, distributive justice occurs mainly within the family and synagogue (Bader et al. 2006:11, 14, 30, 33; Djupe and Sokhey 2003; Greeley and Hout 2006:81, 99–100; Klaff 2006; Sullins 2006:874; Wolfe 2006).

In agreement with most survey evidence, Table 7.6 confirms that Jews and nonaffiliates give the highest support to civil liberties, legal abortion, economic equality, and gender equality; on all issues except economic equality, evangelical Protestants express the lowest

Table 7.6 Impact of religious affiliation on attitudes toward civil liberties, legal abortion, gender equality, and economic equality: mean scores

Religious affiliation	N	Civil liberties (15–30)	Legal abortion (7–14)	Gender equality (4–14)	Economic equality (7–29)
Evangelical Protestants	1,694	23.74	10.44	9.88	19.93
Mainline Protestants	1,647	25.22	11.31	9.96	19.55
Roman Catholics	2,713	25.38	10.91	10.01	19.99
Jews	216	26.51	12.43	10.21	20.83
Nonaffiliates	1,576	26.96	12.50	9.96	21.13
All religious groups	7,846	25.34	11.25	9.96	20.14

preference. Despite their high socioeconomic status, Jews and mainline Protestants take different positions on programs for increasing government services. Whereas mainliners oppose their expansion, Jews back these egalitarian policies. They also display the greatest enthusiasm for gender equality, which the lower-educated nonaffiliated group tends to resist. Mainline Protestants and Catholics share similar policy preferences about civil liberties and gender equality but not toward measures to narrow income inequalities and restrict abortion rights—programs more strongly favored by Catholics.

What explanations clarify the divergent policy preferences that separate evangelical Protestants from Jews and nonaffiliates? As specified in Table 7.7, mainline Protestants and Catholics show intermediate positions between Jews and nonaffiliates on the liberal side and evangelicals on the conservative end. Describing themselves as "conservatives," Protestant evangelicals show the strongest tendency to participate actively in their church, take a literal view of the Bible, perceive God as a patriarchal judge, and place low value on children's independent thinking. By contrast, Jews and nonaffiliates adopt a more "liberal" self-identification. They have limited religious involvement, interpret scripture allegorically, perceive God as an impersonal cosmic force, and uphold children's autonomy. These divergent orientations especially shape attitudes toward procedural justice.

Despite the divergent interpretations of different religious groups, similar variables explain their opinions about justice. Table 7.8 indicates the most important three variables accounting for attitudes held by the four largest religious groups toward civil liberties, legal abortion, gender equality, and economic equality. Ideological orientation assumes primary importance for all issues except civil liberties. Reflecting a nonhierarchical stance toward authority, a high regard for children's autonomy increases support for civil liberties, abortion, and gender equality. Frequent church attendance and prayer raise opposition to civil liberties and abortion, especially among Catholics and evangelical Protestants. Whereas younger age encourages greater enthusiasm for women's equality, higher education exerts a similar positive impact on civil liberties. Preferences for egalitarian income distribution stem mainly from political and class identifications, not from religious participation, children's autonomy, or demography. As individuals become more strongly identified with the Democratic

Table 7.7 Explanations for policy preferences among religious groups: mean scores

		Religious affiliation				
Explanatory variables	Range of scores	Evangelical Protestant	Mainline Protestant	Roman Catholic	Jewish	Nonaffiliate
View of Bible	1–3	1.55	1.84	1.89	2.26	2.44
View of God (1998 only)	3–21	6.86	8.02	8.24	9.07	9.27
Religious participation	2–15	10.55	9.84	9.63	8.41	4.60
Children's autonomy	1–9	5.64	6.40	6.29	7.12	6.98
Personal optimism	5–15	9.99	10.96	10.28	10.95	9.89
Party identification	0–6	2.79	2.80	2.70	2.61	2.84
Ideological identification	1–7	4.43	4.20	4.15	3.62	3.54
Education	1–5	2.26	2.77	2.49	3.61	2.61
Income	1–12	10.75	11.06	11.09	11.67	10.82
Class identification	1–4	2.37	2.64	2.49	2.98	2.46
Age	18–89	48	52	45	51	39

Table 7.8 Explanations for policy preferences among religious groups: regressions

Policy	Explanatory variables[a]	Evangelical Protestant B[b]	Mainline Protestant B	Roman Catholic B	Nonaffiliate B
Civil liberties[c]	Children's autonomy	.320	.338	.300	.305
	Education	.216	.223	.236	.160
	Religious participation	−.231	−.211	−.200	−.134
	Adjusted R²	.369	.479	.419	.443
Legal abortion[d]	Religious participation	−.439	−.442	−.491	−.436
	Ideological identity	−.267	−.135	−.156	−.156
	Children's autonomy	.175	.300	.251	.262
	Adjusted R²	.336	.332	.296	.365
Gender equality[e]	Age	−.139	−.105	−.097	−.060
	Ideological identity	−.098	−.099	−.067	−.089
	Children's autonomy	.061	.061	.066	.078
	Adjusted R²	.127	.120	.083	.076
Economic equality[f]	Partisan identity	−.241	−.219	−.231	−.213
	Ideological identity	−.182	−.217	−.175	−.227
	Class identification	−.082	−.099	−.093	−.102
	Adjusted R²	.678	.708	.653	.614
	Number	1,693	1,646	2,712	1,575

Notes: [a]The explanatory variables include those with the highest regression coefficients in the equations for each religious group. The adjusted R² refers to all the variables in the equation.
[b]B is the unstandardized regression coefficient.
[c]Equations for civil liberties include the following variables: children's autonomy, education, religious participation, party identity, ideological identity, income, age, optimism.
[d]Equations for legal abortion include the following variables: religious participation, ideological identity, children's autonomy, party identity, class identification, education, sex, age, income.
[e]Equations for gender equality include the following variables: age, ideological identity, children's autonomy, view of the Bible, education, sex.
[f]Equations for economic equality include the following variables: partisan identity, ideological identity, class identification, view of Bible, optimism, children's autonomy, age, sex, income, education.

Party, ideological liberalism, and the working class, their commitment to egalitarian public policies rises.

Conclusion

Pundits like traditionalist Catholic Pat Buchanan exaggerate the intensity of the culture wars in America. As we have seen, greater polarization often occurs among factions within the same religious group than among different denominations. Mainline Protestants and Roman Catholics show similar attitudes toward both religion and policies about justice. The major conflicts arise between evangelical Protestants, on the conservative side, and more liberal Jews and nonaffiliates. Even conservative evangelicals, who have achieved high policy unity, have diverged over issue priorities. Whereas evangelical Republican activists want to focus mainly on abortion and homosexuality, other evangelicals seek a more inclusive perspective that has looser ties with the Republican Party. These conservative Protestants believe that poverty, climate change, ecology, human rights, and coercive treatment of U.S. detainees also deserve priority. Among all religious groups, the cultural issues of civil liberties and abortion arouse the greatest controversy. Support for civil liberties stems from well-educated youths who value children's autonomy, rarely pray or attend religious services, and have an optimistic outlook on life and other people. Approval of legal abortion grows stronger when religious involvement declines, priority on children's independence rises, individuals gain more formal education, and people identify themselves as liberal Democrats. Attitudes toward policies to increase government social services and economic equality derive mainly from respondents' economic status and from their identification with a political party and ideology. Low-income, pessimistic women who identify with the working class, the Democratic Party, and a liberal ideology express the highest commitment to economic equality.

Compared with the passive public, political activists in parties and churches view policies through the most comprehensive, systematic ideological lens. Unlike their followers, they take more conservative or liberal stands on all issues, including civil liberties, abortion, gender equality, and egalitarian economic programs. With access to the media, they communicate messages that highlight ideological conflicts.

Cultural polarization increases when activists link general spiritual values to specific policies, the two major parties stress their value differences, and voters find these values salient to their personal lives. Even if Democratic and Republican activists lead the culture war campaigns, ideological polarization does filter down to the American public. Informed voters grasp the connections between religious values and the policies for political justice voiced by party leaders. Yet partisan and ideological identifications, not denominational affiliations, shape most voters' policy preferences (Fiorina 2006; Hunter and Wolfe 2006:10–82, 90–107; Layman 2001; Layman et al. 2006; Mockabee 2007).

To understand more fully the complex ways that religious values influence political attitudes toward justice, researchers should combine sample surveys with focus group interviews and participant observation. This book has explored theological perspectives held by Social Gospelers and New Thought students. Yet membership in Unity and Religious Science churches barely reaches one-tenth of 1 percent of the American population. To understand their political attitudes, we need more surveys that interview larger numbers of New Thought adherents. By designing questions that reflect their religious beliefs as well as those of Social Gospelers, researchers can better explain their opinions about political justice. Focus group interviews with Protestants, Roman Catholics, Jews, and nonaffiliates will explicate the ways that clergy shape attitudes of members who show divergent degrees of involvement in religious activities. The power of social networks, whether in churches or political parties, forms an especially significant predictor of policy preferences. Participant observation in local congregations can help us comprehend the ways that clergy interact with social networks to affect political attitudes.

Social scientists need to conduct more cross-national research on the interaction between religious values and political justice. Survey research on this issue indicates that the same variables explaining democratic attitudes and support for sexual freedom in the United States remain valid for other industrialized nations, such as Austria, Canada, Denmark, France, Germany, Greece, Ireland, Italy, and the Netherlands. If respondents identify with a leftist ideology, have an advanced formal education, perceive few threats from groups, and value children's independence, they will give greater support to political democracy and to freedom for homosexual behavior, abortion, and divorce. In these ten countries, older people who frequently attend religious services show less enthusiasm for sexual freedom than do younger persons and nonaffiliates. Not only in the United States but also in Western Europe, low personal efficacy, limited income, and leftwing ideological identification lead to approval for government policies aimed at expanding economic equality (Andrain and Smith 2006; Nevitte and Cochrane 2006; Scheve and Stasavage 2006; Yuchtman-Yaar and Alkalay 2007).

Cross-national comparisons can also enhance our comprehension of the complex conditions under which diverse religious values produce intense political conflict. Scholars like Amartya Sen (2006) assume that if an individualistic, egalitarian, and nonhierarchical interpretation of justice dominates the political culture, prospects for violent political conflict decline. Society forms an aggregate of individuals, not a homogeneous organic community. Political leaders uphold the individual rights of a citizen, instead of the collective rights of the religious group. Rather than inheriting their identities from past generations, individuals retain extensive freedom to choose which identities take priority. Equality prevails over elitism. An inclusionary, universal ethic based on a shared common humanity supersedes an exclusivist, particularistic notion of justice stressing the need for diverse religious groups to separate from others. Pluralistic attachments discourage a hierarchical approach to justice. Rather than maintain one dominant loyalty to a single religious group, people hold many identities to their religion, ethnicity, occupation, gender, sexual preference, political party, ideology, and even musical tastes. As a result, several affiliations overlap, rather than reinforce each other. Limited governmental control over religious institutions gives them considerable autonomy over their activities. Clergy do not dominate court decisions about law and justice. Under these ideal conditions, a violent culture war becomes unlikely, however important the impact of spiritual values on people's personal lives (Grim and Finke 2007). Along with clergy, political leaders develop procedures for reconciling conflicts—strategies affirmed by the Social Gospel and New Thought. Procedural justice hence emerges from accommodating religious values.

APPENDIX

Measurement of Variables

Variables	No. in 1998–2004 GSS	Questions[a]	Codes	Range	Mean	SD	Alpha
A. Political attitudes							
1. Civil liberties				15–30	25.34	3.38	.91
	76A	Allow atheists free speech.	1 = no, 2 = yes				
	76B	Allow atheists to teach in college.	1 = no, 2 = yes				
	76C	Ban atheist books from public library.	1 = yes, 2 = no				
	78A	Allow free speech to racists.	1 = no, 2 = yes				
	78B	Allow racists to teach in college.	1 = no, 2 = yes				
	78C	Ban racist books from public library.	1 = yes, 2 = no				
	79A	Allow communists free speech.	1 = no, 2 = yes				
	79B	Fire a communist college teacher.	1 = yes, 2 = no				
	79C	Ban communist books from public library.	1 = yes, 2 = no				
	80A	Allow militarists free speech.	1 = no, 2 = yes				
	80B	Allow militarists to teach in college.	1 = no, 2 = yes				
	80C	Ban militarist books from public library.	1 = yes, 2 = no				
	81A	Allow homosexuals free speech.	1 = no, 2 = yes				
	81B	Allow homosexuals to teach in college.	1 = no, 2 = yes				
	81C	Ban books favoring homosexuality from public library.	1 = yes, 2 = no				

				Range	Mean	SD
2. Legal abortion				7–14	11.25	1.83 .90
	206A	Allow pregnant woman a legal abortion if baby has defect.	1 = no, 2 = yes			
	206B	Allow legal abortion if woman wants no more children.	1 = no, 2 = yes			
	206C	Allow legal abortion if pregnancy endangers woman's health.	1 = no, 2 = yes			
	206D	Allow legal abortion if woman comes from poor family.	1 = no, 2 = yes			
	206E	Allow legal abortion if pregnancy resulted from rape.	1 = no, 2 = yes			
	206F	Allow legal abortion if woman is single and declines marriage.	1 = no, 2 = yes			
	206G	Allow legal abortion if woman wants it for any reason.	1 = no, 2 = yes			
3. Gender equality				4–14	9.96	1.52 .68
	202A	Men make better political leaders than do women.	1 = agree 2 = disagree			
	252A	A working mother can establish just as warm a relationship with her children as mothers who do not work for pay.	1 = strongly disagree 2 = disagree 3 = agree 4 = strongly agree			
	252C	If a mother works for pay, her preschool child will likely suffer.	1 = strongly agree 2 = agree 3 = disagree 4 = strongly disagree			

Variables	No. in 1998–2004 GSS	Questions[a]	Codes	Range	Mean	SD	Alpha
3. Gender equality				4–14	9.96	1.52	.68
	252D	Men should concentrate on achieving outside the home while women take care of home and family.	1 = strongly agree 2 = agree 3 = disagree 4 = strongly disagree				
4. Economic equality				7–29	20.14	3.00	.67
	68C	Country spends too much money on health.	1 = agree 2 = about right 3 = disagree (too little)				
	68D	Country grants too much assistance to big cities.	1 = agree 2 = about right 3 = disagree (too little)				
	68H	Country grants too much assistance to blacks.	1 = agree 2 = about right 3 = disagree (too little)				
	68K	Country grants too much assistance to the poor.	1 = agree 2 = about right 3 = disagree (too little)				

74A	Government should take action to reduce income differences between rich and poor.	1 = strongly disagree through 7 = strongly agree			
309A	The federal government should help poor Americans secure a higher standard of living.	1 = strongly disagree (Let people care for themselves.) through 5 = strongly agree			
311A	The federal government should help people pay for doctors and hospital bills.	1 = strongly disagree (Let people care for themselves.) through 5 = strongly agree			

B. Religious beliefs and practices

a. View of Bible

120A	What is your view of the Bible?	1 = literal word of God 2 = inspired but not literal word of God 3 = ancient book of legends, history, and moral concepts recorded by men	1–3	1.93	.62

Variables	No. in 1998–2004 GSS	Questions[a]	Codes	Range	Mean	SD	Alpha
b. View of God (1998 GSS only)				3–21	8.11	3.03	.64
	114A	What is your image of God?	1 = father through 7 = mother				
	114B	What is your image of God?	1 = master through 7 = spouse				
	114C	What is your image of God?	1 = judge through 7 = lover				
c. Religious participation	105	How often do you attend religious services?	1 = never 2 = less than once a year 3 = once or twice a year 4 = several times a year 5 = once a month 6 = 2–3 times a month 7 = nearly every week 8 = every week 9 = several times a week	2–15	8.83	3.31	.64

	110	How often do you pray?	1 = never 2 = less than once a week 3 = once a week 4 = several times a week 5 = once a day 6 = several times a day		

C. Personal values

1. Children's autonomy: stress on independent thinking, not obedience				1–9[b]	6.33	1.69
	170A	How important is obedience as a value taught to children?	1 = least important through 5 = most important			
	170C	How important is independent thinking as a value taught to children?	1 = least important through 5 = most important			
2. Personal optimism				5–15	10.30	2.07
	157	How happy are you?	1 = not too happy 2 = fairly happy 3 = very happy			.63

Variables	No. in 1998–2004 GSS	Questions[a]	Codes	Range	Mean	SD	Alpha
2. Personal optimism				5–15	10.30	2.07	.63
	161	How helpful are people?	1 = not helpful 2 = depends 3 = try to help				
	162	How fair are people?	1 = not fair 2 = depends 3 = try to be fair				
	163A	Can most people be trusted?	1 = no 2 = depends 3 = yes				
	187A	How satisfied are you with your present financial situation?	1 = dissatisfied 2 = fairly satisfied 3 = satisfied				
D. Political identifications							
1. Party self-identification	56	With which party do you identify?	0 = strong Democrat 1 = weaker Democrat 2 = Independent Democrat 3 = Independent 4 = Independent Republican 5 = weaker Republican 6 = strong Republican	0–6	2.76	1.99	

2. Ideological self-identification	66A	What ideological views do you hold?	1 = extremely liberal 2 = liberal 3 = slightly liberal 4 = moderate (centrist) 5 = slightly conservative 6 = conservative 7 = extremely conservative	1–7	4.08	1.23

E. Demographic indicators

1. Age	13	How old are you?	age in years	18–89	46	17
2. Education	19	How much formal education have you attained?	1 = less than high school 2 = high school 3 = junior college 4 = bachelor's degree 5 = graduate degree	1–5	2.55	1.19
3. Sex	23	What is your gender?	1 = male 2 = female			

Variables	No. in 1998–2004 GSS	Questions[a]	Codes	Range	Mean	SD	Alpha
4. Income	37	What was last year's total pretax family income?	01 = under $1,000 02 = $1,000 to $2,999 03 = $3,000 to $3,999 04 = $4,000 to $4,999 05 = $5,000 to $5,999 06 = $6,000 to $6,999 07 = $7,000 to $7,999 08 = $8,000 to $9,999 09 = $10,000 to $14,999 10 = $15,000 to $19,999 11 = $20,000 to $24,999 12 = $25,000 and over	1–12	10.97	2.31	

5. Class self-identification 185A In what social class do you perceive that you belong?

1 = lower class
2 = working class
3 = middle class
4 = upper class

1–4   2.51   .65

Notes: [a] For specific wording of questions, see James A. Davis, Tom W. Smith, and Peter V. Marsden, *General Social Surveys, 1972–2004 Cumulative Codebook*, NORC ed. Chicago: National Opinion Research Center, producer, 2005. Storrs, CT: The Roper Center for Public Opinion Research, University of Connecticut, distributor.

[b] All indices except children's autonomy are additive indices formed by summing scores to several questions. For children's autonomy, after subtracting the 170A score (importance of obedience) from 170C scores (importance of independent thinking), the computer recoded the scores as follows: $4 = 9$, $3 = 8$, $2 = 7$, $1 = 6$, $0 = 5$, $-1 = 4$, $-2 = 3$, $-3 = 2$, $-4 = 1$. The highest score 9 indicates the greatest stress on children's autonomy.

BIBLIOGRAPHY

Aaron, David. 2004. *The Secret Life of God: Discovering the Divine within You*. Boston, MA: Shambala Publications.

Abramowitz, Alan I. 2006. "Disconnected, or Joined at the Hip?" In *Red and Blue Nation?* vol. 1, ed. Pietro Nivola and David W. Brady. Washington, DC: Brookings Institution Press, pp. 72–85, 111–14.

Albanese, Catherine L. 2007. *A Republic of Mind and Spirit: A Cultural History of American Metaphysical Religion*. New Haven, CT: Yale University Press.

Altemeyer, Bob. 1996. *The Authoritarian Specter*. Cambridge, MA: Harvard University Press.

———. 2006. *The Authoritarians*. Winnipeg, Canada: University of Manitoba Department of Psychology. home.cc.umanitoba.ca/~altemey

Alwin, Duane F., Jacob Felson, Edward T. Walker, and Paula A. Tufis. 2006. "Measuring Religious Identities in Surveys." *Public Opinion Quarterly* 70 (winter): pp. 530–64.

Andrain, Charles F., and David E. Apter. 1995. *Political Protest and Social Change: Analyzing Politics*. New York: New York University Press.

Andrain, Charles F., and James T. Smith. 2006. *Political Democracy, Trust, and Social Justice: A Comparative Overview*. Hanover, NH: University Press of New England.

Apter, David E. 2005. "Comparative Sociology: Some Paradigms and their Moments." In *Sage Handbook of Sociology*, ed. Craig Calhoun, Chris Rojek, and Bryan Turner. Thousand Oaks, CA: Sage Publications, pp. 103–26.

———. 2006a. "Duchamp's Urinal: Who Says What's Rational when Things Get Tough?" In *The Oxford Handbook of Contextual Political Analysis*, ed. Robert E. Goodin and Charles Tilly. New York: Oxford University Press, pp. 767–96.

———. 2006b. "Politics as Theatre: An Alternative View of the Rationalities of Power." In *Social Performance: Symbolic Action, Cultural Pragmatics, and Ritual*, ed. Jeffrey C. Alexander, Bernard Giesen, and Jason L. Mast. New York: Cambridge University Press, pp. 218–56.

Apter, David E., and Tony Saich. 1994. *Revolutionary Discourse in Mao's Republic*. Cambridge, MA: Harvard University Press.

Aquinas, Thomas. 1953. *The Political Ideas of St. Thomas Aquinas*. Ed. Dino Bigongiari. New York: Hafner.

———. 1960. *The Pocket Aquinas*. Ed. Vernon J. Bourke. New York: Washington Square Press.

———. 1988. *St. Thomas Aquinas on Politics and Ethics*. Trans. and ed. Paul E. Sigmund. New York: W. W. Norton.

Armor, Reginald C. 1999. *That Was Ernest: The Story of Ernest Holmes and The Religious Science Movement*. Marina del Rey, CA: DeVorss.

Arnold, T. Clay. 2006. "Executive Power, the War on Terrorism, and the Idea of Rights." *Politics and Policy* 34 (December): pp. 670–88.

Aron-Dine, Aviva, and Isaac Shapiro. 2006. "New Data Show Extraordinary Jump in Income Concentration in 2004." Washington, DC: Center on Budget and Policy Priorities. cbpp.org

Augustine. 1984. *City of God*. Trans. Henry Bettenson. Harmondsworth, Middlesex, England: Penguin Books.

Bader, Christopher, Kevin Dougherty, Paul Froese, Byron Johnson, F. Carson Mencken, Jerry Z. Park, and Rodney Stark. 2006. *American Piety in the 21st Century*. Waco, TX: Baylor University Institute of Religion. baylor.edu/isreligion

Barker, David C., and James D. Tinnick III. 2006. "Competing Visions of Parental Roles and Ideological Constraint." *American Political Science Review* 100 (May): pp. 249–63.

BBC. 2006. *World Service Poll: Torture Is Rejected, Even in Struggle against Terrorism*. globescan.com/news_archives/bbctorture06

Belleville, Linda. 2005. "A Re-examination of Romans 16:7 in Light of Primary Source Materials." *New Testament Studies* 51 (April): pp. 231–49.

Bénabou, Roland, and Jean Tirole. 2006. "Belief in a Just World and Redistributive Politics." *Quarterly Journal of Economics* 121 (May): pp. 699–746.

Bender, Thomas. 2006. *A Nation among Nations: America's Place in World History*. New York: Hill and Wang.

Bennett, Stephen Earl. 2006. "Democratic Competence, Before Converse and After." *Critical Review* 18(1–3): pp. 105–41.

Berlinerblau, Jacques. 2005. *The Secular Bible: Why Nonbelievers Must Take Religion Seriously*. New York: Cambridge University Press.

Berryman, Edward. 2005. "Beliefs, Apparitions, and Rationality: The Social Scientific Study of Religion after Wittgenstein." *Human Studies* 28(1): pp. 15–39.

Besecke, Kelly. 2005. "Seeing Invisible Religion: Religion as a Societal Conversation about Transcendent Meaning." *Sociological Theory* 23 (June): pp. 179–96.

Beyerlein, Kraig, and Mark Chaves. 2003. "The Political Activities of Religious Congregations in the United States." *Journal for the Scientific Study of Religion* 42 (June): pp. 229–46.

Beyerlein, Kraig, and John R. Hipp. 2006. "From Pews to Participation: The Effect of Congregation Activity and Context on Bridging Civic Engagement." *Social Problems* 53 (February): pp. 97–117.

Bird, Michael F. 2005. "Jesus and the Gentiles after Jeremias: Patterns and Prospects." *Currents in Biblical Research* 4 (October): pp. 83–108.

Blake, William. 1989. *Blake: The Complete Poems*. 2nd ed. Ed. W. H. Stevenson. New York: Longman.

Blumenfeld, Bruno. 2001. *The Political Paul: Justice, Democracy and Kingship in a Hellenistic Framework.* London: Sheffield Academic Press.

Bolzendahl, Catherine, and Clem Brooks. 2005. "Polarization, Secularization, or Differences as Usual? The Denominational Cleavage in U.S. Social Attitudes since the 1970s." *Sociological Quarterly* 46 (winter): pp. 47–78.

Bolzendahl, Catherine, and Daniel J. Myers. 2004. "Feminist Attitudes and Support for Gender Equality: Opinion Change in Women and Men, 1974–1998." *Social Forces* 83 (December): pp. 759–90.

Bourdieu, Pierre. 1986. "The Forms of Capital." In *Handbook of Theory and Research for the Sociology of Education*, ed. John G. Richardson. Westport, CT: Greenwood Press, pp. 241–58.

———. 1998a. *Acts of Resistance: Against the Tyranny of the Market.* Trans. Richard Nice. New York: New Press.

———. 1998b. *Practical Reason: On the Theory of Action.* Stanford, CA: Stanford University Press.

Bowman, Matthew. 2007. "Sin, Spirituality, and Primitivism: The Theologies of the American Social Gospel, 1885–1917." *Religion and American Culture: A Journal of Interpretation* 17 (winter): pp. 95–126.

Brenner, Robert. 2007. "Structure vs. Conjuncture: The 2006 Elections and the Rightward Shift." *New Left Review*, no. 43 (January/February): pp. 33–59.

Brooks, Clem, and Jeff Manza. 2007. *Why Welfare States Persist: The Importance of Public Opinion in Democracies.* Chicago, IL: University of Chicago Press.

Brooks, Thom. 2006. "Knowledge and Power in Plato's Political Thought." *International Journal of Philosophical Studies* 14 (March): pp. 51–77.

Cady, H. Emilie. 1995. *Complete Works of H. Emilie Cady: Lessons in Truth, How I Used Truth, God a Present Help.* Unity Village, MO: Unity Books.

Calvin, John. 1982. *Treatises against the Anabaptists and against the Libertines.* Trans. and ed. Benjamin Wirt Farley. Grand Rapids, MI: Baker Book House.

———. 1996. *The Bondage and Liberation of the Will.* Trans. G. I. Davies, ed. A. N. S. Lane. Grand Rapids, MI: Baker Books, 1996.

———. 2001. *Calvin's Institutes.* Abridged ed. Ed. Donald K. McKim. Louisville, KY: Westminster John Knox Press.

Campbell, Colin. 2006. "Do Today's Sociologists Really Appreciate Weber's Essay *The Protestant Ethic and the Spirit of Capitalism*?" *Sociological Review* 54 (May): pp. 207–23.

Campbell, David E. 2006. "Religious 'Threat' in Contemporary Presidential Elections." *Journal of Politics* 68 (February): pp. 104–15.

Campbell, John L. 2002. "Ideas, Politics, and Public Policy." In *Annual Review of Sociology*, vol. 28, ed. Karen S. Cook and John Hagan. Palo Alto, CA: Annual Reviews, pp. 21–38.

———. 2004. *Institutional Change and Globalization.* Princeton, NJ: Princeton University Press.

Carlson, Matthew, and Ola Listhaug. 2006. "Public Opinion on the Role of Religion in Political Leadership: A Multi-level Analysis of Sixty-three Countries." *Japanese Journal of Political Science* 7 (December): pp. 251–71.

Carsey, Thomas M., and Geoffrey C. Layman. 2006. "Changing Sides or Changing Minds? Party Identification and Policy Preferences in the American Electorate." *American Journal of Political Science* 50 (April): pp. 464–77.

Carter, Susan B., Scott Sigmund Gartner, Michael R. Haines, Alan L. Olmstead, Richard Sutch, and Gavin Wright, eds. 2006. *Historical Statistics of the United States*, vols. 2, 3, 5. New York: Cambridge University Press.
Catechism of the Catholic Church. 1997. New York: Doubleday.
Cesari, Jocelyne. 2005. "Religion and Politics: Interaction, Confrontation and Tensions." *History and Anthropology* 16 (March): pp. 855–95.
Chittister, Joan. 2004. *In the Heart of the Temple: My Spiritual Vision for Today's World.* New York: BlueBridge.
———. 2005. *The Way We Were: A Story of Conversion and Renewal.* Maryknoll, NY: Orbis Books.
Clifton, Brett M. 2004. "Romancing the GOP: Assessing the Strategies Used by the Christian Coalition to Influence the Republican Party." *Party Politics* 10 (September): pp. 475–98.
Clydesdale, Timothy T. 1999. "Toward Understanding the Role of Bible Beliefs and Higher Education in American Attitudes toward Eradicating Poverty, 1964–1996." *Journal for the Scientific Study of Religion* 38 (March): pp. 103–18.
Cochran, John K., Mitchell B. Chamlin, Leonard Beeghley, and Melissa Fenwick. 2004. "Religion, Religiosity, and Nonmarital Sexual Contact: An Application of Reference Group Theory." *Sociological Inquiry* 74 (February): pp. 102–27.
Coffin, William Sloane. 1977. *Once to Every Man: A Memoir.* New York: Atheneum.
———. 1993. *A Passion for the Possible: A Message to U.S. Churches.* Louisville, KY: Westminster John Knox Press.
———. 1999. *The Heart Is a Little to the Left: Essays on Public Morality.* Hanover, NH: University Press of New England.
———. 2004. *Credo.* Louisville, KY: Westminster John Knox Press.
———. 2005. *Letters to a Young Doubter.* Louisville, KY: Westminster John Knox Press.
Coffin, William Sloane, and Morris I. Leibman. 1972. *Civil Disobedience: Aid or Hindrance to Justice?* Washington, DC: American Enterprise Institute for Public Policy Research.
Cohen, Steven M., and Charles S. Liebman. 1997. "American Jewish Liberalism: Unraveling the Strands." *Public Opinion Quarterly* 61 (fall): pp. 405–30.
Collins, Randall. 1993. "Liberals and Conservatives, Religious and Political: A Conjuncture of Modern History." *Sociology of Religion* 54 (fall): pp. 127–46.
Converse, Philip E. 1964. "The Nature of Belief Systems in Mass Publics." In *Ideology and Discontent*, ed. David E. Apter. New York: The Free Press of Glencoe, pp. 206–61.
———. 2006. "Democratic Theory and Electoral Reality." *Critical Review* 18(1–3): pp. 297–329.
Cook, Michael L. 2003. *Justice, Jesus, and the Jews: A Proposal for Jewish-Christian Relations.* Collegeville, MN: Liturgical Press.
Corley, Kathleen E. 2002. *Women and the Historical Jesus: Feminist Myths of Christian Origins.* Santa Rosa, CA: Polebridge Press.
Cotter, Wendy. 2005. "The Parable of the Feisty Widow and the Threatened Judge (Luke 18:1–8)." *New Testament Studies* 51 (July): pp. 328–43.
Crossan, John Dominic. 2007. *God and Empire: Jesus against Rome, Then and Now.* New York: HarperCollins.
Crossan, John Dominic, and Jonathan L. Reed. 2004. *In Search of Paul: How Jesus's Apostle Opposed Rome's Empire with God's Kingdom.* New York: HarperCollins.

Crouter, Richard. 2005. *Friedrich Schleiermacher: Between Enlightenment and Romanticism.* Cambridge: Cambridge University Press.

Crowson, H. Michael, Stephen J. Thoma, and Nita Hestevold. 2005. "Is Political Conservatism Synonymous with Authoritarianism?" *Journal of Social Psychology* 145 (October): pp. 571–92.

Curry, Evans W., Jerome R. Koch, and H. Paul Chalfant. 2004. "Concern for God and Concern for Society: Religiosity and Social Justice." *Sociological Spectrum* 24 (November–December): pp. 651–66.

Daily Word. 2006. "World Peace." 7 December, p. 21.

D'Antonio, William V. 2005. "American Catholics and Party Politics: Demography, Commitment and Social Teachings." *National Catholic Reporter*, 30 September, pp. 17, 19.

D'Antonio, William V., James D. Davidson, Dean R. Hoge, and Mary L. Gautier. 2007. *American Catholics Today: New Realities of Their Faith and Their Church.* Lanham, MD: Rowman and Littlefield.

Davis, Darren W. 2007. *Negative Liberty: Public Opinion and the Terrorist Attacks on America.* New York: Russell Sage Foundation.

Davis, Nancy J., and Robert V. Robinson. 1996. "Are the Rumors of War Exaggerated? Religious Orthodoxy and Moral Progressivism in America." *American Journal of Sociology* 102 (November): pp. 756–87.

Day, Dorothy. 1988. "The Roots of Radicalism." *Catholic Worker* 55 (May): pp. 1–2.

———. 1997. *The Long Loneliness.* New York: HarperCollins.

———. 2005. *Dorothy Day: Selected Writings.* Ed. Robert Ellsberg. Maryknoll, NY: Orbis Books.

———. 2006. *From Union Square to Rome.* Maryknoll, NY: Orbis Books.

Deutsch, Morton. 2006. "A Framework for Thinking about Oppression and Its Change." *Social Justice Research* 19 (March): pp. 7–41.

DeVries, Dawn, and B. A. Gerrish. 2005. "Providence and Grace: Schleiermacher on Justification and Election." In *The Cambridge Companion to Friedrich Schleiermacher*, ed. Jacqueline Mariña. Cambridge: Cambridge University Press, pp. 189–207.

Dewhurst, J. Frederic and Associates. 1955. *America's Needs and Resources: A New Survey.* New York: Twentieth Century Fund.

Dillon, Michele, and Paul Wink. 2007. *In the Course of a Lifetime: Tracing Religious Belief, Practice, and Change.* Berkeley: University of California Press.

Dionne, E. J. 2006. "Polarized by God? American Politics and the Religious Divide." In *Red and Blue Nation?* vol. 1, ed. Pietro S. Nivola and David W. Brady. Washington, DC: Brookings Institution Press, pp. 175–205.

Djupe, Paul A., and Anand E. Sokhey. 2003. "American Rabbis in the 2000 Elections." *Journal for the Scientific Study of Religion* 42 (December): pp. 563–76.

Douglas, Mary, and Steven Ney. 1998. *Missing Persons: A Critique of Personhood in the Social Sciences.* Berkeley: University of California Press.

Duckitt, John. 2006. "Differential Effects of Right Wing Authoritarianism and Social Dominance Orientation on Outgroup Attitudes and Their Mediation by Threat from and Competitiveness to Outgroups." *Personality and Social Psychology Bulletin* 32 (May): pp. 684–96.

Durkheim, Émile. 1972. *Émile Durkheim: Selected Writings.* Ed. Anthony Giddens. London: Cambridge University Press.

Eagly, Alice H., and Amanda B. Diekman. 2006. "Examining Gender Gaps in Sociopolitical Attitudes: It's Not Mars and Venus." *Feminism and Psychology* 16 (February): pp. 26–34.
Edwards, Linda. 2001. *A Brief Guide to Beliefs: Ideas, Theologies, Mysteries, and Movements.* Louisville, KY: Westminster John Knox Press.
Eisenach, Eldon J. 2004. "Emerging Patterns in America's Political and Religious Self-Understanding." *Studies in American Political Development* 18 (spring): pp. 44–59.
Eisenstein, Marie A. 2006. "Rethinking the Relationship between Religion and Political Tolerance in the US." *Political Behavior* 28 (December): pp. 327–48.
Ellison, Christopher G., Samuel Echevarría, and Brad Smith. 2005. "Religion and Abortion Attitudes among U.S. Hispanics: Findings from the 1990 Latino National Political Survey." *Social Science Quarterly* 86 (March): pp. 192–208.
Ellsberg, Robert. 2005. "Introduction." In *Dorothy Day: Selected Writings*, ed. Robert Ellsberg. Maryknoll, NY: Orbis Book, pp. xvii–xliii.
Elwood, Christopher. 2002. *Calvin for Armchair Theologians.* Louisville, KY: Westminster John Knox Press.
Emerson, Michael O. 1996. "Through Tinted Glasses: Religion, Worldviews, and Abortion Attitudes." *Journal for the Scientific Study of Religion* 35 (March): pp. 41–55.
Emerson, Ralph Waldo. 1929. *The Complete Works of Ralph Waldo Emerson.* Vol. 6, *Conduct of Life*; vol. 8, *Letters and Social Aims.* New York: William H. Wise.
———. 1981. *The Portable Emerson.* Ed. Carl Bode and Malcolm Cowley. New York: Penguin Books.
———. 1983. *Selected Writings of Ralph Waldo Emerson.* Ed. William H. Gilman. New York: Penguin Books.
———. 2004. *The Political Emerson: Essential Writings on Politics and Social Reform.* Ed. David M. Robinson. Boston, MA: Beacon Press.
Engberg-Pedersen, Troels. 2006. "Paul's Stoicizing Politics in Romans 12–13: The Role of 13:1–10 in the Argument." *Journal for the Study of the New Testament* 29 (December): pp. 163–72.
Engler, Steven. 2003. "Modern Times: Religion, Consecration and the State in Bourdieu." *Cultural Studies* 17 (May–July): pp. 445–67.
Esquith, Stephen L. 2001. "Power, Poise, and Place: Toward an Emersonian Theory of Democratic Citizenship." In *The Emerson Dilemma: Essays on Emerson and Social Reform*, ed. T. Gregory Garvey. Athens: University of Georgia Press, pp. 234–54.
Evans, Christopher H. 2004. *The Kingdom Is Always but Coming: A Life of Walter Rauschenbusch.* Grand Rapids, MI: William B. Eerdmans.
Evans, John H. 2002. "Polarization in Abortion Attitudes in U.S. Religious Traditions, 1972–1998." *Sociological Forum* 17 (September): pp. 397–422.
Everton, Sean F. 2005. "Mainline Evangelical Renewal Movements: A Preliminary Inquiry." In *Research in the Social Scientific Study of Religion*, vol. 15, ed. Ralph L. Piedmont and David O. Moberg. Leiden, the Netherlands: Brill, pp. 189–206.
Felix, David. 1965. *Protest: Sacco-Vanzetti and the Intellectuals.* Bloomington: Indiana University Press.
Felson, Jacob, and Heather Kindell. 2007. "The Elusive Link between Conservative Protestantism and Conservative Economics." *Social Science Research* 36 (June): pp. 673–87.

Fernandes, Deepa. 2007. *Targeted: Homeland Security and the Business of Immigration.* New York: Seven Stories Press.
Fillmore, Charles. 1967. *Dynamics for Living.* Ed. Warren Meyer. Unity Village, MO: Unity Books.
———. 1989. *Talks on Truth.* Unity Village, MO: Unity School of Christianity.
———. 1998a. *Mysteries of Genesis.* Unity Village, MO: Unity Books.
———. 1998b. *Prosperity.* Unity Village, MO: Unity Books.
———. 1999a. *The Essential Charles Fillmore: Collected Writings of a Missouri Mystic.* Ed. James Gaither. Unity Village, MO: Unity Books.
———. 1999b. *The Twelve Powers of Man.* Unity Village, MO: Unity Books.
———. 2005. *Christian Healing.* 2nd ed. Unity Village, MO: Unity Books.
Fillmore, Myrtle. 1988. *Myrtle Fillmore's Healing Letters.* Ed. Frances W. Foulks. Unity Village, MO: Unity School of Christianity.
———. 2006. *How to Let God Help You.* 4th ed. Unity Village, MO: Unity House.
Fiorina, Morris P., with Samuel J. Abrams and Jeremy C. Pope. 2006. *Culture War? The Myth of a Polarized America.* 2nd ed. New York: Pearson Longman.
Fiorina, Morris P., and Matthew S. Levendusky. 2006. "Disconnected: The Political Class versus the People." In *Red and Blue Nation?* ed. Pietro S. Nivola and David W. Brady. Washington, DC: Brookings Institution Press, pp. 49–71, 95–111.
Fishburn, Janet Forsythe. 2003. "Walter Rauschenbusch and 'The Woman Movement': A Gender Analysis." In *Gender and the Social Gospel*, ed. Wendy J. Deichmann Edwards and Carolyn De Swarte Gifford. Urbana: University of Illinois Press, pp. 71–86.
Foner, Eric. 1998. *The Story of American Freedom.* New York: W. W. Norton.
Francia, Peter L., John C. Green, Paul S. Hernson, Lynda W. Powell, and Clyde Wilcox. 2005. "Limousine Liberals and Corporate Conservatives: The Financial Constituencies of the Democratic and Republican Parties." *Social Science Quarterly* 86 (December): pp. 761–78.
Frankfurter, Marion Denman, and Gardner Jackson, eds. 1928. *The Letters of Sacco and Vanzetti.* New York: The Viking Press.
Freyne, Sean. 2004. *Jesus, A Jewish Galilean: A New Reading of the Jesus-Story.* London: T and T Clark International.
Friedman, Jeffrey. 2006. "Democratic Competence in Normative and Positive Theory: Neglected Implications of 'The Nature of Belief Systems in Mass Publics.'" *Critical Review* 18(1–3): pp. i–xliii.
Friesen, Steven J. 2005. "Injustice or God's Will: Explanations of Poverty in Proto-Christian Texts." In *A People's History of Christianity*, vol. 1, *Christian Origins*, ed. Richard A. Horsley. Minneapolis, MN: Fortress Press, pp. 240–60.
Gallagher, Sally K. 2004a. "The Marginalization of Evangelical Feminism." *Sociology of Religion* 65 (fall): pp. 215–37.
———. 2004b. "Where Are the Antifeminist Evangelicals? Evangelical Identity, Subcultural Location, and Attitudes toward Feminism." *Gender and Society* 18 (August): pp. 451–72.
Galsworthy, John. 1984. *Five Plays: Strife, Justice, The Eldest Son, The Skin Game, Loyalties.* London: Methuen.
Gerhards, Jürgen. 1995. "Framing Dimensions and Framing Strategies: Contrasting Ideal- and Real-Type Frames." *Social Science Information* 34 (June): pp. 225–48.

Gilbert, Armida. 2001. "'Pierced by the Thorns of Reform': Emerson on Womanhood." In *The Emerson Dilemma*, ed. T. Gregory Garvey. Athens: University of Georgia Press, pp. 93–114.

Glaeser, Edward L., Giacomo A. M. Ponzetto, and Jesse M. Shapiro. 2004. *Strategic Extremism: Why Republicans and Democrats Divide on Religious Values.* Discussion Paper number 2044. Cambridge, MA: Harvard Institute of Economic Research. post.economics.harvard.edu/hier/2004papers/2004list/html

Goldstein, Warren. 2004. *William Sloane Coffin Jr.: A Holy Impatience.* New Haven, CT: Yale University Press.

Gornick, Janet C. 2007. "Atlantic Passages: How Europe Supports Working Parents and Their Children." *American Prospect* 18 (March): pp. A19–A22.

Gougeon, Len. 1998. "Emerson and the Woman Question: The Evolution of His Thought." *New England Quarterly* 71 (December): pp. 570–92.

Grafton, Carl, and Anne Permaloff. 2005. "Liberal and Conservative Dissensus in Areas of Domestic Public Policy Other than Business and Economics." *Policy Sciences* 38 (March): pp. 45–67.

Grassi, Joseph A. 2000. "Matthew's Concept of Justice." *The Bible Today* 38 (July): pp. 234–38.

Greeley, Andrew. 2004. *The Catholic Revolution: New Wine, Old Wineskins, and the Second Vatican Council.* Berkeley: University of California Press.

Greeley, Andrew, and Michael Hout. 2006. *The Truth about Conservative Christians: What They Think and What They Believe.* Chicago: University of Chicago Press.

Green, John C. 2003. "A Liberal Dynamo: The Political Activism of the Unitarian-Universalist Clergy." *Journal for the Scientific Study of Religion* 42 (December): pp. 577–90.

———. 2006. *The American Religious Landscape and Political Attitudes: A Baseline for 2004.* Akron, OH: Bliss Institute of Applied Politics. uakron.edu/bliss

———. 2007. "Religion and Torture: A View from the Polls." *Review of Faith and International Affairs* 5 (summer): pp. 23–27.

Green, John C., Kimberly H. Conger, and James L. Guth. 2006. "Agents of Value: Christian Right Activists in 2004." In *The Values Campaign? The Christian Right and the 2004 Elections*, ed. John C. Green, Mark J. Rozell, and Clyde Wilcox. Washington, DC: Georgetown University Press, pp. 22–55.

Grendstad, Gunnar. 2003. "Comparing Political Orientations: Grid-Group Theory versus the Left-Right Dimension in the Five Nordic Countries." *European Journal of Political Research* 42 (January): pp. 1–21.

Grim, Brian J., and Roger Finke. 2007. "Religious Persecution in Cross-National Context: Clashing Civilizations or Regulated Religious Economies?" *American Sociological Review* 72 (August): pp. 633–58.

Gura, Philip F. 2007. *American Transcendentalism: A History.* New York: Hill and Wang.

Gushee, David P., and Justin Phillips. 2006. "Moral Formation and the Evangelical Voter: A Report from the Red States." *Journal of the Society of Christian Ethics* 26 (fall/winter): pp. 23–60.

Gylfason, Thorvaldur. 2007. "Why Europe Works Less and Grows Taller." *Challenge* 50 (January–February): pp. 21–39.

Hacker, Jacob S. 2006. *The Great Risk Shift.* New York: Oxford University Press.

Hacker, Jacob S., Suzanne Mettler, and Dianne Pinderhughes. 2005. "Inequality and Public Policy." In *Inequality and American Democracy: What We Know and What We Need to Learn*, ed. Lawrence R. Jacobs and Theda Skocpol. New York: Russell Sage Foundation, pp. 156–213.

Hacker, Jacob S., and Paul Pierson. 2006. *Off Center: The Republican Revolution and the Erosion of American Democracy*. New Haven, CT: Yale University Press.

Hall, H. Lark. 1994. *V. L. Parrington: Through the Avenue of Art*. Kent, OH: Kent State University Press.

Harley, Gail M. 2002. *Emma Curtis Hopkins: Forgotten Founder of New Thought*. Syracuse, NY: Syracuse University Press.

Hays, Samuel P. 1995. *The Response to Industrialism: 1885–1914*. 2nd ed. Chicago: University of Chicago Press.

Hearn, Kathy. 2007. "Step by Step on the Path of Abraham." *Science of Mind* 80 (March): pp. 90–96.

Hedges, Chris. 2006. *American Fascists: The Christian Right and the War on America*. New York: Free Press.

Heen, Erik M. 2004. "The Role of Symbolic Inversion in Utopian Discourse: Apocalyptic Reversal in Paul and in the Festival of the Saturnalia/Kronia." In *Hidden Transcripts and the Arts of Resistance: Applying the Work of James C. Scott to Jesus and Paul*, ed. Richard A. Horsley. Leiden, the Netherlands: Brill, pp. 123–44.

Hellerman, Joseph H. 2000. "Wealth and Sacrifice in Early Christianity: Revisiting Mark's Presentation of Jesus' Encounter with the Rich Young Ruler." *Trinity Journal* 21 (fall): pp. 143–64.

Helm, Paul. 2004. *John Calvin's Ideas*. Oxford: Oxford University Press.

Helmer, Christine. 2005a. "Biblical Theology: Bridge over Many Waters." *Currents in Biblical Research* 3 (April): pp. 169–96.

———. 2005b. "Biblical Theology: Reality and Interpretation across Disciplines." In *Biblical Interpretation: History, Context, and Reality*, ed. Christine Helmer with Taylor G. Petrey. Atlanta, GA: Society of Biblical Literature, pp. 1–13.

———. 2005c. "Is It True? Hermeneutical Reading of the Present." In *Reading the Present in the Qumran Library: The Perception of the Contemporary by Means of Scriptural Interpretations*, ed. Kristin De Troyer and Armin Lange. Atlanta, GA: Society of Biblical Literature, pp. 3–19.

———. 2005d. "Schleiermacher's Exegetical Theology and the New Testament." In *The Cambridge Companion to Friedrich Schleiermacher*, ed. Jacqueline Mariña. Cambridge: Cambridge University Press, pp. 229–47.

———. 2006. "A Review of *Chrislicher Glaube im Pluralismus. Studien zu einer Theologie der Kultur* by Christoph Schwöbel." *Harvard Theological Review* 99 (January): pp. 111–15.

Hendricks, Obery M., Jr. 2005. "Class, Political Conservatism and Jesus." *Crosscurrents* 55 (fall): pp. 304–21.

———. 2006. *The Politics of Jesus*. New York: Doubleday.

Hennessy, Martha. 2005. "Idolatry and Nationalism: Interview with William Sloane Coffin." *Catholic Worker* 72 (August–September): p. 3.

Herzog, William R. II. 2000. *Jesus, Justice, and the Reign of God: A Ministry of Liberation*. Louisville, KY: Westminster John Knox Press.

———. 2004. "Onstage and Offstage with Jesus of Nazareth: Public Transcripts, Hidden

Transcripts, and Gospel Texts." In *Hidden Transcripts and the Arts of Resistance*, ed. Richard A. Horsley. Leiden, the Netherlands: Brill, pp. 41–60.

———. 2005a. *Prophet and Teacher: An Introduction to the Historical Jesus*. Louisville, KY: Westminster John Knox Press.

———. 2005b. "Why Peasants Responded to Jesus." In *A People's History of Christianity*, vol. 1, *Christian Origins*, ed. Richard A. Horsley. Minneapolis, MN: Fortress Press, pp. 47–70.

Hester, J. David. 2005. "Eunuchs and the Postgender Jesus: Matthew 19:12 and Transgressive Sexualities." *Journal for the Study of the New Testament* 28 (September): pp. 13–40.

Hetherington, Marc J. 2005. *Why Trust Matters: Declining Political Trust and the Demise of American Liberalism*. Princeton, NJ: Princeton University Press.

Holmes, Ernest. 1936. *It's Up to You!* Los Angeles, CA: Institute of Religious Science.

———. 1938. *Creative Mind*. New York: Robert M. McBride and Company.

———. 1970. *Know Yourself! You Are More than You Think*. Ed. Willis Kinnear. Los Angeles, CA: Science of Mind Publications.

———. 1988. *The Science of Mind*. Fiftieth Anniversary Ed. New York: G. P. Putnam's Sons.

———. 1991. *Living the Science of Mind*. Marina del Rey, CA: DeVorss Publishers.

———. 1999a. *How to Change Your Life*. 2nd ed. Deerfield Beach, FL: Health Communications.

———. 1999b. *Words That Heal Today*. 3rd ed. Deerfield Beach, FL: Health Communications.

———. 2002. *The Essential Ernest Holmes*. Ed. Jesse Jennings. New York: Jeremy P. Tarcher/Putnam.

———. 2005. *What Religious Science Teaches: A New Thought Primer*. Burbank, CA: Science of Mind Publishing.

———. 2006. *The Hidden Power of the Bible: What Science of Mind Reveals about the Bible and You*. New York: Jeremy P. Tarcher/Putnam.

Holmes, Fenwicke L. 1970. *Ernest Holmes: His Life and Times*. New York: Dodd, Mead and Company.

Hood, M. V. III, and Mark Caleb Smith. 2002. "On the Prospect of Linking Religious-Right Identification with Political Behavior: Panacea or Snipe Hunt?" *Journal for the Scientific Study of Religion* 41 (December): pp. 697–710.

Hook, Janet. 2007. "Poll Gives Congress Mixed Grades." *Los Angeles Times*, 19 January, p. A18.

Hoover, Dennis R., Michael D. Martinez, Samuel H. Reimer, and Kenneth D. Wald. 2002. "Evangelicalism Meets the Continental Divide: Moral and Economic Conservatism in the United States and Canada." *Political Research Quarterly* 55 (June): pp. 351–74.

Hopkins, Emma Curtis. 1884. "God's Omnipresence." *Journal of Christian Science* 2 (5 April): p. 5.

———. 1888. *Class Lessons 1888*. Ed. Elizabeth C. Bogart. Repr., Marina del Rey, CA: DeVorss, 1977.

———. 1891a. *All is Divine Order:* Bible Lesson 1. Pittsfield, MA: Sun Printing Company.

———. 1891b. *The Bread of Life:* Bible Lesson 6.

———. 1891c. *Christ is All in All:* Bible Lesson 22.

———. 1891d. *In Retrospection:* Bible Lesson 11.
———. 1891e. *Mary and Martha:* Bible Lesson 12.
———. 1891f. *Power of the Mind:* Bible Lesson 15.
———. 1891g. *The Real Kingdom:* Bible Lesson 10.
———. 1891h. *Scourge of Tongues:* Bible Lesson 20.
———. 1891i. *Simplicity of Faith:* Bible Lesson 21.
———. 1892a. *God and Man Are One:* Bible Lesson 34. Pittsfield, MA: Sun Printing Company.
———. 1892b. *Heaven Around Us:* Bible Lesson 31.
———. 1892c. *Justice of Jehovah:* Bible Lesson 33.
———. 1892d. *Spiritual Ideas:* Bible Lesson 35.
———. 1892e. *True Ideal of God:* Bible Lesson 30.
———. 1893a. *The New Doctrine Brought Out:* Bible Lesson 90. Repr., Bevercreek, OH: Desert Church of the Learning Light, 2005.
———. 1893b. *The Resurrection.* Repr., Bevercreek, OH: Desert Church of the Learning Light, 2005.
———. 1893c. *Universal Energy:* Bible Lesson 88. Repr., Bevercreek, OH: Desert Church of the Learning Light, 2005.
———. 1894a. *The Genesis Series: Bible Interpretations of 1894.* Repr., Bevercreek, OH: Desert Church of the Learning Light, 2005.
———. 1894b. *Twelve Powers of the Soul.* Repr., Bevercreek, OH: Desert Church of the Learning Light, 2004.
———. 1901. *Spiritual Law in the Natural World.* Chicago: Purdy Publishing Company.
———. 1925. *High Mysticism: A Series of Twelve Studies in the Wisdom of the Sages of the Ages.* 6th ed. New York: E. S. Gorham.
———. 1928. *Résumé: Practice Book for the Twelve Chapters in High Mysticism.* Cornwall Bridge, CT: Emma Curtis Hopkins Fund.
———. 2003a. *Ministry of the Holy Mother.* Repr., Bevercreek, OH: Desert Church of the Learning Light.
———. 2003b. *Scientific Christian Mental Practice.* Repr., Camarillo, CA: DeVorss Publications.
———. 2005a. *According to Thy Faith.* Repr., Bevercreek, OH: Desert Church of the Learning Light.
———. 2005b. *Esoteric Philosophy in Spiritual Science.* Repr., Bevercreek, OH: Desert Church of the Learning Light.
———. 2005c. *Judgment Series in Spiritual Science.* Repr., Bevercreek, OH: Desert Church of the Learning Light.
Horrell, David G. 2002. "Paul." In *The Biblical World*, vol. 2, ed. John Barton. New York: Routledge, pp. 258–83.
Horsley, Richard A. 2005a. "Jesus and Empire." *Union Seminary Quarterly* 59(3–4): pp. 44–74.
———. 2005b. "Jesus Movements and the Renewal of Israel." In *A People's History of Christianity*, vol. 1, *Christian Origins*. Minneapolis, MN: Fortress Press, pp. 23–46.
Horsley, Richard A., and Neil Asher Silberman. 1997. *The Message and the Kingdom.* New York: Grosset/Putnam.
Hudnut-Beumler, James. 2004. "The Riverside Church and the Development of Twentieth-Century American Protestantism." In *The History of the Riverside Church*

in the City of New York, ed. Peter J. Paris. New York: New York University Press, pp. 7–53.

Hunt, Matthew O. 2002. "Religion, Race/Ethnicity, and Beliefs about Poverty." *Social Science Quarterly* 83 (September): pp. 810–31.

Hunter, James Davison, and Alan Wolfe. 2006. *Is There a Culture War? A Dialogue on Values and American Public Life*. Washington, DC: Brookings Institution Press.

Hurtado, L. W. 2004. "Jesus' Death as Paradigmatic in the New Testament." *Scottish Journal of Theology* 57 (November): pp. 413–33.

Hutchings, Vincent L. 2003. *Public Opinion and Democratic Accountability: How Citizens Learn about Politics*. Princeton, NJ: Princeton University Press.

International New Thought Alliance. 2006. *International New Thought Alliance: Declaration of Principles*. Amended January 2000. Mesa, AZ: International New Thought Alliance. newthoughtalliance.org/about.htm

Inter-Parliamentary Union. 2007. "Women in National Parliaments as of 31 March 2007." Geneva, Switzerland: Inter-Parliamentary Union. ipu.org/wmn-e/classif.htm.

Iversen, Torben, and David Soskice. 2006. "Electoral Institutions and the Politics of Coalitions: Why Some Democracies Redistribute More than Others." *American Political Science Review* 100 (May): pp. 165–81.

Jacobs, David, and Richard Kleban. 2003. "Political Institutions, Minorities, and Punishment: A Pooled Cross-National Analysis of Imprisonment Rates." *Social Forces* 80 (December): pp. 725–55.

Jacobson, Gary C. 2007. *A Divider, Not a Uniter: George W. Bush and the American People*. New York: Pearson Longman.

Jacoby, William G. 2006. "Value Choices and American Public Opinion." *American Journal of Political Science* 50 (July): pp. 706–23.

Jasper, James M. 2006. *Getting Your Way: Strategic Dilemmas in the Real World*. Chicago: University of Chicago Press.

Jeffers, James S. 2002. "Slaves of God: The Impact of the Cult of the Roman Emperor on Paul's Use of the Language of Power Relations." *Fides et Historia* 34 (winter/spring): pp. 123–39.

Jelen, Ted G. 2003. "Catholic Priests and the Political Order: The Political Behavior of Catholic Pastors." *Journal for the Scientific Study of Religion* 42 (December): pp. 591–604.

———. 2005. "Political Esperanto: Rhetorical Resources and Limitations of The Christian Right in the United States." *Sociology of Religion* 66 (fall): pp. 303–21.

Jelen, Ted G., and Clyde Wilcox. 2003. "Causes and Consequences of Public Attitudes toward Abortion: A Review and Research Agenda." *Political Research Quarterly* 56 (December): pp. 489–500.

Jennings, Jesse. 2006. "Who's Running the Show? New Thought's Hidden Agenda." *Science of Mind* 79 (August): pp. 6–14.

———. 2007. "We *Do* Have a Hammer: Thoughts on Global Change." *Science of Mind* 80 (January): pp. 22–30.

Jervis, Robert. 2006. "Understanding Beliefs." *Political Psychology* 27 (October): pp. 641–63.

Johnson, Chalmers. 2006. *Nemesis: The Last Days of the American Republic*. New York: Metropolitan Books.

Johnston, David Cay. 2007. "Income Gap Is Widening, Data Shows." *New York Times* 29 March, pp. C1, C10.

Kam, Cindy D., and Donald R. Kinder. 2007. "Terror and Ethnocentrism: Foundations of American Support for the War on Terrorism." *Journal of Politics* 69 (May): pp. 320–38.

Kellstedt, Lyman A., Corwin E. Smidt, John C. Green, and James L. Guth. 2007. "A Gentle Stream or a 'River Glorious'? The Religious Left in the 2004 Election." In *A Matter of Faith: Religion in the 2004 Presidential Election*, ed. David E. Campbell. Washington, DC: The Brookings Institution Press, pp. 232–56.

King, Karen L. 2003. *The Gospel of Mary of Magdala: Jesus and the First Woman Apostle*. Santa Rosa, CA: Polebridge Press.

———. 2006. *The Secret Revelation of John*. Cambridge, MA: Harvard University Press.

Klaff, Vivian. 2006. "Defining American Jewry from Religious and Ethnic Perspectives: The Transitions to Greater Heterogeneity." *Sociology of Religion* 67 (winter): pp. 415–38.

Knauth, Robin J. DeWitt. 2004. "The Jubilee Transformation: From Social Welfare to Hope of Restoration to Eschatological Salvation." Ph.D. dissertation. Harvard University.

Knuckey, Jonathan. 2005. "A New Front in the Culture War? Moral Traditionalism and Voting Behavior in U.S. House Elections." *American Politics Research* 33 (September): pp. 645–71.

———. 2006. "Explaining Recent Changes in the Partisan Identifications of Southern Whites." *Political Research Quarterly* 59 (March): pp. 57–70.

Kohut, Andrew. 2007. *Trends in Political Values and Core Attitudes: 1987–2007*. Washington, DC: Pew Research Center for the People and the Press. people-press.org.

Kohut, Andrew, John C. Green, Scott Keeter, and Robert C. Toth. 2000. *The Diminishing Divide: Religion's Changing Role in American Politics*. Washington, DC: Brookings Institution Press.

Krause, Deborah. 2005. "Keeping It Real: The Image of God in the New Testament." *Interpretation* 59 (October): pp. 358–68.

Krugman, Paul. 2006. "Left Behind Economics." *New York Times* 14 July, p. A19.

Kull, Steven. 2005. *The Federal Budget: The Public's Priorities*. College Park, MD: Program on International Policy Attitudes. worldpublicopinion.org.pipa

Lakoff, George. 2002. *Moral Politics: How Liberals and Conservatives Think*. 2nd ed. Chicago: University of Chicago Press.

———. 2004. *Don't Think of an Elephant! Know Your Values and Frame the Debate*. White River Junction, VT: Chelsea Green Publishing.

———. 2006a. *Thinking Points: Communicating Our American Values and Vision*. New York: Farrar, Straus and Giroux.

———. 2006b. *Whose Freedom? The Battle over America's Most Important Idea*. New York: Farrar, Straus and Giroux.

Larson, Martin A. 1985. *New Thought or a Modern Religious Approach: The Philosophy of Health, Happiness, and Prosperity*. New York: Philosophical Library.

Layman, Geoffrey. 2001. *The Great Divide: Religious and Cultural Conflict in American Party Politics*. New York: Columbia University Press.

Layman, Geoffrey C., Thomas M. Carsey, and Juliana Menasce Horowitz. 2006. "Party

Polarization in American Politics: Characteristics, Causes, and Consequences." In *Annual Review of Political Science*, vol. 9, ed. Nelson Polsby. Palo Alto, CA: Annual Reviews, pp. 83–110.

Layman, Geoffrey C., and John C. Green. 2006. "Wars and Rumours of Wars: The Contexts of Cultural Conflict in American Political Behaviour." *British Journal of Political Science* 36 (January): pp. 61–89.

Leo, Marilyn. 2006. *In His Company: Ernest Holmes Remembered.* Camarillo, CA: M. Leo Presents.

Lerner, Michael. 1994. *Jewish Renewal: A Path to Healing and Transformation.* New York: G. P. Putnam's Sons.

———. 2005. "When the Right Breaks the Barrier, How Should a Spiritual Left Respond?" *Tikkun* 20 (July–August): pp. 33–35.

———. 2007. *The Left Hand of God: Healing America's Political and Spiritual Crisis.* Revised ed. New York: HarperCollins.

Leustean, Lucian N. 2005. "Towards an Integrated Theory of Religion and Politics." *Method and Theory in the Study of Religion* 17(4): pp. 364–81.

Levesque, Paul L., and Stephen M. Siptroth. 2005. "The Correlation between Political and Ecclesial Ideologies of Catholic Priests: A Research Note." *Sociology of Religion* 66 (winter): pp. 419–29.

Lichter, Daniel T., Zhenchao Qian, and Martha L. Crowley. 2005. "Child Poverty among Racial Minorities and Immigrants: Explaining Trends and Differentials." *Social Science Quarterly* 86 (December): pp. 1037–59.

Lichterman, Paul. 2005. *Elusive Togetherness: Church Groups Trying to Bridge America's Divisions.* Princeton, NJ: Princeton University Press.

Locke, John. 2003. *Two Treatises of Government* and *A Letter Concerning Toleration.* Ed. Ian Shapiro. New Haven, CT: Yale University Press.

Lockhart, Charles. 2003. *The Roots of American Exceptionalism: History, Institutions and Culture.* New York: Palgrave Macmillan.

London, Jack. 1986. *To Build a Fire and Other Stories.* New York: Bantam Books.

Lotke, Eric, Robert Gerson, Paul Waldman, and Andrew Seifter. 2007. *The Progressive Majority: Why a Conservative America Is a Myth.* Washington, DC: Campaign for America's Future and Media Matters for America. ourfuture.org

Lübker, Malte. 2007. "Inequality and the Demand for Redistribution: Are the Assumptions of the New Growth Theory Valid?" *Socio-Economic Review* 5 (January): pp. 117–48.

Lynn, Barry W. 2005. "Politics and Proof-Texts: Why I Disagree with Jim Dobson and Jim Wallis." *Church and State* 58 (March): p. 23.

Maddison, Angus. 1995. *Monitoring the World Economy 1820–1992.* Paris: Organisation for Economic Cooperation and Development Development Centre.

———. 2003. *The World Economy: Historical Statistics.* Paris: Organisation for Economic Cooperation and Development Development Centre.

Magnani, Laura, and Harmon L. Wray. 2006. *Beyond Prisons: A New Interfaith Paradigm for Our Failed Prison System.* Minneapolis, MN: Fortress Press.

Mamiya, Lawrence H. 2004. "Congregations within a Congregation: Contemporary Spirituality and Change at the Riverside Church." In *The History of the Riverside Church in the City of New York*, ed. Peter J. Paris. New York: New York University Press, pp. 279–343.

Mansbach, Richard. 2006. "Calvinism as a Precedent for Islamic Radicalism." *Brown Journal of World Affairs* 12 (winter/spring): pp. 103–15.

Mansbridge, Jane. 2005. "Cracking through Hegemonic Ideology: The Logic of Formal Justice." *Social Justice Research* 18 (September): pp. 335–47.

Manza, Jeff, and Christopher Uggen. 2006. *Locked Out: Felon Disenfranchisement and American Democracy*. New York: Oxford University Press.

Mariña, Jacqueline. 2004. "Schleiermacher on the Outpourings of the Inner Fire: Experiential Expressivism and Religious Pluralism." *Religious Studies* 40 (June): pp. 125–43.

———. 2005. "Christology and Anthropology in Friedrich Schleiermacher." In *The Cambridge Companion to Friedrich Schleiermacher*, ed. Jacqueline Mariña. Cambridge: Cambridge University Press, pp. 151–70.

Martin, Darnise C. 2005. *Beyond Christianity: African Americans in a New Thought Church*. New York: New York University Press.

McCarty, Nolan, Keith T. Poole, and Howard Rosenthal. 2006. *Polarized America: The Dance of Ideology and Unequal Riches*. Cambridge, MA: MIT Press.

McConkey, Dale. 2001. "Whither Hunter's Culture War? Shifts in Evangelical Morality, 1988–1998." *Sociology of Religion* 62 (summer): pp. 149–74.

McDonald, Michael D., Silvia M. Mendes, and Myunghee Kim. 2007. "Cross-temporal and Cross-national Comparisons of Party Left–Right Positions." *Electoral Studies* 26 (March): pp. 62–75.

McDowell, Frederick P. W. 1987. "Heaven, Hell, and Turn-of-Century-London." In *George Bernard Shaw's Man and Superman*, ed. Harold Bloom. New York: Chelsea House Publishers, pp. 35–47.

McGerr, Michael. 2003. *A Fierce Discontent: The Rise and Fall of the Progressive Movement in America, 1870–1920*. New York: Free Press.

McGrath, Joanna Collicutt. 2006. "Post-traumatic Growth and the Origins of Early Christianity." *Mental Health, Religion and Culture* 9 (June): pp. 291–306.

McNamara, Martin. 2005. "Some Reflections on Covenant and Towards a Theology of the Absurd." *Milltown Studies* 55 (summer): pp. 65–81.

Meeks, Wayne A. 2005. "Why Study the New Testament?" *New Testament Studies* 51 (April): pp. 155–70.

Melville, Herman. 1961. *Moby Dick or The White Whale*. New York: New American Library.

———. 2002. *White-Jacket or The World in a Man-of-War*. New York: The Modern Library.

Meulemann, Heiner. 2004. "Enforced Secularization—Spontaneous Revival? Religious Belief, Unbelief, Uncertainty, and Indifference in East and West European Countries 1991–1998." *European Sociological Review* 20 (February): pp. 47–61.

Meyer, Marvin. 2005. *The Gnostic Gospels of Jesus*. New York: HarperCollins.

Minkenberg, Michael. 2002. "Religion and Public Policy: Institutional, Cultural, and Political Impact on the Shaping of Abortion Policies in Western Democracies." *Comparative Political Studies* 35 (March): pp. 221–47.

Mishel, Lawrence, Jared Bernstein, and Sylvia Allegretto. 2007. *The State of Working America 2006/2007*. Ithaca, NY: Cornell University Press.

Mockabee, Stephen T. 2007. "A Question of Authority: Religion and Cultural Conflict in the 2004 Election." *Political Behavior* 29 (June): pp. 221–48.

Monson, J. Quin, and J. Baxter Oliphant. 2007. "Microtargeting and the Instrumental Mobilization of Religious Conservatives." In *A Matter of Faith: Religion in the 2004 Presidential Election*, ed. David E. Campbell. Washington, DC: Brookings Institution Press, pp. 95–119.

Moore, Laura M., and Seth Ovadia. 2006. "Accounting for Spatial Variation in Tolerance: The Effects of Education and Religion." *Social Forces* 84 (June): pp. 2205–22.

Moore, Laura M., and Reeve Vanneman. 2003. "Context Matters: Effects of the Proportion of Fundamentalists on Gender Attitudes." *Social Forces* 82 (September): pp. 115–39.

Moran, Timothy Patrick. 2006. "Statistical Inference and Patterns of Inequality in the Global North." *Social Forces* 84 (March): pp. 1799–1818.

Mosley, Glenn R. 2006. *New Thought, Ancient Wisdom: The History and Future of the New Thought Movement*. Philadelphia, PA: Templeton Foundation Press.

Mühlhäusler, Peter, and Adrian Peace. 2006. "Environmental Discourses." In *Annual Review of Anthropology*, vol. 35, ed. William H. Durham and Jane Hill. Palo Alto, CA: Annual Reviews, pp. 457–79.

Mulligan, Kenneth. 2006. "Pope John Paul II and Catholic Opinion toward the Death Penalty and Abortion." *Social Science Quarterly* 87 (September): pp. 739–53.

Nevitte, Neil, and Christopher Cochrane. 2006. "Individualization in Europe and America: Connecting Religious and Moral Values." *Comparative Sociology* 5(2–3): pp. 203–30.

Newport, Frank, Jeffrey M. Jones, Lydia Saad, and Joseph Carroll. 2006. "Democrats' Election Strength Evident across Voter Segments." *Gallup Poll Briefing*, 9 November, pp. 35–38.

New York Times. 2006. "Stop the Slaughter in Lebanon, Israel and the Occupied Territories!" 31 July, p. A9.

Nightingale, Benedict. 1984. "Introduction" to John Galsworthy, *Five Plays*. London: Methuen, pp. ix–xxiv.

Noakes, John A., and Hank Johnston. 2005. "Frames of Protest: A Road Map to a Perspective." In *Frames of Protest: Social Movements and the Framing Perspective*, ed. Hank Johnston and John A. Noakes. Lanham, MD: Rowman and Littlefield, pp. 1–29.

Nossiff, Rosemary. 2007. "Gendered Citizenship: Women, Equality, and Abortion Policy." *New Political Science* 29 (March): pp. 61–76.

Nunberg, Geoffrey. 2006. *Talking Right*. New York: Public Affairs.

Ochs, Peter. 2005. "Covenant." In *Modern Judaism: An Oxford Guide*, ed. Nicholas de Lange and Miri Freud-Kandel. New York: Oxford University Press, pp. 290–300.

O'Donovan, Oliver, and Joan Lockwood O'Donovan, eds. 1999. *From Irenaeus to Grotius: A Sourcebook in Christian Political Thought*. Grand Rapids, MI: William B. Eerdmans.

Ohlander, Julianne, Jeanne Batalova, and Judith Treas. 2005. "Explaining Educational Influences on Attitudes toward Homosexual Relations." *Social Science Research* 34 (December): pp. 781–99.

Oldmixon, Elizabeth Anne. 2005. *Uncompromising Positions: God, Sex, and the U.S. House of Representatives*. Washington, DC: Georgetown University Press.

Oliner, Samuel P., and Jeffrey R. Gunn. 2006. "Manifestations of Radical Evil: Structure and Social Psychology." *Humboldt Journal of Social Relations* 30(1): pp. 108–43.

Olson, Laura R. 2007. "Whither the Religious Left? Religiopolitical Progressivism in Twenty First-Century America." In *From Pews to Polling Places: Faith and Politics in the American Religious Mosaic,* ed. J. Matthew Wilson. Washington, DC: Georgetown University Press, pp. 53–79.

Osberg, Lars, and Timothy Smeeding. 2006. "'Fair' Inequality? Attitudes toward Pay Differentials: The United States in Comparative Perspective." *American Sociological Review* 71 (June): pp. 450–73.

Owen, J. Judd. 2007. "Locke's Case for Religious Toleration: Its Neglected Foundation in the *Essay Concerning Human Understanding*." *Journal of Politics* 69 (February): pp. 156–68.

Page, Cristina. 2006. *How the Pro-Choice Movement Saved America: Freedom, Politics, and the War on Sex.* New York: Basic Books.

Palier, Bruno, and Yves Surel. 2005. "Les 'Trois I' et l'Analyse de l'État en Action." *Revue Française de Science Politique* 55 (February): pp. 7–32.

Parrington, Vernon Louis. 1930. *Main Currents in American Thought.* 3 vols. New York: Harcourt, Brace.

Pelikan, Jaroslav. 2005. *Whose Bible Is It? A Short History of the Scriptures.* New York: Penguin Books.

Pellerin, Daniel. 2003. "Calvin: Militant or Man of Peace?" *Review of Politics* 65 (winter): pp. 35–59.

Permaloff, Anne, and Carl Grafton. 2003. "The Behavioural Study of Political Ideology and Public Policy: Testing the Janda, Berry, and Goldman Model." *Journal of Political Ideologies* 8 (June): pp. 185–208.

Petersen, Larry R. 2001. "Religion, Plausibility Structures, and Education's Effect on Attitudes toward Elective Abortion." *Journal for the Scientific Study of Religion* 40 (June): pp. 187–203.

Piketty, Thomas, and Emmanuel Saez. 2003. "Income Inequality in the United States, 1913–1998." *Quarterly Journal of Economics* 118 (February): pp. 1–39.

———. 2006. "The Evolution of Top Incomes: A Historical and International Perspective." *American Economic Review* 96 (May): pp. 200–05.

———. 2007. "How Progressive Is the U.S. Federal Tax System? A Historical and International Perspective." *Journal of Economic Perspectives* 21 (winter): pp. 3–24.

Pitchford, Susan, Christopher Bader, and Rodney Stark. 2001. "Doing Field Studies of Religious Movements: An Agenda." *Journal for the Scientific Study of Religion* 40 (September): pp. 379–92.

Plato. 2003. *The Republic.* 2nd ed. Trans. Desmond Lee. London: Penguin Books.

Pontifical Council for Justice and Peace. 2004. *Compendium of the Social Doctrine of the Church.* Washington, DC: United States Conference of Catholic Bishops.

Pottenger, John R. 2007. *Reaping the Whirlwind: Liberal Democracy and the Religious Axis.* Washington, DC: Georgetown University Press.

Pyle, Ralph E. 2006. "Trends in Religious Stratification: Have Religious Group Socioeconomic Distinctions Declined in Recent Decades?" *Sociology of Religion* 67 (spring): pp. 61–79.

Rasmussen, Claire, and Michael Brown. 2005. "The Body Politic as Spatial Metaphor." *Citizenship Studies* 9 (November): pp. 469–84.

Rasor, Paul. 2003. "The Postmodern Challenge to Liberal Theology." *Unitarian Universalist Christian* 58:5–56.

Rauschenbusch, Walter. 1896. "The Ideals of Social Reformers." *American Journal of Sociology* 2 (September): pp. 202–19.
———. 1897. "The Stake of the Church in the Social Movement." *American Journal of Sociology* 3 (July): pp. 18–30.
———. 1912. *Christianizing the Social Order*. New York: Macmillan.
———. 1913. "Some Moral Aspects of the 'Woman Movement.' " *Biblical World* 42 (October): pp. 195–99.
———. 1991. *Christianity and the Social Crisis*. Louisville, KY: Westminster John Knox Press.
———. 1997. *A Theology for the Social Gospel*. Louisville, KY: Westminster John Knox Press.
Reese, Stephen D. 2001. "Prologue—Framing Public Life: A Bridging Model for Media Research." In *Framing Public Life: Perspectives on Media and Our Understanding of the Social World*. Mahwah, NJ: Lawrence Erlbaum, pp. 7–31.
Reimer, Sam, and Jerry Z. Park. 2001. "Tolerant (In)civility? A Longitudinal Analysis of White Conservative Protestants' Willingness to Grant Civil Liberties." *Journal for the Scientific Study of Religion* 40 (December): pp. 735–45.
Richardson, Robert D., Jr. 1995. *Emerson: The Mind on Fire*. Berkeley: University of California Press.
Riegle, Rosalie G. 2003. *Dorothy Day: Portraits by Those Who Knew Her*. Maryknoll, NY: Orbis Books.
Robinson, David M. 2001. "Emerson's 'American Civilization': Emancipation and the National Destiny." In *The Emerson Dilemma*, ed. T. Gregory Garvey. Athens: University of Georgia Press, pp. 221–33.
———. 2003. "Introduction: Emerson's Spiritual Principles." In *The Spiritual Emerson: Essential Writings*, ed. David M. Robinson. Boston, MA: Beacon Press, pp. 1–20.
Roof, Wade Clark, and William McKinney. 1987. *American Mainline Religion: Its Changing Shape and Future*. New Brunswick, NJ: Rutgers University Press.
Rose, Or N. 2006. "Righteous Indignation: An Interview with William Sloane Coffin." *Tikkun* 21 (March/April): pp. 41–43.
Rosen, Stanley. 2005. *Plato's Republic: A Study*. New Haven, CT: Yale University Press.
Rudolph, Thomas J., and Jillian Evans. 2005. "Political Trust, Ideology, and Public Support for Government Spending." *American Journal of Political Science* 49 (July): pp. 660–71.
Sager, Ryan. 2006. *The Elephant in the Room: Evangelicals, Libertarians, and the Battle to Control the Republican Party*. Hoboken, NJ: John Wiley.
Santos, Michael G. 2006. *Inside: Life Behind Bars in America*. New York: St. Martin's Press.
Schaffner, Brian, and Nenad Senic. 2006. "Rights or Benefits? Explaining the Sexual Identity Gap in American Political Behavior." *Political Research Quarterly* 59 (March): pp. 123–32.
Schaller, Thomas F. 2006. *Whistling Past Dixie: How Democrats Can Win without the South*. New York: Simon and Schuster.
Scheve, Kenneth, and David Stasavage. 2006. "Religion and Preferences for Social Insurance." *Quarterly Journal of Political Science* 1(3): pp. 255–86.
Schleiermacher, Friedrich. 1963. *The Christian Faith*. Ed. H. R. Mackintosh and J. S. Stewart. New York: Harper and Row.

———. 2003. *Fifteen Sermons of Friedrich Schleiermacher Delivered to Celebrate the Beginning of a New Year.* Trans. and ed. Edwina Lawler. Lewiston, NY: Edwin Mellen Press.

Schneider, Saundra K., and William G. Jacoby. 2005. "Elite Discourse and American Public Opinion: The Case of Welfare Spending." *Political Research Quarterly* 58 (September): pp. 367–79.

———. 2007. "Reconsidering the Linkage between Public Assistance and Public Opinion in the American Welfare State." *British Journal of Political Science* 37 (July): pp. 555–66.

Scholz, Susanne. 2005. "Review Essay: The Christian Right's Discourse on Gender and the Bible." *Journal of Feminist Studies in Religion* 21 (spring): pp. 81–100.

Schwarz, Frederick A. O., Jr., and Aziz Z. Huq. 2007. *Unchecked and Unbalanced: Presidential Power in a Time of Terror.* New York: The New Press.

Segal, Alan F. 2006. "The Resurrection: Faith or History?" In *The Resurrection of Jesus: John Dominic Crossan and N. T. Wright in Dialogue*, ed. Robert B. Stewart. Minneapolis, MN: Fortress Press, pp. 121–38.

Sen, Amartya. 2006. *Identity and Violence: The Illusion of Destiny.* New York: W. W. Norton.

Shapiro, Rami. 2004. *The Hebrew Prophets: Selections Annotated and Explained.* Woodstock, VT: Skylight Paths Publishing.

Shaw, George Bernard. 1946. *Man and Superman: A Comedy and a Philosophy.* Harmondsworth, Middlesex, England: Penguin Books.

Sinclair, Barbara. 2006. *Party Wars: Polarization and the Politics of National Policy Making.* Norman: University of Oklahoma Press.

Smeeding, Timothy M. 2005. "Public Policy, Economic Inequality, and Poverty: The United States in Comparative Perspective." *Social Science Quarterly* 86 (December): pp. 955–83.

———. 2006. "Poor People in Rich Nations: The United States in Comparative Perspective." *Journal of Economic Perspectives* 20 (winter 2006): pp. 69–90.

Smidt, Corwin E. 2007. "Evangelical and Mainline Protestants at the Turn of the Millennium: Taking Stock and Looking Forward." In *From Pews to Polling Places: Faith and Politics in the American Religious Mosaic*, ed. J. Matthew Wilson. Washington, DC: Georgetown University Press, pp. 29–51.

Smith, Christian, and Robert Faris. 2005. "Socioeconomic Inequality in the American Religious System: An Update and Assessment." *Journal for the Scientific Study of Religion* 44 (March): pp. 95–104.

Smith, M. Brewster, Jerome S. Bruner, and Robert W. White. 1956. *Opinions and Personality.* New York: John Wiley.

Smith, Robert B. 2003. "Political Extremism—Left, Center, and Right." *American Sociologist* 34 (spring/summer): pp. 70–80.

Sojourners/Call to Renewal. 2006. *A Covenant for a New America: From Poverty to Opportunity.* Washington, DC: Sojourners/Call to Renewal. covenantforanewamerica.org

Spickard, James V. 2005. "Ritual, Symbol, and Experience: Understanding Catholic Worker House Masses." *Sociology of Religion* 66 (winter): pp. 337–57.

Spong, John Shelby. 1977. *The Living Commandments.* New York: Seabury Press.

———. 1988. *Living in Sin? A Bishop Rethinks Human Sexuality.* New York: HarperCollins.

———. 1991. *Rescuing the Bible from Fundamentalism: A Bishop Rethinks the Meaning of Scripture*. New York: HarperCollins.
———. 1993. *This Hebrew Lord: A Bishop's Search for the Authentic Jesus*. New York: HarperCollins.
———. 1994. *Resurrection: Myth or Reality? A Bishop's Search for the Origins of Christianity*. New York: HarperCollins.
———. 1996. *Liberating the Gospels: Reading the Bible with Jewish Eyes*. New York: HarperCollins.
———. 1998. *Why Christianity Must Change or Die: A Bishop Speaks to Believers in Exile*. New York: HarperCollins.
———. 1999. *The Bishop's Voice: Selected Essays*. Ed. Christine M. Spong. New York: Crossroad Publishing Company.
———. 2000. *Here I Stand: My Struggle for a Christianity of Integrity, Love, and Equality*. New York: HarperCollins.
———. 2001. *A New Christianity for a New World: Why Traditional Faith Is Dying and How a New Faith Is Being Born*. New York: HarperCollins.
———. 2005. *The Sins of Scripture: Exposing the Bible's Texts of Hate to Reveal the God of Love*. New York: HarperCollins.
———. 2007. *Jesus for the Non-Religious: Recovering the Divine at the Heart of the Human*. New York: HarperCollins.
Spong, John Shelby, and Jack Daniel Spiro. 1999. *Dialogue: In Search of Jewish–Christian Understanding*. Haworth, NJ: Christianity for the Third Millennium.
Stanton, Timothy. 2006. "Locke and the Politics and Theology of Toleration." *Political Studies* 54 (March): pp. 84–102.
Stark, Rodney. 2006. *Cities of God: The Real Story of How Christianity Became an Urban Movement and Conquered Rome*. New York: HarperCollins.
Starks, Brian, and Robert V. Robinson. 2005. "Who Values the Obedient Child Now? The Religious Factor in Adult Values for Children, 1986–2002." *Social Forces* 84 (September): pp. 343–59.
Steensland, Brian. 2006. "Cultural Categories and the American Welfare State: The Case of Guaranteed Income Policy." *American Journal of Sociology* 111 (March): pp. 1273–1326.
Steensland, Brian, Jerry Z. Park, Mark D. Regnerus, Lynn D. Robinson, W. Bradford Wilcox, and Robert D. Woodberry. 2000. "The Measure of American Religion: Toward Improving the State of the Art." *Social Forces* 79 (September): pp. 291–318.
Stenger, Katherine E. 2005. "The Underrepresentation of Liberal Churches: Mobilization Strategies of Religious Interest Groups." *Social Science Journal* 42(3): pp. 391–403.
Stenner, Karen. 2005. *The Authoritarian Dynamic*. New York: Cambridge University Press.
Stevens, Mitchell L. 2002. "The Organizational Vitality of Conservative Protestantism." In *Social Structure and Organizations Revisited*, ed. Michael Lounsbury and Marc J. Ventresca. New York: JAI, pp. 337–60.
Stopler, Gila. 2005. "The Liberal Bind: The Conflict between Women's Rights and Patriarchal Religion in the Liberal State." *Social Theory and Practice* 31 (April): pp. 191–231.
Street, Debra, and Jeralynn Sittig Cossman. 2006. "Greatest Generation or Greedy

Geezers? Social Spending Preferences and the Elderly." *Social Problems* 53 (February): pp. 75–96.
Sullins, D. Paul. 1999. "Catholic/Protestant Trends on Abortion: Convergence and Polarity." *Journal for the Scientific Study of Religion* 38 (September): pp. 354–69.
———. 2006. "Gender and Religion: Deconstructing Universality, Constructing Complexity." *American Journal of Sociology* 112 (November): pp. 838–80.
Sutton, John R. 2004. "The Political Economy of Imprisonment in Affluent Western Democracies, 1960–1990." *American Sociological Review* 69 (April): pp. 170–89.
Swain, Glenn. 2007. "La Adelita: The Life of Dolores Huerta." *Science of Mind* 80 (September): pp. 12–18.
Swain, Virginia. 2006. "Turning to the Light of God Within." *Daily Word* 144 (December): pp. 6–12.
Talbott, Rick. 2006. "Imagining the Matthean Eunuch Community: Kyriarchy on the Chopping Block." *Journal of Feminist Studies in Religion* 22 (spring): pp. 21–43.
Taussig, Hal. 2006. *A New Spiritual Home: Progressive Christianity at the Grass Roots.* Santa Rosa, CA: Polebridge Press.
Temkin, Moshik. 2007. "Sacco and Vanzetti Today." *The Nation* 285 (August 27/September 3): pp. 7–8.
Thagard, Paul. 2000. *Coherence in Thought and Action.* Cambridge, MA: MIT Press.
Thandeka. 2005. "Schleiermacher, Feminism, and Liberation Theologies: A Key." In *The Cambridge Companion to Friedrich Schleiermacher,* ed. Jacqueline Mariña. Cambridge: Cambridge University Press, pp. 287–305.
Therborn, Göran. 2007. "After Dialectics: Radical Social Theory in a Post-Communist World." *New Left Review,* no. 43 (January–February): pp. 63–114.
Thompson, Michael, Marco Verweij, and Richard J. Elli. 2006. "Why and How Culture Matters." In *The Oxford Handbook of Contextual Political Analysis,* ed. Robert E. Goodin and Charles Tilly. New York: Oxford University Press, pp. 319–40.
Thurber, James, and Elliott Nugent. 1941. *The Male Animal: A New Comedy.* New York: Samuel French.
Tice, Terrence. 2006. *Schleiermacher.* Nashville, TN: Abingdon Press.
Tisdale, Leonora Tubbs. 2004. "Preachers for All Seasons: The Legacy of Riverside's Free Pulpit." In *The History of the Riverside Church in the City of New York,* ed. Peter J. Paris. New York: New York University Press, pp. 55–135.
Toner, Robin, and Janet Elder. 2007. "Most Support U.S. Guarantee of Health Care." *New York Times* 2 March, pp. A1, A15.
Trine, Ralph Waldo. 1910. *Land of Living Men.* New York: Dodge Publishing Company.
———. 2002. *In Tune with the Infinite.* Richmond, VA: Oaklea Press.
Tumber, Catherine. 2002. *American Feminism and the Birth of New Age Spirituality: Searching for the Higher Self, 1875–1915.* Lanham, MD: Rowman and Littlefield.
Tuntiya, Nana. 2005. "Fundamentalist Religious Affiliation and Support for Liberties: A Critical Reexamination." *Sociological Inquiry* 75 (May): pp. 153–76.
Unnever, James D., and Francis T. Cullen. 2006. "Christian Fundamentalism and Support for Capital Punishment." *Journal of Research in Crime and Delinquency* 43 (May): pp. 169–97.
U.S. Bureau of the Census. 1975. *Historical Statistics of the United States: Colonial Times to 1970.* Washington, DC: U.S. Department of Commerce.

Vahle, Neal. 1993. *Open at the Top: The Life of Ernest Holmes*. Mill Valley, CA: Open View Press.
———. 1996. *Torch-Bearer to Light the Way: The Life of Myrtle Fillmore*. Mill Valley, CA: Open View Press.
———. 2002. *The Unity Movement: Its Evolution and Spiritual Teachings*. Philadelphia, PA: Templeton Foundation Press.
Verter, Bradford. 2003. "Spiritual Capital: Theorizing Religion with Bourdieu against Bourdieu." *Sociological Theory* 21 (June): pp. 150–74.
Vial, Theodore. 2005. "Schleiermacher and the State." In *The Cambridge Companion to Friedrich Schleiermacher*, ed. Jacqueline Mariña. Cambridge: Cambridge University Press, pp. 269–85.
Volscho, Thomas W., Jr., and Andrew S. Fullerton. 2005. "Metropolitan Earnings Inequality: Union and Government-Sector Employment Effects." *Social Science Quarterly* 86 (December): pp. 1324–37.
Von Rautenfeld, Hans. 2005. "Thinking for Thousands: Emerson's Theory of Political Representation in the Public Sphere." *American Journal of Political Science* 49 (January): pp. 184–97.
Voskuilen, Thijs. 2005. "Operation Messiah: Did Christianity Start as a Roman Psychological Counterinsurgency Operation?" *Small Wars and Insurgencies* 16 (June): pp. 192–215.
Wade, Robert Hunter. 2006. "Should We Worry about Income Inequality?" *International Journal of Health Sciences* 36(2): pp. 271–94.
Wakefield, Dan. 2006. *The Hijacking of Jesus*. New York: Nation Books.
Wald, Kenneth D., Adam L. Silverman, and Kevin S. Fridy. 2005. "Making Sense of Religion in Political Life." In *Annual Review of Political Science*, vol. 8, ed. Nelson W. Polsby. Palo Alto, CA: Annual Reviews, pp. 121–43.
Wallis, Jim. 1994. *The Soul of Politics*. New York: The New Press and Maryknoll, NY: Orbis Books.
———. 2005a. *The Call to Conversion: Why Faith Is Always Personal But Never Private*. Revised ed. New York: HarperCollins.
———. 2005b. *God's Politics*. New York: HarperCollins.
———. 2005c. "The Message Thing." *New York Times* 4 August, p. A23.
———. 2007. "What to Do." In Walter Rauschenbusch, *Christianity and the Social Crisis in the 21st Century*, ed. Paul Raushenbush. New York: HarperOne.
Wallis, Jim, and Chuck Gutenson. 2006. *Living God's Politics: A Guide to Putting Your Faith into Action*. New York: HarperCollins.
Watson, Bruce. 2007. *Sacco and Vanzetti: The Men, the Murders, and the Judgment of Mankind*. New York: Viking Penguin.
Weber, Lori. 2003. "Rugged Individuals and Social Butterflies: The Consequences of Social and Individual Political Participation for Political Tolerance." *Social Science Journal* 40(2): pp. 335–42.
Weber, Max. 1958. *From Max Weber: Essays in Sociology*. Trans. and ed. H. H. Gerth and C. Wright Mills. New York: Oxford University Press Galaxy.
———. 2002. *The Protestant Ethic and the Spirit of Capitalism*. 3rd ed. Trans. Stephen Kalberg. Los Angeles, CA: Roxbury.
Weeden, Kim A., and David B. Grusky. 2005. "The Case for a New Class Map." *American Journal of Sociology* 111 (July): pp. 141–212.

Weiler, Jonathan, and Marc J. Hetherington. 2006. *The Democratic Strategist: A Journal of Public Opinion and Political Strategy* 1 (August): pp. 1–5. thedemocraticstrategist.org/0609.weilera.php

Weisenfeld, Judith. 2004. "Universal in Spirit, Local in Character: The Riverside Church and New York City." In *The History of the Riverside Church in the City of New York*, ed. Peter J. Paris. New York: New York University Press, pp. 179–239.

Westen, Drew. 2007. *The Political Brain: The Role of Emotion in Deciding the Fate of the Nation*. New York: Public Affairs.

Wilcox, Clyde. 2003. "Evangelicals and Abortion." In *A Public Faith: Evangelicals and Civic Engagement*, ed. Michael Cromartie. Lanham, MD: Rowman and Littlefield, pp. 101–15.

Wilcox, W. Bradford. 2004. *Soft Patriarchs, New Men: How Christianity Shapes Fathers and Husbands*. Chicago: University of Chicago Press.

Wildavsky, Aaron. 1998. *Culture and Social Theory*. Ed. Sun-Ki Chai and Brendon Swedlow. New Brunswick, NJ: Transaction Publishers.

Williams, Rhys H. 1998. "Political Theology on the Right and Left." *Christian Century* 115 (July 29–August 5): pp. 722–24.

Wills, Garry. 2006. *What Paul Meant*. New York: Viking.

Winer, Mark L. 2006. "Dialogue on Holocaust Theology: A Response to Bob Reiss." *Theology* 109 (September–October): pp. 334–42.

Wintrobe, Ronald. 2006. *Rational Extremism: The Political Economy of Radicalism*. New York: Cambridge University Press.

Witherington, Ben III. 2000. *Jesus the Sage: The Pilgrimage of Wisdom*. Minneapolis, MN: Fortress Press.

Witherspoon, Thomas E. 2000. *Myrtle Fillmore: Mother of Unity*. 3rd ed. Unity Village, MO: Unity Books.

Wolfe, Alan. 2006. "Free Speech, Israel, and Jewish Illiberalism." *Chronicle of Higher Education* 53 (17 November): pp. B6–B8.

Wolin, Sheldon S. 2004. *Politics and Vision: Continuity and Innovation in Western Political Thought*. Expanded ed. Princeton, NJ: Princeton University Press.

Wright, N. T. 2005. *Paul in Fresh Perspective*. Minneapolis, MN: Fortress Press.

Wyman, Walter E., Jr. 2005. "Sin and Redemption." In *The Cambridge Companion to Friedrich Schleiermacher*, ed. Jacqueline Mariña. Cambridge: Cambridge University Press, pp. 129–49.

Yamane, David. 2007. "Beyond Beliefs: Religion and the Sociology of Religion in America." *Social Compass* 54 (March): pp. 33–48.

Yuchtman-Yaar, Ephraim, and Yasmin Alkalay. 2007. "Religious Zones, Economic Development and Modern Value Orientations: Individual versus Contextual Effects." *Social Science Research* 36 (June): pp. 789–807.

INDEX

Abraham Path Initiative 148
Acton, John 1
Affiliated New Thought Network 146
agape (spiritual love) 13, 35, 58
American Baptist Churches (U.S.A.) 82, 180
American Civil Liberties Union 72
American Enterprise Institute 151
Americans United for Separation of Church and State 72, 147
anarchism 54, 90, 158–9, 161
Apostles' Creed 18, 20, 45, 69–70, 82–3, 106, 108, 183
Aquinas, Thomas 14–16, 18
Assembly of God 180
Association of Global New Thought 146, 148
Association of Unity Churches International 120, 146
Augustine 16, 18, 45–6

baptism 42, 82
Baptists 76
Batterham, Forster 93
Ben Sira 47
Bernardin, Joseph (Cardinal) 73
Blake, William 27–9
Boff, Leonardo 85, 91
Buchanan, Pat 178, 190

Buddhists 89, 99, 114, 126, 146
Bunyan, John 83
Bush, George H. W. 82
Bush, George W. 63–4, 82, 137–8, 146, 149, 151

Cady, H. Emilie 118–19, 125
Caesar 33, 35, 40
Call to Renewal movement 74, 89, 146
Calvin, John 16–17, 29–30, 46, 144
Calvinism 105–6, 110
Campolo, Tony 74, 99
Canada 153–5
capitalism 16–17, 73, 119, 131, 159
Cardenal, Ernesto 91
Carter, Jimmy 148
Catechism of the Catholic Church 18
Catholic Worker movement 20, 65, 89–94
Center for Progressive Christianity 147
Central Intelligence Agency (CIA) 69, 75, 137
Chávez, César 147
Chittister, Joan 99
Christ, indwelling Spirit 77, 115–16, 118, 121, 126–7
Christian Coalition 144, 148, 151
Christian Science 114, 125
Churchill, Winston 135
Church of Christ 180

Church Women United 147
class identification 169, 172, 179, 187–90
class structure 28, 33, 40–1
Clinton, William 148
Coffin, William Sloane 19, 26, 65–9, 75–82, 85–6, 89, 92–4, 98; abortion 80; Bible 77–8; capitalism 78; children's independence 78; church's role 77, 79; civil liberties 79, economic equality 78, 81; fatalism 79; gender equality 78–9; God 76; government expenditures and taxes 78, 81; hierarchy 77–8; individualism 80; Jesus 76–7, 82; Kingdom of God 77; prison reform 81; sexual freedom 79–81; world peace 75, 79–81
cognitive worldviews 138
Colemon, Johnnie 133
communism 54, 90, 160
Communist Party 90
Compendium of the Social Doctrine of the Church 18
comunidades eclesiales de base (Christian base communities) 11
Concerned Women for America 144
Confucianism 126
Congregational Church 25, 69, 76, 82, 89, 125, 131, 150, 156, 180, 182; *see also* United Church of Christ
Congress of Industrial Organizations (CIO) 161
conservatism: beliefs 5, 10, 14, 18–20, 143–4, 163–4, 180; influence 26, 150–2; organization 144–6
Constantine 45
Coolidge, Calvin 122
corporations, power of 52, 58, 63–5, 67, 91, 99, 145, 153
Council for National Policy 144
covenant 33, 36–7, 42, 95
Covenant for a New America 73–4
Creative Thought 126, 130
crucifixion 32, 38–9, 41, 44, 72, 93, 159
culture war 159, 178, 190, 192
Curran, Charles 85

Daily Word 123, 125, 147–8
Day, Dorothy 20, 26, 65–7, 89–94, 96, 98, 147; abortion 93; capitalism 90–1; church's role 90–2; civil liberties 91; economic equality 92; fatalism 93; gender equality 92; God 91; government expenditures 93; hierarchy 90; individualism 92–3; Jesus 91–2; prison reform 91; sexual freedom 92–3; world peace 90, 92
Democratic Party 23; activists 165, 190–1; influence 62, 149; organization 148; policy preferences 73, 75, 100, 145, 148–50, 152–4, 165, 170–2, 174–8, 187–91
dialectical method 22–3, 29–30
Disciples of Christ 74, 99, 156, 180
discourse 21–2, 24, 29, 139, 160, 163
Distributive Justice 62
Divine Science 114–15, 146
Dobson, James 20, 72, 99, 106
dominionist movement 144
Domitian 44
Douglas, Mary 10
Durkheim, Émile 166

economic equality: attitudes toward 65, 150, 156; levels of 52, 63–4, 67, 154
economic growth 51
ecumenism 58, 69, 72, 86, 92, 143–4, 147
Eddy, Mary Baker 114–15, 119
education, impact 170–1, 174–5, 177–9, 183, 185, 187–90
Emerson, Ralph Waldo 101, 106, 109–14, 119, 124–5, 127–8; Bible 111; capitalism 114; church's role 111; civil liberties 112; fatalism 112–13; economic equality 113–14; gender equality 110, 112; God 110–11; government expenditures 113, hierarchy 112; individualism 109–12; Jesus 110; prison reform 111; socialism 114
Engels, Friedrich 59
Enlightenment values 22, 30, 56, 124

entrepreneurial values 140
Episcopal Church 68, 82, 85, 89, 99, 131, 180, 182
Episcopalians 69, 76, 87, 89, 92, 144, 150, 152, 156
Equality League of Self-Supporting Women 53
ethnic group inequalities 51, 53, 57, 71, 75, 78–9, 110–11, 133, 137
Eucharist 42–3, 82, 84, 91, 111, 184
Europe, West 61, 64, 137, 153–6, 167, 191–2
Everlasting Gospel 28
evil, concept of 40, 44, 46, 55, 70, 77, 91, 100, 108, 111, 114, 132

Falwell, Jerry 151
family models 163–5, 178
Family Research Council 144
family values 74
FBI (Federal Bureau of Investigation) 137
Feminist Alliance 53
Fillmore, Charles 118–23, 125, 131; capitalism 122–3; church's role 120; economic equality 123; gender equality 121; God 121–2; hierarchy 119–20; individualism 119–21; Kingdom of God 120; prison reform 121; sexual attitudes 121–2; world peace 121
Fillmore, Myrtle 101, 118–19, 125, 131; gender equality 121; God 121; presidential preferences 122; private property 122; sexual attitudes 122
Focus on the Family 144
Fosdick, Harry Emerson 76, 80
Fourier, Charles 114
Fox, Matthew 85
frames 38, 162–3, 179
Friends Committee on National Legislation 143
Fuller, Margaret 113–14
fundamentalism 20, 22–3, 54, 56, 70, 72, 74, 82, 168
Fundamentals, The 22

Galsworthy, John 134–6
Gandhi, Mohandas 80, 97
General Social Survey (GSS) 26, 157, 168
Gentiles 35–9, 42, 44, 107
George, Henry 60
Global Heart Vision 148
globalization 8, 63
Global Marshall Plan 99
Gnosticism 106–7
Gospel of Mary 101, 106–9
government expenditures and taxes, level of 62–4, 154–5
Green Party 97, 100

Harrington, Michael 93
heaven 83, 93, 101, 105–6, 110, 129
Hegel, G. W. F. 114
hell 75, 83, 101, 110
Hendricks, Obery M. 134
Heritage Foundation 151
Herodian dynasty 32–4
Heschel, Abraham Joshua 94
Hinduism 114, 119, 126
Holmes, Ernest 102, 118, 125–31; capitalism 130; civil liberties 128–9; economic equality 131; fatalism 128; gender equality 130; God 126–8, 130; hierarchy 128; individualism 128–31; Jesus 126–7, 130; Kingdom of God 129; law 128–30; sexual freedom 129–30; world peace 129
Holmes, Fenwicke 125
Homes of Truth 114
Hoover, Herbert 122
Hopkins, Emma Curtis 101, 106, 114–19, 125; children's independence 116; civil liberties 117; economic equality 118; fatalism 116–17; gender equality 118; God 115, 118; hierarchy 116; individualism 115; influence 115, 118; Jesus 115–16; prison reform 117; sexual attitudes 117–18; world peace 115–17
Hopkins Metaphysical Association 115

House Committee on Un-American Activities (HUAC) 161
Huerta, Dolores 147–8

idealism 101–2, 107–8, 110–11, 115, 127
ideological identifications 163–5, 175–9, 187–91; conservative 75, 150, 155, 163–4, 169, 173, 176–9, 187; liberal 149–50, 152, 156, 164–5, 169, 172, 175–9, 185, 187–90
immigrants' rights 96, 137, 150, 159, 161, 167
Industrial Workers of the World 54
Institute of Religious Science and Philosophy 126
Interfaith Alliance 147
International Association of Religious Science Churches (IARSC) 126
International Divine Science Association 118
International Metaphysical League 118
International New Thought Alliance (INTA) 118, 120, 126, 133, 146
inversionary discourse 21–2, 25, 35–6, 41, 122
Irenaeus 107
Isaiah 34, 83
Islam 114, 126
Israel, modern state 97–100, 145, 186

Jesus 2, 25, 27–40, 124, 136, 183–4; beliefs 34–8, 67; influence 32, 45–6, 97, 100; roles 33–4, 46–7, 107–8, 131–2
Jesus Seminar 124, 133
Jews 25, 99–100, 132, 146, 150, 152, 165, 178–9, 185–7; Conservative 186; liberal 61, 69, 99, 144; Orthodox 145, 185–6; Reconstructionist 185–6; Reform 89, 144, 185–6; Renewal 185
Johnson, Lyndon 82
Journal of Christian Science 115
Judaism 126
Jung, Carl 127
Justice 134–5

Kant, Immanuel 103, 127
Kennedy, John F. 23, 82
King, Martin Luther Jr. 25, 80, 97
Küng, Hans 85

labor unions, power of 52, 62, 64, 131, 137, 148–9, 153–4
LaHaye, Tim 20, 99
Lakoff, George 162–4, 178
Leo XII (Pope) 62
Lerner, Michael 19, 26, 65–7, 74, 94–100, 132, 143, 146, 156, 185–6; abortion 97; church's role 95–6; civil liberties 97; economic equality 96, 98; fatalism 97; gender equality 97; God 95–7; government expenditures 98–9; hierarchy 96; individualism 95–7; prison reform 97; sexual freedom 98; world peace 97
Lessons in Truth 119, 125
liberalism: beliefs 5, 17–19, 142–3, 164–5, 180, 185; influence 25–6, 152–3; organization 146–9
liberation theology 11, 46
libertarianism 10, 90, 122, 165
Liberty University 151
Living Wage 62
Locke, John 15, 17, 142
London, Jack 48–50, 90
Luther, Martin 29, 46
Lutherans: Evangelical Lutheran Church in America 74, 89, 99, 156, 180; Missouri Synod 180; Wisconsin Synod 180

Male Animal 159, 161
McCarthy, Joseph 87, 161
McLaren, Brian 74
Maritain, Jacques 90
Man and Superman 101
Marx, Karl 59
mass media 21, 24, 47, 74, 97–8, 141–2, 144–5, 148, 161–3, 181, 190–1
materialism 101–2, 107, 110, 113–14, 127
Maurin, Peter 89

Melville, Herman 1–2
Merton, Thomas 90
Messiah 38–9, 41, 44
Methodists 69, 74, 76, 82, 89, 92, 99, 131, 156, 180
Micah 34, 83, 95
Mill, John Stuart 158, 167, 175
mobilization 24–5, 141, 143, 146, 150–1, 160
Moby Dick 1
modernization 8, 22, 24, 50–2, 153–4, 166–7
Moise, Lionel 93
Moses 33, 95
Muslims 89, 137, 146, 161

National Coalition on Religion and the Environment 147
National Council of Churches 23, 147
National Federation of Independent Business 151
nationalism 2, 54, 58, 71, 76, 80–1, 97, 121
National Security Agency 137
Nazarene 180
neoliberalism 8
Nero 44
Network of Spiritual Progressives 65, 94, 97–9, 146, 148
New Deal 62, 89
Nicene Creed 18, 20, 45, 69, 82–3, 106–8, 183
Niebuhr, H. Richard 75, 77
Niebuhr, Reinhold 77
nonaffiliates' attitudes 150, 178–9, 186–9
normative frameworks 138
Nugent, Elliott 159

Oliver, Elouise 133
optimism 103, 105, 108, 169–75, 177–8, 190
organic community 12, 43–4, 55, 58
Owen, Robert 114

Palabra Diaria, La 123
Palestinians 97–100, 145, 148, 186

Parrington, Vernon Louis 67, 78, 161
Patrick Henry College 151
patron/client ties 40
Paul 25, 28, 38–47, 82, 108; influence 86, 107, 119; teachings 39–44, 116
Pentecostal 180
personalism 92
Pietism 50, 68, 88
Plato 103–5, 107, 109–10, 114, 127
Plymouth Brethren Church 68
polarization, cultural 23, 178–9, 190–2
policy frames 138–9
political activism and participation 111–12, 133, 139–40
political influence 133, 138–41
political organization 133, 144–9
political party identifications 149, 151–2, 155, 165, 169–72, 174–8, 187–91
populism 11, 22, 51, 67, 96, 112
Presbyterians 69, 74, 76, 89, 99, 131, 150, 156, 180, 182
prison conditions 59, 73, 135–7, 154
programmatic solutions 139
Progressive movement 22, 51–4, 57, 60
Protestants 152, 180; black 152, 180; evangelical 23, 25, 74, 106, 133, 140, 144, 151–2, 154–6, 165–7, 171–2, 178–82, 185–90; fundamentalist 82, 85–7, 89, 105–6; liberal 68, 89, 94, 99, 180; mainline 69, 145, 152, 156, 166, 178–9, 182–3, 187–90
psychoanalysis 127, 167–8
public opinion: abortion 150, 173–8, 186–9, 191; civil liberties 150, 173–8, 186–9; economic equality 150, 177–8, 186–9, 192; gender equality 176–8, 186–9

Quimby, Phineas 127

Rauschenbusch, Walter 12, 15–16, 25, 48, 50, 52, 54–65, 67, 73, 77–9, 81, 93–6, 122, 131–2; Bible 56; capitalism 49, 56–63; children's independence 61; church's role 55–8; civil liberties 59;

economic equality 56–7, 60; fatalism 58–9; gender equality 56–7, 61; God 55, 61; government expenditures and taxes 59–60; hierarchy 57–8; individualism 58; Jesus 55–6, 61; Kingdom of God 58–9; prison reform 59; sexual freedom 60–1
Reagan, Ronald 63, 82
"Red Scare" 54, 65, 159, 161
Regent University 151
Religious Science 26, 114–15, 118, 191; activities 133, 148; beliefs 12, 20, 100, 104, 106, 131, 148, 177; leadership 125–6, 130, 133; organization 106, 125–6, 143
Religious Science International 126, 146
Republic, The 103
Republican Party 23; activists 133, 145–6, 165, 190–1; influence 149–51; organization 145, 149–51; policy preferences 63–4, 73–5, 100, 146, 151, 154, 165, 170–2, 174–8, 188–90
Rerum Novarum 62
Ripley, George 109
Riverside Church of New York City 68, 75–6, 81
Robertson, Pat 20, 72, 99, 106, 151, 178
Roman Catholic Church 12–15, 20, 45–6, 51, 57, 62, 90–3, 107, 144, 184
Roman Catholics 17, 152, 156, 178, 183–90; liberal 69, 89, 99, 144, 156, 183–5; orthodox/traditional 23, 25, 82, 86–7, 89, 105–6, 140, 145, 155, 167, 183–5
Roman Empire 32–6, 38–41, 43–6, 72, 108–9
Roosevelt, Theodore 52
Ryan, John A. 62

Sacco, Nicolas 158–9
Schleiermacher, Friedrich 29–32, 47, 55, 57, 105, 109
Science of Mind (magazine) 125–6, 130, 147
Science of Mind, The (book) 125

Sen, Amartya 192
Seventh Day Adventists 180
Shaw, George Bernard 101
sin 30, 40, 44, 70, 77, 84, 95, 108
Sinclair, Upton 90
slavery 40, 43, 57, 109–11
Social Democrats 12
socialism 49–50, 54, 73, 131, 159–60; Christian 16, 50, 59, 78, 81; scientific 59
social networks 141, 151, 153, 166, 191
Society of Friends 74, 111, 156
sociohermeneutics 29
Sojourners (magazine) 74, 148
Sojourners (organization) 20
Southern Baptists 20, 82, 144, 180
Spirit, Holy 31, 77, 91, 117
Spiritual Covenant with America 94, 98
Spinoza, Benedict de 114
Spong, John Shelby 19, 26, 65–9, 82–92, 94, 143;abortion 87; Bible 82–3, 85–6; church's role 83–7; civil liberties 87; economic equality 83, 88–9; fatalism 86–7; gender equality 88; God 83–4, 87; government expenditures and taxes 89; hierarchy 85; individualism 86; Jesus 83–4, 86–7; prison reform 88; sexual freedom 83, 87–8; world peace 83, 88
subsidiarity 90
Swain, Virginia 123
Swedenborg, Emanuel 114

Taoism 126
terror 137, 139, 150, 155
Tertullian 107
Theology for the Social Gospel 55
Thérèse of Lisieux 90
Thurber, James 159, 161
Tiberius Caesar 35
tikkun (world renewal and transformation) 95–6, 132
Tikkun (magazine) 97, 148
Torah 32, 94–5, 185–6
torture 137, 167
Transcendentalism 109–10, 115

transubstantiation 91
Trine, Ralph Waldo 13, 127, 131
Troward, Thomas 127
Tumkin, Mary A. 133
Tyndale, William 29

Unitarianism 109–11, 124
Unitarian Universalists 25, 69, 82, 89, 99, 124, 131, 144, 152, 156
United Centers for Spiritual Living 126
United Church of Christ 82, 99, 180; see also Congregational Church
United Church of Religious Science 99, 126, 146
United Farm Workers (UFW) 147
United Nations 73, 123, 129
Unity Magazine 123, 125
Unity School of Christianity 26, 99, 114–15, 118–21, 123–5, 130, 191; activities 123; beliefs 12, 20, 100, 104, 106, 131, 177; leadership 133; organization 106, 143
Universal Foundation for Better Living 133, 146
utilitarianism 10, 126

Vanzetti, Bartolomeo 158–60
Vatican 18, 57, 85, 91, 167, 184–5

Vatican II Council 20, 183–4
vision, religious 133, 142–4

Wallis, Jim 20, 25, 65–76, 79–81, 85–6, 88–9, 93, 98–9, 143, 146; abortion 73–4; capitalism 73; church's role 70, 74; civil liberties 73; economic equality 72–3; fatalism 72; gender equality 71; God 70; government expenditures and taxes 73; hierarchy 71; individualism 71–2; Jesus 70–2, 74; Kingdom of God 70; prison reform 73; sexual freedom 72–4; world peace 72–3
Weiss, Cora 82
Westar Institute 124, 133
White Jacket 1
Wildavsky, Aaron 10
Wilson, Randy 78
Wilson, Woodrow 52, 54
Winer, Mark 132–3, 156
Woman's Federal Labor Union 118
World Council of Churches 147
world peace 58, 68–9, 71–2
World Union for Progressive Judaism 132

Yahweh 33–4, 37
Yale 68, 75, 81

Zoroastrianism 114